Working Class Credit and Community since 1918

Working Class Credit and Community since 1918

Avram Taylor

First Published 2002 by
PALGRAVE MACMILLAN
Houndmills, Basingstoke, Hampshire RG21 6XS and
175 Fifth Avenue, New York, N.Y. 10010
Companies and representatives throughout the world

PALGRAVE MACMILLAN is the global academic imprint of the Palgrave Macmillan division of St. Martin's Press, LLC and of Palgrave Macmillan Ltd. Macmillan® is a registered trademark in the United States, United Kingdom and other countries. Palgrave is a registered trademark in the European Union and other countries.

ISBN 0–333–96232–X

This book is printed on paper suitable for recycling and made from fully managed and sustained forest sources.

A catalogue record for this book is available from the British Library.

Library of Congress Cataloging-in-Publication Data
Taylor, Avram, 1962–
    Working class credit and community since 1918 / by Avram Taylor.
        p.   cm.
    Includes bibliographical references and index.
    ISBN 0–333–96232–X
    1. Loans, Personal—Great Britain—History—20th century.   2. Consumer credit—Great Britain—History—20th century.   3. Working class—Great Britain—History—20th century.   I. Title.
HG3756.G7 T39 2002
332.7′43′09410904—dc21

                                                                    2002072307

10   9   8   7   6   5   4   3   2   1
11   10   09   08   07   06   05   04   03   02

Printed and bound in Great Britain by
Antony Rowe Ltd, Chippenham and Eastbourne

To my father

'Your letter in the "Chronicle" made me smile because it indicated that tick was a thing of the past, well it is still prevalent here especially with families on Social Security or the Dole . . . Tick still lives on here. In fact I myself have more tick than Big Ben!'

Extract from a letter to the author from a Tyneside resident

Contents

Abbreviations

APR   Annual Percentage Rate
CAB   Citizens' Advice Bureau
CDP   Community Development Project
CPAG   Child Poverty Action Group
DHSS   Department of Health and Social Security
LETS   Local Exchange Trading System
MAC   Money Advice Centre
NCC   National Consumer Council
PSI   Policy Studies Institute

Acknowledgements

I have many people to thank for their help with this research, in fact too many to list here. However, I would like to acknowledge the contribution of just a few of those who helped. Firstly, I would like to thank the Economic and Social Research Council for funding this research. I would like to thank my supervisor, Ian Roberts at the University of Durham, for all his help. Also Richard Brown and David Byrne, his colleagues in the department. Thanks are also due to Bill Lancaster at the University of Northumbria for help with locating sources. I would like to thank all those who gave so freely of their time, and put up with my persistent questioning, I hope you approve of the use I have made of your stories. I would like to record my particular thanks to all those involved in the credit union movement on Tyneside, you made me feel very welcome. I would like to thank Paul Summers and David Wilkinson for listening to and discussing my ideas. Thanks are also due to Duncan Fuller, Lorna Goldsmith and Don MacRaild at the University of Northumbria, and Tim Kirk at the University of Newcastle, whose comments on earlier drafts of this work have proved invaluable. Finally, I would like to thank Jimmy Forsyth and West Newcastle Local Studies Centre for allowing me to use the cover photograph.

Introduction

The society we live in today runs on credit. We have all become accustomed to adopting a 'buy now pay later' attitude in our everyday lives. Most people in regular employment have access to overdraft facilities, bank loans, credit cards, store cards, and various other forms of credit. Indeed, much credit is used to fund a consumer lifestyle. It enables people to pay for a variety of goods and services without using cash. People use credit to pay for clothes, washing machines, stereos, cinema tickets, holidays and countless other items. However, in the past, the poor had to resort to credit to furnish themselves with the basic necessities of life. Regular visits to the pawnshop, asking for credit at the corner shop, and weekly visits from a tallyman or 'ticket' man were all part of the fabric of working class life in most areas. For those of us who did not live through the period ourselves, it is hard for us to imagine the extent of the poverty that existed during the 1920s and 1930s. Some survival strategies hinged on the merest objects and were dealt with by particular types of pawn shop, such as those which existed on Tyneside at the time. One woman, speaking of Tyneside during the 1920s, said,

> There was a penny pawn shop, you could put your frying-pan in to get your kettle out! Mind you a penny went a lot further in them days.[1]

This book is the story of the types of credit that have traditionally been associated with the working class: how they began, how they became an established part of working class life, what they were used for, and what happened to them in the new period of post-war affluence. We need to remember that, even as society became generally more prosperous after the Second World War, there have always been parts of

1

the country where people were experiencing poverty, as well as sectors of society which remained more or less permanently on, or below, the poverty line. So, for those on low incomes today, there is often still a need to turn to some of those older forms of credit to furnish themselves with the basic necessities of life.

This book seeks to assess the effect of credit on working class communities, and attempts to relate this to the debate about the decline of the working class community and possible changes in the working class after 1945. There is a large body of literature on the decline of the working class community in the post-war period which presents the issue in terms of 'before' and 'after.' This study also attempts to look at the use of credit in this way, by asking how changes in the use of credit by the working class, after 1945, relate to wider changes that may have taken place within the class itself. It is not, therefore, appropriate to include forms of credit that either did not exist before 1945 (such as credit cards) or, if they did exist, were not used by the working class before that date (for instance, bank overdrafts). The other feature of the type of credit offered by commercial banks is that it involves either no social relationships at all, in the case of plastic cards, or very little social interaction (overdrafts can be arranged over the telephone).

The use of credit by working class communities during the pre-war period had a paradoxical effect: it involved a potential loss of respectability and status, but also created and enforced mutuality. This mutuality found expression in a number of ways, a good example being the money or 'diddlum club' organised by local communities themselves. So, the central question this raises for the period after 1945 is to what extent does the use of credit by the working class continue to involve a degree of mutuality in saving and borrowing?

Previous studies of this area of working class life have tended to fall into two main categories: general historical surveys of the subject area, or purely empirical contemporary surveys. Melanie Tebbutt's *Making Ends Meet: Pawnbroking and Working Class Credit* and Paul Johnson's *Saving and Spending* are the two most prominent examples of the first type of study.[2] As for the second, there have been countless recent surveys of the extent of indebtedness, not least: *Consumers and Credit* (published by the NCC in 1980) and *Credit and Debt: the PSI Report* (published in 1992).[3] There has been little attempt to compare the pre- and post-war periods, or to place this type of credit within a theoretical framework. As well as being a local study of working class credit, this book is also a comparative study of the workings of this type of credit in both time periods, before and after 1945. As it is neither possible nor desirable to write history or sociology in a vacuum, the research has also been related to issues of social theory on which the evidence may shed some light.

Each chapter of the book explores the development of a specific form of credit. Chapter 1 examines the issues that confront us in a discussion of the working class over the period from 1918 to the present. In particular, it addresses the question of whether or not there has been a change in the working class since the Second World War, as some have suggested. It also examines the practical workings of mutuality in particular areas through the use of oral history. It is argued that where mutuality (or sharing) was a feature of working class life, there was also an element of self-interest. Working class social networks are based upon both kinship and locality. This chapter examines those social networks and concludes that the type of neighbourhood sharing that they engaged in is best seen as a form of credit in itself. It is therefore suggested that neighbourhood sharing was not wholly altruistic, and was based upon a norm of reciprocity in which there was an exchange of goods or services that was not necessarily immediate.

Chapter 2 examines illegal moneylending, which is a practice that often takes place within the working class itself. This is another way in which the close relationships that existed within the working class can also be seen to contain an element of self-interest. The central aim of this is to demonstrate that illegal moneylending within working class communities forms an area of life in which the laws of calculated economic action and the ethics of the working class community interpenetrate. The work of Richard Munch on the interpenetration of different types of action is introduced here to explain this phenomenon.[4]

Chapter 3 explores the relationship between small shopkeepers and working class communities. It is argued that this relationship is conditioned by the contradictory class location of small shopkeepers.[5] Several commentators have made the point that shopkeepers in working class areas tend to be drawn from the skilled working class. This was true of shopkeepers on Tyneside, which meant they tended to be viewed as part of the communities they exploited. This makes it difficult to explain the relationship between shopkeepers and their customers purely in terms of naked self-interest, or the cash nexus, as Marx would have it.[6] The argument raised in this chapter is that the commercial relationships involved in the use of credit by the working class are rarely of a totally economic nature, and this is further explored in the subsequent chapter.

Chapter 4 and 5 deal with the relationship between agents of credit firms and their customers. One consistent feature of the use of credit by the working class is that those companies who offer them credit tend to rely upon 'agents' or collectors to mediate between themselves and their customers. An examination of the relationship between the customer and the agent shows that there is often an emotional tie involved, as was also the case with shopkeeper and customer. These later chapters explore the dynamics of that relationship, as well as considering the extent to which the companies involved in this type of trading have become bureaucratised, as Weber argues.[7] It was found that although there had been a gradual process of bureaucratisation within these companies, the use of personal evaluation and personal contact was still maintained at various organisational levels. Finally, we look at the conclusions that can be drawn from the above discussion of the use of credit by the working class.

The approach adopted here allies history and sociology.[8] The past and the present have both been investigated through the use of primary and secondary source materials. The study draws on a wide range of documentary evidence and a number of open-ended interviews. In sociological terms, this is a piece of qualitative research. As many of the interviews deal with events that happened a long time ago the end product could also be described as 'oral history'. It can be argued that, since we can interview people only about events that have already taken place, there is no meaningful distinction between oral history and qualitative social research in this sense.

The type of study presented here rests upon source materials that are elusive or partial; in many cases, the only evidence we have comes from the mouths of the people themselves. There are very few primary sources, either published or unpublished, that deal with these particular types of credit. Many of the forms of credit investigated vanished without leaving any written record. In the case of illegal moneylending, for example, it was not necessary or desirable for the participants that there should be written records of transactions at all. Corner shops usually kept 'tick books' at the time, recording how much customers owed for groceries. However none seem to have survived to the present. So, oral sources, one of the few means of investigating this topic, are the only way we can gain an understanding of the social relationships involved in the use of credit by the working class. The sources employed are valuable, but they are also problematic. Some issues of evidence and interpretation require consideration.

The first is to do with the fact that the evidence is not actually written down. Historians are used to dealing with written evidence in various forms. They can even acquire what E.H. Carr has called 'a fetishism of documents'. This amounts to the belief, 'If you find it in the documents, it is so.'[9] Because oral evidence, by definition, does not take the form of a document, it thus feels less 'reliable' to some historians. As Carr points out though,

> No document can tell us more than what the author of the document thought—what he thought had happened, what he thought ought to happen or would happen, or perhaps only what he wanted others to think he thought, or even only what he himself thought he thought.[10]

In this sense, oral sources are no better or worse than written ones, as long as we do not exchange a 'fetishism of documents' for a 'fetishism of audio tapes'.

The second problem with using this type of source is the respondents' chronological distance from the events they are describing. This can obviously be quite great in some cases. It is not at all uncommon for oral historians to interview retired people about events that had happened during their childhood, for example. It would be wrong to deny that people's recollections can become distorted over a long period of time. They can and do so. On the other hand, as has been pointed out above, written documents are often subject to the same problem. Of course they are unlikely to be written fifty or sixty years after the events they describe, but they are often written after the fact. If they are minutes of a meeting they may have been recorded at the time, but they are still only one person's version of events. All historical sources have their advantages and their disadvantages. It is the historian's responsibility to approach a particular source with an awareness of the problems associated with it. With oral history, there is the dual problem of bias and distance to contend with. However, if the researcher begins aware of these problems, oral history can be as valuable and reliable as other sources.[11] Sixty people were interviewed during the course of this research. They included customers of credit firms, credit traders, advice workers, and credit union members. These respondents were located by a variety of means, including an appeal for information in the local daily paper, credit union visits, and personal introductions. The research also draws on letters from various Tyneside residents, written in response to the newspaper appeal.

Context

Tyneside, the geographical focus of the research, has historically had a large industrial working class based on coal mining, heavy engineering and shipbuilding. Thus it is an area with different types of occupational communities in close proximity. Tyneside has historically contained a number of different types of established working class communities, and this study includes examples of colliery villages, shipbuilding communities, and both 'rough' and 'respectable' working class areas. The size of the industrial working class in the area also led to the growth of a considerable network of credit firms (many of which were based in Newcastle) that sold to them. Tyneside also had a wide variety of credit firms operating within the area. Finally, the type of credit trading that took place on Tyneside is representative of the type of credit trading that took place in other areas, and this should also become apparent during the course of the book. Many of the changes in working class communities and in credit trading that took place on Tyneside were also happening nationally. The pattern of events I describe at a local level reflects wider national trends. The focus on Tyneside allows us to see the way in which broader national trends shape the lives of individuals, as well as the way in which individuals themselves shape the course of events. There is continual reference to developments in other parts of the country, to allow the similarities in working class life nationally to be drawn. It is therefore important to discuss the economic context in which working class credit is given.

The fundamental fact of working class life in twentieth century Britain is a gradual and general increase in living standards over the course of the century, even though this has been accompanied by the persistence of both absolute and relative poverty. As Joanna Bourke puts it,

> In the twentieth century, absolute levels of poverty fell. In part, this was the effect of improvements in real wages. Historians differ on when real wages started to increase, and the magnitude of the increase, but one of the most reliable estimates suggests that real incomes increased by 90 per cent between 1850 and the First World War, and there were even more dramatic improvements between 1924 and 1935.[12]

However, as she says, the findings from social surveys of poverty have been less optimistic. Benjamin Seebohm Rowntree's first social survey of York in 1899 showed that 'at least one-third of the poor had too little money to buy enough even for physical existence, let alone for social participation.'[13] Rowntree's repetition of this survey, usually referred to as 'the 1936 survey', used different methods, and a different poverty line to take into account the greater expectations of the time, as the definition of what constituted 'obvious want and squalor' had changed since then.[14] J.H. Veit-Wilson has done much to correct misrepresentations of Rowntree, and demonstrates that Rowntree's figures are often misquoted. Veit-Wilson points out that Rowntree did see an improvement in the economic condition of workers in York between 1899 and 1936 in terms of absolute poverty, 'a fall from roughly one in ten of the population of York to around one in twenty-five', while relative poverty remained relatively constant at about 40 per cent of the working class population in York in 1936, as compared to 43.4 in 1899.[15] Other interwar studies showed that poverty had declined, and that poverty was mainly the result of unemployment; the number of families living in poverty due to inadequate wages had dropped dramatically.[16]

Of course, a consideration of such studies brings us face-to-face with questions of how to define poverty, whether this should be by absolute or relative criterion, and what constitutes acceptable standards of living at any given time. These are all difficult questions to answer, and it is impossible to resolve them here. In a useful discussion of definitions of poverty, one which illustrates the complexity of this issue, George and Howards identify four distinct definitions that appear in the literature, based on: starvation, subsistence, social coping and social participation.[17] A consideration of the evidence presented in social surveys shows that there have always been parts of our society where people were experiencing poverty, relatively speaking, as well as sectors of society which remained more or less permanently on, or below, the poverty line.

After the Second World War, Britain entered into the period of the 'long boom', and levels of poverty continued to fall. Full employment was achieved in 1951 along with a rise in the level of real wages and an unprecedented rise in mass consumption.[18] In the decade after 1951, the personal consumption of manual workers increased by roughly 25 per cent.[19] Rowntree's third social survey of York, in 1951, found that only 2.8 per cent of the working class population of York was living in 'primary poverty', and that there was not a single family in York whose poverty was due to the unemployment of an able-bodied wage earner.[20] However, as Kent points out, this work was 'very short and perhaps unduly optimistic'.[21] Eric Hopkins says that during the period from 1951–74, the cost of living rose, but weekly money wages increased by a greater amount, so that real wages just about doubled.[22] Sidney Pollard comes to a very similar conclusion about the slightly longer period of 1950–80, asserting that average real weekly wage and salary earnings just failed to double during this time.[23] At the same time, though, there were still residual pockets of poverty, as Hopkins points out. These pockets became more noticeable, with the increase of mass unemployment and the spread of insecure low-paid employment in the 1980s.[24] The redistribution of income, begun by the Edwardian Liberal governments from the rich to the poor, was reversed after 1979, as Martin Pugh demonstrates. During the 1980s there was not only a rise in poverty, but also a widening of the gap between the rich and the poor.

> Whereas in 1979 the top 20 per cent of wage earners had enjoyed 37 per cent of all income after tax, by 1988 they had 44 per cent; conversely, the poorest 20 per cent of the population, who had received 9.5 per cent of income in 1979, earned a mere 6 per cent by 1988.[25]

In fact, the 'poor' are always being 'rediscovered'. In 1995, Carl Chinn noted that the contemporary debate about poverty had been sharpened by the recognition that deep inequalities persisted in England. However, it was during the 1960s that full employment began to disappear, and the poor were 'rediscovered' by a number of social investigators. Commentators such as Ken Coates, Richard Silburn, Richard Titmuss, Brian Abel-Smith and Peter Townsend have drawn attention to the continued existence of poverty amid affluence.[26] Taking their cue from Rowntree, more recent studies have measured poverty in 'relative' rather than 'absolute' terms. This has led to the establishment of a number of minimum standards of living, or competing poverty lines. Those falling below what is held to be a reasonable minimal standard of living are defined as poor. Of course, there is no generally accepted criterion for a reasonable minimal standard of living, and this fact will always bedevil such attempts at quantifying poverty. An alternative approach to that of a poverty line is to measure poverty as a proportion of average or disposable incomes. Piachaud begins his 1988 study of poverty in Britain by asserting that, although absolute poverty has undoubtedly declined over the course of the past century, poverty must be defined in relative terms. Thus a poverty level should rise (or fall) in step with incomes generally — defined as personal disposable income per capita — this would give a constant relative poverty level.[27] This was then used to rework the findings of previous studies of that poverty, from Rowntree onwards, which provides possibly the best historical overview of changes in the level of poverty. He concludes that a major reduction in poverty took place between 1899 and 1953, but it increased after 1973 as a result of unemployment, changes in family structure, and the ageing of the population.[28]

The reality of what it means to be poor in post-war Britain is documented in the many reports and social surveys that describe the experience of individuals who do not have what most people would consider a reasonable minimal standard of living. This literature has shown how poverty continues to have an impact on every aspect of the lives of the poor.[29] The consequences of poverty for the individual are not only material, but psychological and social as well. If we just take the most obvious material aspects of continued poverty, inadequate food and clothing, then even a superficial survey of the evidence indicates that many of those at the bottom of our society have continued to struggle with inadequate financial resources.

It has been noted that cutting back on food as a way of making ends meet was very common in surveys of those with low incomes, but that the reasons for this were varied, and the extent of the cut-backs was difficult to determine exactly, due to the lack of comparative figure with families on higher incomes.[30] A consistent theme in such studies is that mothers often deny themselves food in order to feed their children. One mother quoted in a study of poverty in the 1990s said that,

> I only eat once a day, usually at tea-time, if I feel like it. But I've got to the stage I say to myself I'm not hungry, I can go for days without nothing. [Q. Is that to save money?] It's because I want to put a bit decent in my bairns' stomach.[31]

Ashley also noted that most people on low incomes also experienced problems with clothing for both utilitarian and social reasons.[32] This can be seen in works such as Hilary Land's study of 86 large families in London in the mid-1960s, which showed that parents would deprive themselves of clothing in order to provide for their children, and some mothers did not own any shoes other than a pair of slippers.[33]

Another focus of controversy, and source of poverty, has been the inadequacy of levels of benefit.[34] In their study of poverty during the period of Margaret Thatcher's Government, Andrews and Jacobs capture the case of a couple from the North-East of England.

> She is six months pregnant. When they got married they moved into a council house, she from a bedsitter, he from his mother's. They have no furniture at all and are sleeping on the floor in a sleeping bag. They have all their meals out in cafes as they have no cooker. This also costs in bus fares. Her doctor has written saying this is dangerous to her health, but the DHSS refused payment and said they should obtain credit.[35]

It is through stories such as these that we can appreciate what it means to be poor in post-war Britain, and why there is a continuing need for credit to provide life's necessities amongst the poor. We should now turn to consider how we organise discussion of these issues.

Theoretical framework

The theoretical approach of this work draws on several traditions in order to offer an explanation that can function at both the macro and micro levels. At the broadest level it is based on a materialist conception of history which can be reduced to the basic proposition: 'that social classes, class conflict and class consciousness exist and play a role in history', to borrow a phrase from Hobsbawm.[36] This perspective forms the basis for the whole study. In addition, it is also informed by Weber's ideas about the rationalisation of social life, Ferdinand Tönnies' notion of Gemeinschaft and Gesellschaft, as well as the more recent work of Anthony Giddens on the nature of modernity. Finally, it employs the work of Philip Abrams, Erving Goffman, Arlie Russell Hochschild and others to explain social interaction at the level of the individual and the community. We can now consider how this approach will be used in the study.

There is probably no single existing explanation that adequately deals with the changes that have occurred within communities during this period. This study has employed a conceptual framework utilising ideas drawn from three sociologists, which indicates the broad direction of social change. The three concepts in question are: Ferdinand Tönnies' notion of Gemeinschaft and Gesellschaft, Philip Abram's notion of modern neighbourhoodism, and Anthony Giddens' work on trust. The basic direction of the change in social relations can be described in terms of the movement from Gemeinschaft to Gesellschaft. These terms are first used by Tönnies in *Gemeinschaft und Gesellschaft* (1887). As Larry Lyon puts it,

> Tönnies contrasted the types of human relationships appearing typic-
> ally in extended families or rural villages (Gemeinschaft) with those
> found in modern, capitalist states (Gesellschaft). Gemeinschaft-like
> relationships are based on a natural will (wesenwille) that includes
> sentiment, tradition, and common bonds as governing forces . . . In
> contrast, Gesellschaft-like relationships are based upon a rational will
> (kurwille) that includes, of course, rationality, as well as individualism
> and emotional disengagement as key elements. The basis for this

rational will is urban, industrial capitalism. Gesellschaft is characterised
by little or no identification with the community ... [37]

Tönnies saw Gemeinschaft and Gesellschaft as ideal types. No society
will contain relations that are solely dominated by one of these types. All
'real' societies will exist somewhere between these two extremes. I would
argue that not only is this a useful way of depicting change within
urban society, but that it is also the fundamental direction of change
outlined by subsequent social theorists.

To be more specific, this is the underpinning 'meta-narrative' behind
much of the writings on this subject. To take two (highly significant)
examples, it is very similar to the transformation of society that Max
Weber saw as resulting from increasing 'rationalization', Gemeinschaft
and Gesellschaft also bear a striking similarity to Emile Durkheim's
concepts of 'mechanical' and 'organic' solidarity. Larry Lyon notes
these similarities, and also points to the same implication in Marx's
work.[38] This is expressed in Marx's notion of the increasing dominance
of the cash nexus. This tendency is well-represented within the classical
tradition. It is also still being continued today in the work of Anthony
Giddens who, in works such as *The Consequences Of Modernity* and *Modernity and Self-Identity* is, arguably, still exploring the same basic movement
between these two ideal types as Tönnies was over a century ago. His
work on the decline of trust in contemporary society provides a useful
explanation of recent changes within communities.

Giddens defines trust as 'the vesting of confidence in persons or in
abstract systems, made on the basis of a 'leap into faith' which brackets
ignorance or lack of information'.[39] He says that there were four main foci
of trust in pre-modern cultures: kinship relations, the local community,
religious cosmologies and tradition. I would argue that this is also true
of working class communities throughout much of the modern period.
In fact, it is only in conditions Giddens calls 'late modernity' that this
begins to break up. This is not inconsistent with Giddens' belief that
the period of late modernity is one in which the consequences of
modernity become more radicalised and more universalised than they
previously were.[40] Giddens argues that in the modern period the locality
is no longer the source of security that it previously was. In certain
contexts, there is a delay in this process. In the case of working class
communities, it does not so much denote a difference between pre-
modernity and modernity, as between modernity and late modernity.

The unifying problem for this study is the different ways that the
various forms of credit investigated can be explained in terms of the

interpenetration of rationalities. It will be argued that neighbourhood sharing was, as Abrams suggests, governed by the norm of reciprocity, and thus contained an instrumental element. Such neighbourhood sharing appears in three guises: as an exchange between equals, as a form of 'charity' (which can be seen as simply involving a highly delayed and generalised repayment), and as an exploitative use of the norm of reciprocity (for example, illegal moneylending). In the relationship between formal credit-givers and customers there is also an element of 'performance' in Goffman's sense of the word.

1
Credit, Kinship and Community: the Impact of Credit upon Working Class Social Networks

The debate about community

The term 'community' is both controversial and difficult to define, but I can offer a working definition of it, as the social networks that exist within a given locality. These networks function at an accessible level of geography. In talking about 'community' we are inevitably discussing something which is 'sub-class'; that is, a smaller entity than class itself. The basic point is that 'community' is a multifarious and complex phenomenon. Does the term refer to a geographical space, or some vague sense of belonging? Or, does it encompass not only locality and social networks, but also the meanings that people construct for themselves of the place and social relationships they are a part of?[1] The notion of community, as it is commonly used, implies social integration, solidarity and mutuality. As Raymond Williams said some years ago, community, unlike all other terms of social organisation, never seems to be used unfavourably.[2]

Recently, Joanna Bourke has questioned the positive manner in which communities have been depicted, by historians, and by working class writers themselves. Bourke feels that nostalgia has resulted in conflict within communities being overlooked in working class autobiographies, while historians of the Left have seen community as conducive to class consciousness.[3] She has suggested that the closeness to both kin and neighbours was not either as welcome or as widespread as has often been assumed, as 'proximity did not necessarily breed intimacy'.[4] For Bourke, communities were not only characterised by social harmony, but were also sources of conflict and division. It is particularly important to recognise the importance of gender divisions within communities, as it was women who were the most important actors in both kinship and neighbourhood networks.[5] Several authors have pointed to the role that women played in local networks, with Trevor Lummis going so far as to claim that '... the greater part of what is subsumed under the heading of "community" is simply the class experience of women.'[6]

The degree of overlap between those social networks based upon neighbourhood and those based upon kinship is so great that they need to be considered together. This point emerges from several accounts of working class communities in the period before 1945. In her study of lower working class life in inner London during the late 1880s, Ellen Ross says, 'Neighbourhood relationships in many London districts overlapped with kinship, though to an extent which it is probably impossible to determine.'[7] Carl Chinn comes to a similar conclusion in his study of a working class district in Birmingham between 1880 and 1939. He says that both daughters and sons favoured matrilocal residence during this period.[8]

The use of credit by working class communities during the interwar years had a paradoxical effect, as it involved a potential loss of respectability and status, as well as creating mutuality. This mutuality found expression in a number of ways, a good example being the money or diddlum club local communities organised themselves. Another manifestation of this was the way women lent each other articles to pawn. Many commentators have made the point that this type of mutuality was characteristic of the working class during this period. It is part of the stereotype of the 'traditional' working class, that it led a communal lifestyle and lived in close-knit occupational communities. However, this stereotype has proven to be of limited usefulness, and in many places it has been contradicted by empirical data.[9]

The image of the 'traditional' working class community is well-known and appears in a number of studies.[10] However, it needs to be rehearsed here. In *Coal is Our Life* Dennis Henriques and Slaughter describe a mining community they call Ashton, in which solidarity is said to be strongly developed. The home-work link is important in forming a close-knit community, as are common hardships and shared experiences.[11] Thus, the 'traditional' working class was supposed to have led a communal lifestyle, a point captured by Brian Jackson.

> Without money to fall back on, men must turn to each other for help. And out of that necessary habit of mutuality grow not only the friendly societies, the unions, the co-ops, but all those groupings of community.[12]

By 'groupings of community' he means various clubs, and the brass bands: 'the familiar interlocking cells of community'.[13]

Examples of Jackson's 'necessary habit of mutuality' are not hard to find. Here is an account from the 1920s. The words are a woman's:

> You wouldn't go hungry not if next door had got any bread...You'd get a piece, if it was only a piece of bleedin' stale bread. There was some very hungry times. We was poor as bleedin' church mice, poorer than that...[14]

When times were hard people helped each other. Such a message was also conveyed by the Tynesiders interviewed for this study. Their story was one of sharing and co-operation.

Many observers have pointed to fundamental changes in the character of the British working class after the Second World War. Much writing on this subject has concerned itself with the 'corruption' of the post-war working class, and implies that it has deviated from some former purity. This idea is often expressed in a dichotomy between the 'traditional' life of the working class before the war, and the 'non-traditional' nature of life after it. However, the concept of a 'traditional' way of life is in itself problematic, and raises a number of issues. What were the principle ways that working class life has been said to alter after the Second World War?

The fundamental change in working class life has been that of greater affluence. This has caused many to question Marx's theory of society, as Marx expected there to be a 'polarisation' of classes under capitalism, with the progressive impoverishment of the proletariat. Instead, each successive generation of the working class has been told 'It wasn't like this when I was a lad,' and for the most part it usually was not. There were advances in the living standards of the working class after the First World War, for example, but for many these were comparatively short-lived. After the Second World War we entered into the period of the long boom, and living standards reached levels that previous generations could not even have dreamed of. Although some sections of the working class have remained comparatively poor, the working class as a whole has experienced greater prosperity during the post-war period.

The greater affluence of workers has led to attitudinal changes in the working class, according to some observers. These are often listed under the general heading of 'embourgeoisement' (the adoption of middle-class values and habits by the working class), or they are attributed to an increase in materialism and individualism among workers. With the growth of individualism, the concept of 'community' is said to have disappeared, and working class lives are said to have become 'privatised'. The widespread ownership of consumer durables has also led to the belief that there is no longer a working class in the way that it existed during the nineteenth century. This is the ultimate claim of those who preach the doctrine of post-war social revolution.

The idea of the disappearance of the working class in contemporary Britain is explored by Goldthorpe *et al* in *The Affluent Worker in the Class Structure*, which challenges the whole thesis of embourgeoisement. However Goldthorpe *et al* did see several differences between the workers they studied and the 'traditional' working class. These included an increasingly instrumental attitude to work, and an increasingly home-centred (or privatised) social life.[15] This seems to suggest that the distinction between an old 'traditional' and a new 'non-traditional' working class would appear to be more useful (and open) than that of a 'traditional' proletariat and an embourgeoised working class. So how has the erosion of traditional working class values been depicted?

Richard Hoggart was one of the first writers to become concerned with the disappearance of the 'traditional' working class. Hoggart addresses himself to the cultural change that the post-war working class was experiencing. Hoggart distinguishes between what he calls 'older' and 'newer' attitudes. The older attitudes he describes are those from his childhood, spent as part of the northern working class during the interwar years. He begins by pointing out that older attitudes have not completely disappeared and newer attitudes were not completely unknown in the previous generation.[16] Hoggart's central concern is how traditional working class values have been transformed in the era of mass consumption. He does not question the fact that working people became better off materially than they were before the war, but he feels that 'the accompanying cultural changes' were not always an improvement.[17] He says that the labour movement is in danger of losing the material improvements that it has gained because '. . . material improvements can be used so as to incline the body of working-people to accept a mean form of materialism as a social philosophy.'[18]

Blackwell and Seabrook take Hoggart's argument onboard, but they begin by offering two criticisms of Hoggart's view. One is that the 'older' values he describes are seen as the essence of the class itself. The other is that he is describing only one section of the working class at one particular moment.[19] However, they also echo Hoggart in asking, 'What need is there of socialism when capitalism can provide everything which was once deemed to be necessary . . . ?'[20] They feel that it was natural for the working class to want the consumer goods that became available for the first time in the 1950s. The working class thus has not been corrupted by affluence, but transformed by it. The core of their argument is that acceptance of consumer goods involves acceptance of the logic of capitalism itself, 'wherever it may lead us'.[21] They point to the decay of community as part of the price of consumerism. This is a recurrent theme in Seabrook's work.[22]

So what about community? What happened to it after 1945? Some of these writers would have us believe that every old working class district was torn down after the war, and that the old residents were moved to an inhospitable council estate on the edge of town. In the process, the community spirit of the inhabitants was irreparably damaged. What actually happened? What did happen was far more complex. Firstly, not all the old inner city areas were demolished at once — there was often a delay of 10 or 20 years between one area and another being cleared. Secondly, some are quite visibly still there! They have not been redeveloped, they have just deteriorated. Bill Williamson says that, during the 1950s,

> In some of the older industrial areas, in South Wales, the north east, Yorkshire, Lancashire and central Scotland, workers in mines and docks and shipyards and heavy engineering factories continued to live their lives in densely populated areas of terraced housing, and often, as in the case of miners, in sharply segregated communities. Within such communities older working class values, attitudes and life-styles held firm.[23]

Some mining villages, in areas such as the Durham coalfield for example, would seem to have survived intact both physically and socially to the present day.

Brian Jackson and Dennis Marsden show that much of the old, independent working class culture of Huddersfield 'survived the first wave of television'.[24] The description they give of working class life in post-war Huddersfield brings out the continued importance of old working class institutions such as the Co-op, the club and the brass band. This older culture was, however, being threatened by changes in the wider society. People were moving away from the old working class areas and, consequently, from their local clubs. The brass bands had now to compete with school orchestras for younger players. Jackson concludes that it is rehousing which is the most serious challenge to the continued existence of the old patterns of life. The new housing estates offered nothing that could take the place of what Jackson calls 'the familiar interlocking cells of community', because, as he puts it, 'Community centres are no substitute for community.'[25]

The classic study of the effects of rehousing, based upon research carried out in Bethnal Green and Dagenham between 1953 and 1955 by Willmott and Young, demonstrated the continued importance of the extended family and kinship networks to the working class during the 1950s. They also found that strong family ties did not exclude outsiders, but acted as a bridge between the individual and the community.[26] According to them, however, the centrality of the wider family to people's daily lives was being undermined by the effects of rehousing. When Bethnal Green residents moved to Greenleigh (a new housing estate in Dagenham) they suffered the loss of the old family and kinship networks. People living on Greenleigh were isolated, not just from their kin, but from fellow residents as well. Willmott and Young point out, 'One reason people have so little to do with their neighbours is the absence of places to meet them.'[27]

A woman in Sunderland, who moved onto a new council estate in 1954, also makes this point. The woman describes the estate like this,

> All there was on our estate was houses for families. There were no shops, no church no pavements...There was nothing for women and children and nowhere for women to go. It was a long time before I did anything or went anywhere, and then I got involved in the church.[28]

The physical conditions on such estates worked against the establishment of community. High-rise blocks offered even less opportunity for social contact. As Campbell points out, despite architects' attempts to build community spirit into them, streets in the air do not engender a sense of community. She says, 'This brave new world of social engineering produces the opposite of community contact,' — that is, isolation. The truth of this statement is undeniable, but is there always such a complete lack of social life on the new estates?

In Willmott's follow-up study of Dagenham, published in 1963, he looked at an estate that had been settled in the 1920s and 30s. In this study Willmott asked,

> Are the isolation from kin and the aloofness from neighbours part of a new way of life altogether, or are they merely transitional? What

social patterns evolve on housing estates when place and people have had time to settle down; how do they then compare with the 'traditional' communities?[29]

He found that the experience of the first people to move to Dagenham was very similar to those who migrated to new council estates after 1945. In fact, there was probably even less attention paid to the social needs of the residents on the pre-war estate. Not surprisingly, then, it took a long time for the population of the estate to become stable, but by the late 1950s it appeared to have become relatively settled. Willmott found that matrilocality was almost as marked at Dagenham as in the East End. In fact, 44 per cent of their sample of married people had parents on the estate (in Bethnal Green 54 per cent of the parents of married people were in the same borough).

Willmott's findings were in many ways, though, quite ambiguous as he detected several patterns of residence. Many people who had been brought up in Dagenham stayed there and established 'extended families' like those of 'traditional' communities. On the other hand, some people who grew up on the estate moved away from it. Those who moved to the estate after their marriage tended to leave their parents behind them in the old district. In some cases, though, their relatives were able to follow them onto the estate. The effect of all this was that, although some people on the estate were just as isolated as the residents of Greenleigh, others were part of a similar kinship system to that in Bethnal Green.[30] Willmott drew a similar conclusion about the relationships between neighbours on the estate. He claimed, 'A set of relationships very similar to that of the traditional East End community has developed for some people on the estate, but not for others.'[31] This presents a curious paradox, but it does show how communities can develop over time, and warns us against the adoption of an overly dogmatic approach to the subject. Willmott concluded that despite the lack of collective facilities the 'fundamental regularities of working-class life will re-assert themselves'.[32] He felt, 'In part, Dagenham is the East End reborn', even though this process had taken about a generation. Willmott demonstrated that communities are not static entities, but constantly evolving. This conclusion is also borne out by Fiona Devine in her follow-up to the original *Affluent Worker* study, where she found that many of those who moved to Luton followed, or were followed by, kin and friends resulting in the regrouping of social networks over time.[33]

We can add a further dimension to Seabrook's picture of urban decay, by focusing on the new communitarian spirit seen on even the worst council estates around the country. Credit unions are just one example of this phenomenon. Paul Harrison says,

> The seventies saw the blossoming of new concepts of community action, of neighbourhood self-help, of the value of collective pressure, through lobbying, demonstrations, publicity, to achieve a better deal for disadvantaged groups.[34]

Beatrix Campbell describes how the tenants' action against the council created a new community spirit on an estate in Sheffield pointing out,

> Though the tenants did not like living there they grew into a community in the course of their campaigns: 'We're like old friends now, in and out of each other's houses,' said one of their organisers. 'We don't want to be separated from each other.'[35]

The fact that such groups often organise against a Labour Council, does not mean the participants no longer vote Labour, a fact Campbell underlines.

For every successful tenants' group, such as the one described above, there is one that has suffered from a lack of success. Campbell also describes a tenants' association on a large estate in Coventry that has been totally demoralised by its lack of success.[36] Where community action is successful it can do much to bring people together, but there are many failed attempts. Harrison feels that tenants' associations in Hackney are good at providing social activities for their members, but they are not very effective pressure groups. Very few people are involved in the campaigning side of their activities, so it is left up to the leaders to shoulder the burden. In some places, though, there may be no individuals willing to take on such an onerous task. Harrison says that this is why community workers have been unable to form associations on some of the worst estates. Even where groups are successfully created, their continued existence is usually dependent upon the continued involvement of a few active individuals. As Harrison puts it,

> Often it is only the dedication and ability of one, two, or three individuals that keeps things going, and when they move on — as the most able often do, to better housing elsewhere, or to a seat on the council — the tenants' association may collapse unless it can find a replacement.[37]

This brings us to a central issue in the discussion of community in the post-war period: the fact that many people living in deprived areas do not want to live in them! An individual solution to the poor housing conditions, high crime rates and lack of amenities that exist in certain inner city areas is, simply to leave. As one of Campbell's informants from a council estate in Coventry put it, '. . . anybody here with get-up and go gets up and goes.'[38] This is quite a complex issue, as some people may wish to leave an area but be unable to do so. They can, therefore, become trapped in a place they may not have wanted to move to in the first place, and are now unable to leave. This is not conducive to the formation of close community ties. On the other hand, as Campbell points out above, even in areas where people are reluctant to live, at first, community spirit can develop. Finally, it would seem that there are areas that may be quite hard to let to outsiders, but are still sought by local people who wish to remain in the area they were brought up in. This brings us back, full circle, to the continued importance of local ties that was such a marked feature of areas such as Bethnal Green.

As well as the problem of a constantly shifting population, one of the main difficulties community organisations face is the apathy of the men in many communities. Harrison remarked on the fact that most of the community activists he met were women.[39] Not only are men not usually active in community organisations, but they can often be opposed to their wives becoming involved. These are recurring themes in Campbell's work. As a female respondent told her, 'The first hurdle you have to get over is your husband.'[40] Those women who do overcome opposition at home (and not all do) then have to face a further conflict with men, outside the home, over the form and content of their organisation. What happens to those individual women who do go through this process? As Campbell points out, their whole selves change. They can gain much in terms of self-confidence. She says,

> These women were changed by their politics, but most of them have nowhere to pursue their own development save through self-improvement — through further education, acquiring skills which they return to their community.[41]

However, for some women, the acquisition of skills can lead to a decisive break with their community. Campbell acknowledges that 'self-improvement puts these women's class belonging in jeopardy', but she still does not talk about those women who leave their communities as a result of it. The women she discusses have all managed to combine self-improvement with continued involvement in their own communities. For those who leave their communities — to do a degree course, or whatever — there is often no going back. So, ironically both total withdrawal from the community and total involvement in it can have the same effect: the concerned individuals leave.

In *Goliath*, Campbell continues her analysis of the divisions in contemporary working class communities, going a stage further. She describes other divisions that exist in what she calls, 'Britain's Dangerous Places'. In this she looks at the scene of riots in 1991. In investigating the causes of the riots, though, she indicates how the communities involved are fractured. For example, racism, particularly against Asian shopkeepers, was a feature of the disturbances in Ely (in Wales) and on the Meadow Well estate (in North Tyneside). Blackbird Leys, on the periphery of Oxford, was the scene of joyriding performances (or 'hotting' displays). These displays had been going on for some time and Campbell points out that the displays '... divided the community between those who wanted to watch and those who felt tormented by the night noise'.[42] In Scotswood (in Newcastle) the community was divided clearly along gender lines. Campbell says that it was women who were 'Scotswood's most active citizens and yet also its most exposed targets'.[43] Campbell's argument is quite complex. She looks at several factors that have contributed to the situation. However, her analysis is perhaps best summed up in the phrase used in *The Guardian*'s review of the work, 'The lads are at war with their community.'[44] This is the case in Scotswood, as pointed out above, and also in the other areas she visited.

Campbell feels that such estates are split into two communities: a criminal and a communitarian element. She feels that, on Meadow Well, the communitarian element suffered from a lack of local authority funding (for whatever reason), and was also attacked by the criminal element in its own community. The men in such communities had completely abdicated all responsibility, not only for their families, but for themselves as well. They were doing whatever they wanted, and leaving all the coping to the women. The lawless behaviour of the men was facilitated by the attitude of the police, who had abandoned those communities. It could take police up to two hours to respond to calls in Scotswood, for example, and they had been known to tell victims, 'What do you expect? You're in Scotswood.'[45] The recent police initiatives to deal with crime, Neighbourhood Watch and community policing, have not helped these communities either.

What are the implications of this for 'community'? Is Campbell justified in calling the areas she describes 'Britain's Dangerous Places'?

Is this even a new problem? There have always been 'respectable' and 'rough' areas, and the latter have often had a reputation for being 'dangerous places'. However, it would certainly seem as if 'rough' areas are a whole lot 'rougher' than they have ever been, as a result of the current recession. Broken windows are still broken windows, even if their cause is acute social deprivation. Campbell feels that the only thing that marked the riots out from everyday life was their scale, as '... they were simply larger displays of what these neighbourhoods had to put up with much of the time'.[46]

Campbell's analysis of the different responses of men and women to long-term unemployment is quite categorical. Her argument is, 'Crime and coercion are sustained by men. Solidarity and self-help are sustained by women. It is as stark as that.'[47] She does not allow for any individual responses that may occur to the common problem of poverty. There are other responses to this situation, even if only apathy or despair to what extent are the activities she describes (that is, crime and community action) only the most visible responses to acute social deprivation? This is a question difficult to answer. There is a lack of social research on this topic. What we do know about areas like Scotswood and Meadow Well tends to come from the police, who see only the worst side of a district, or the community activists, who are not representative of the population as a whole. When Campbell visits Meadow Well, she talks to the handful of women who form the core group of the local Credit Union. These women are not even typical members of the Credit Union, let alone typical residents of the estate. Only a small proportion of the people on the estate are members of the Credit Union, and only a few play an active role in it. Similarly, we can ask: what proportion of the men on the estate are involved in criminal activities? These objections are not raised to dismiss the analysis presented in *Goliath*, but to qualify it. The strength of Campbell's argument is that the responses to poverty it depicts are indicative, even if they are not completely typical. It would seem that it is women who have the task of coping with the problems long-term poverty creates, while many men have given up. Not all the men in places like Meadow Well are criminals, though, just as not all the women are community activists.

Female self-help is not only provided by Food Co-ops and Credit Unions; women have other ways of providing mutual aid for themselves. Campbell quotes one community worker who says,

The lasses have the bairns. The relationship with the lad has broken down, but the relationship with his mother will remain.

It's amazing. The responsibility bypasses the son, who does nothing, but his mother will be helpful, passing on a cot, or some clothes. Often the lasses will still go to see his mother, and go round for Sunday dinner.[48]

This suggests that, in some respects, not a lot has changed. Women are still dependent on help from female relatives living nearby to bring up their children, just as they were in Bethnal Green during the 1950s. The only difference is that the men are perhaps doing even less than they used to. The lads have their own community of men who they hang around with. The young women, if they have children, will be more isolated, but may still be part of a female network of mutual aid. So neither men nor women are living what could be termed a 'privatised' lifestyle.

Broadly speaking, we have distinguished three types of community. These can be labelled: established/'traditional'; newly settled; regrouped/partially regrouped. Willmott and Young showed how Bethnal Green remained an established/'traditional' community during the 1950s. However, those Bethnal Green residents who moved to Greenleigh were moving into the second type of community (that is, newly settled) and they experienced the isolation that can result from such a move. Willmott's follow-up study of Dagenham, and Fiona Devine's work, both show how communities can regroup over time. The places described in those studies are examples of the third type of community: regrouped/partially regrouped. All three types of community existed during the the long boom, and it is perhaps only more recently, with the destruction of heavy industry, that the established/'traditional' type of community has become more scarce.

We can now move on to consider working class communities on Tyneside.

Working class communities during the interwar period

The experience of one respondent, a miner's son, born in South Shields in 1928, perhaps typifies the delicate balance of a family and their earnings. His mother was a tailoress but, when he was five years old, his father left home, which meant that his family was considerably worse off than many others in the neighbourhood. His mother survived by taking in sewing from the neighbours, as well as through their charity. He said,

The people upstairs were working. He was a labourer in the shipyard, that was real luxury that. So they had a large family and she would make, say a pan of broth, and she would bring it down. She would say, 'Oh, I've made too much'. That's the way the generosity worked. Everybody kept an eye on everybody else and made sure everybody was alright.[49]

Another respondent (born in 1925 in Howdon) offered this detailed and vivid account of neighbourhood sharing during the 1930s:

> Well when me mother baked, I mean everybody baked then...Then when I used to come in from school she used to have all this stuff that she had baked and she would maybe give you a little tart on a saucer. All the old women were [known as] grannies. They weren't any relation but it was granny this and granda that. She would say, 'Run down to granny Sayers and give her that'. It was a little apple tart or something. She give everybody that was on their own a little bit for all we didn't have a lot of money...[50]

She goes on to describe how her mother, in turn, benefited from the generosity of one of her neighbours,

> The lady who lived further along the street she was a real store woman. Everything she got at the store, the Co-op you know. When her dividend came she would knock on the door, 'Are you there?' and she used to give me mother half-a-crown. And me mother would say, 'Eeh no, I don't want your half crown.' Then she [the neighbour] would say, 'Go on, get yourself a few cakes.' In her eyes it was a little treat for my mother to have for herself.[51]

The direct gift of a sum of money was rare, as Chinn says of Birmingham:

> Money was obviously a scarce commodity in the slums and neighbourly help usually took other, more readily available forms, the most common of which was the lending of food or belongings.[52]

The other examples cited here bear out this point.

However, it is not so easy to agree with what Chinn says about the motivation behind neighbourhood sharing. He maintains that communal sharing and self-help was not motivated by selfishness but was carried out with little thought of profit or reward.[53] Here Chinn is responding to Anderson's point that the working class employed a 'calculative orientation towards kin'.[54] Ellen Ross has a different view of the motivation behind working class sharing to that expressed by Chinn. She says,

> The bulk of women's day-to-day sharing was exchange; in theory at least, reciprocity was the rule. 'You always got it [what you lent] back,' one woman recalled. To be thought of as untrustworthy as a borrower was one of the worst accusations that could be brought by neighbourhood gossip against a woman, threatening an important part of her livelihood... Services were often compensated by money payments: childcare, maternity nursing, sitting up with the sick, running errands. These payments constituted a significant element in the survival of those in precarious circumstances — often widows or old women — who lived through serving neighbours.[55]

There was then a degree of mutuality present in working class neighbourhoods during the period before the Second World War. We now need to decide which is the correct interpretation of this neighbourhood sharing — the one proposed by Chinn or the version that Ross offers us? Or, are the reasons for this type of mutuality just too complex to be subsumed by categories such as 'unconditional giving' or a 'calculative attitude' towards family and friends?

The idea that, 'You wouldn't go hungry, not if next door had got any bread,' is but one viewpoint. One interviewee described what she had to do as a child when there was no food in the house:

> I mean I used to go, this is in the 1930s and 1940s, and ask a lady over the road ('cause her husband worked in a factory, well I mean that was a good job in a factory) if I could wash her dishes. For the simple reason that I knew I would get something to eat, and you know she used to give me brown bread and bramble jelly and, you know, I can still taste that bramble jelly today... My mother just sent me, 'Go over and ask Mrs so-and-so if you can wash her dishes,' knowing that she would give me something to eat.[56]

The man from South Shields, quoted above, whom we shall call Mr Lewis, felt that neighbourhood sharing was itself a form of credit. Although several respondents discussed working class mutuality during this period, Mr Lewis gave the most detailed account of it. It is worth quoting him at length on this subject. In the earlier quotation he made the point, 'Everybody kept an eye on everybody else.' He then expanded upon this,

> The community looked after itself. So if somebody was a miner, for example, if you helped them to put the coal in they would give you a couple of buckets of coal. Or, like me mother, they would let her have some coal very cheaply. You know, coppers a bucket. So we didn't buy coal from a coalman. There were enough miners around to buy coal from.[57]

A recurrent feature of Mr Lewis's account is that there was an exchange of goods and/or services. When I asked Mr Lewis if people usually received something in exchange this became more apparent.

> It would be, yes, but not immediately but you knew it was there. I mean in some cases it would be. I mean if you wanted some coal from a pitman you paid him tuppence a bucket for the coal...But a lot of other things...I don't know where they drew lines...Some things you paid for other things you didn't. So if you wanted ginger beer from the ginger beer lady across the road, you paid her...If somebody was baby-sitting, I mean they never got paid.[58]

Equally, the same man also gave a positive account of the motivation behind neighbourhood sharing.

> Well it was a kind of goodwill everywhere. So it was part of this community spirit. In other words, people knew that you would do anything for me. So I would do anything for you. So you knew if my mother was ill the neighbours would look after me...Also she was a member of a large family. It was like belonging to an extended family being in the working class in those days.[59]

I then asked him how far had this 'spirit of goodwill' extended? He replied,

> Oh, I would say half a street and it spilled over because of relationships you see. So me mother had a friend in the next street who she went to church with and knew since she was a little girl. So she was part of our [group]. So there'd be a hard core where everybody belonged, cause you were all neighbours, then everybody would have their own fringe groups. Some members of which would coincide with others, others wouldn't.[60]

The social networks involved in this type of sharing were based upon both kinship and neighbourhood. Mr Lewis clearly felt that the type of activity the members were engaged in was itself a form of credit, but not one involving an immediate repayment. He says that although repayment (in whatever form) was not immediate, 'You knew you could call on it.'[61] This is why he feels it was like having money in the bank. In fact, in one phrase, he adopts the language of banking: 'It was an understanding that you could draw on that.'[62]

From this description, working class mutuality in the interwar period sounds very much like the 'LETS' system operating in some areas today. The 'LETS INFO PACK' offers this definition of a LETS system,

> 'LETS' stands for 'Local Exchange Trading System.' It gives people and businesses the opportunity to acquire or sell goods and services without traditional cash. It also provides a communication network through which members of the community can meet their other needs for education, recreation and social interaction.[63]

As another introductory leaflet puts it, 'It enables local people to give and receive all kinds of services from one another, without the need to spend money.'[64] Of course, even from this cursory description of the system, it differs in several ways from the neighbourhood sharing that was described above. Firstly, there sometimes was an exchange of cash in the pre-war period. Secondly, the LETS scheme is usually run through a central database, listing services and goods on offer in the area, and it involves the keeping of accounts and so on. In other words, it is a highly bureaucratised form of exchange; neighbourhood sharing in working class areas was completely informal. Finally, it cannot seriously be argued that the LETS system has been adopted by the contemporary working class as an alternative to previous forms of sharing, as the system has had a very limited, and localised, impact. It is also, at present, more concerned with middle-class notions of 'The Green Pound' and ecologically sound ways of using resources than it is with reaching working class communities. Nevertheless, the comparison with pre-war forms of sharing is instructive in that it draws our attention to the fact that this was not wholly altruistic and was based upon the idea of a norm of reciprocity. We shall return to this point later, but first we should consider whether there was mutuality involved in the use of credit by the working class during the interwar period.

Melanie Tebbutt describes how, before the Second World War, 'bundle women' or 'runners' used to pawn goods for their neighbours for a few pence commission. Women made use of these agents if they were either employed in mill or factory work, in which case they had little time to visit the pawnbroker, or if they wanted to avoid the shame that would result from their neighbours knowing they had used a pawnbroker.[65] So in this case, a 'neighbourly' act could become quite profitable. Tebbutt says that,

> For some the business of collecting such bundles was a casual affair rewarded with a glass of whisky but for others it provided a regular living. Commission in the Black Country during the 1890s was 'rigidly fixed' at a 1/2 d. in the shilling or part of a shilling, another payment becoming due if the pledge was also redeemed. A 'popper' in a good district with a fair connection was said to earn between £1 and 25s. a week.[66]

One respondent told me,

> I never went to the pawnshop, for the simple reason that I had the bairns. I couldn't go but me neighbour went, and if you wanted anything in the pawnshop, she'd put it in for you.[67]

In this case there was no direct payment involved in visiting the pawnshop for a neighbour. However this 'favour' could well become part of the type of exchange of goods and services described above. So could obtaining tickets from a credit agent for a neighbour. One woman said that not only did her mother obtain tickets for those women who were refused them because they owed too much, but she would also pay the ticket agent for women who did not want him to call when their husband was at home.[68]

The collective organisation of savings clubs would seem to be a classic example of the type of mutuality in saving and borrowing held to be characteristic of working class communities during this period. These were usually known as 'diddly' or 'diddlum' clubs, and they could exist for general saving or for a specific goal. Members paid a weekly sum which could either be constant or progressively increasing. One informant described the diddlum club like this:

> A woman got 20 friends to pay a shilling a week for 21 weeks. At the start the names were put in a hat and as they were drawn out they claimed £1. First out got first week and so on, then the one that ran it got the last week for running it.[69]

Again we can see that, although there was a degree of mutuality involved in this arrangement, the woman who ran it did not do so for nothing. Another woman described a diddlum club that ran in a small pit village near Stanley during the interwar years. She said that an old woman, called Mrs Brown, used to run a money club (or diddlum) in the village.

> You paid a shilling a week for 21 weeks, and the 21st week was hers for doing the club. Everyone paid their shilling in, those 20 people, and the 20 numbers were put in a hat and you drew out of the hat to see whether you got it the first week or the last week... and in a way this was helping this old Mrs Brown who was a widow, because in those days the widow's pension was very little.[70]

There was often a profit to be made from helping one's neighbours and nowhere is this more apparent than in the type of moneylending that took place within working class communities during this period.

An examination of the type of lending that took place within working class communities also shows that there was often an instrumental element (that is, an element of calculation) involved in the solidaristic relationships (that is, the community of interest) that existed within the working class itself. Women may have lent each other money, but there was usually some interest charged on a loan. Similarly, there was also sometimes a charge for borrowing items to pawn.[71] This research did not reveal any examples of women charging for borrowed items, but did throw up women who had bought pawn tickets from their neighbours. One respondent said,

> Another thing I remember about the pawnshops was this old woman used to come knocking and say, 'Do you want to buy a ticket for half-a-crown or 2s?' And like somebody would buy it off them, well me mother used to do it. She would say, 'Well what's in?' [The other woman replied] 'Well there's a pair of nice curtains and there's a tablecloth.' And it would be worth the money.[72]

The point about this transaction was that it was carried out only after careful investigation of the value of the pawned goods, as this woman went on to explain. It could provide some people with the opportunity to acquire articles cheaply at the expense of their neighbours.

A final way in which women exploited their neighbours was through the sale of shop tokens on the black market. Two shops played an important role in providing for working class communities on Tyneside during the interwar years. These were Parrish's of Byker and Shephard's of Gateshead. Both of these were large department stores in working class areas that operated mainly on credit, both with their own currency. To obtain Shephard's or Parrish's money, the customer had to first obtain a ticket from an agent of that shop. The tickets were sold in multiples of a pound, and the interest charged on them was a shilling to the pound.[73] The tickets were then exchanged for that shop's own currency (this was sometimes called 'Monopoly Money' or 'Funny Money' by those that used it).[74] These shops were able to attract customers from all over Tyneside, so they were an important source of credit for the working class of Tyneside during this period. Neither of these shops would exchange their own tokens for cash, so a substantial black market in Shephard's and Parrish's money arose.

The evidence collected on this suggests that the 'street value' of the tokens was usually 14 shillings to the pound. It could also be more or less than this, depending on the circumstances in which the tokens were changed. The sale of tokens for cash seems to have been carried out on several levels. Firstly, between neighbours. Secondly, they could be exchanged at some corner shops. Thirdly, they were sometimes sold to professional people, such as doctors, who could make a considerable profit this way. One woman seems to suggest that 'black market' trading in tokens could almost become a small business.

> I remember a dealer in Parrish's checks in our street. She would buy a pound's worth of checks for, say, 12s. and 6d. and resell them for 15s. Making a profit of 2s. and 6d. to the pound. She always had checks for sale. Of course the poor unfortunate person selling them got deeper and deeper into debt.[75]

Like illegal moneylending, this practice took place within working class communities but it was not always approved of by the community itself. Another respondent said,

> People used to get so many Parrish's checks and sell them to somebody else a lot cheaper. They still had that debt to pay off. People were hard up and they used to sell them . . . I used to think it was terrible for them people to go and buy them because it was creating a bigger debt for the people who were selling them.[76]

Many of the mass-produced consumer goods which first became widely available during the interwar period were bought on hire-purchase.[77]

Working class consumers were among those who made use of hire-purchase during this period. However, the conditions under which it was offered to working class consumers were often unfavourable to them. This was because of the abuses of the hire-purchase system perpetrated by unscrupulous vendors, who took advantage of the fact that this type of credit remained unregulated until 1938.[78] Working class consumers were the principal victims of these credit traders. This can be ascertained from contemporary accounts and the fact that the Bill to remedy the abuses of the system was proposed by Ellen Wilkinson, the Labour MP for Jarrow who led the Jarrow March in 1936, out of concern for her constituents. The *Hire Purchase Act* of 1938 was the first piece of hire-purchase legislation, and became law in July of that year.[79]

During the Bill's second reading, Ellen Wilkinson gave examples of the type of practices that she was attempting to combat. The most notorious was that of 'snatch-back'. This is where a hire-purchase firm takes the goods from the hire-purchaser, after a considerable proportion of the cost has already been paid, in order to resell them. Ellen Wilkinson pointed out that this abuse was the result of a loophole in the existing law, which was 'the cancer in the whole system'.[80] She gives the example of a woman who has obtained furniture worth £27 1s. 9d. and had paid £25 16s. 9d. when she fell behind with her payments. She was then prosecuted and the court ordered her to pay £6 8s. 9d. for costs. While she was out cleaning, a van called and took all the furniture away as well as £5 worth of goods to pay for the court costs.[81] Ellen Wilkinson also read a letter from a Justice of the Peace in Manchester describing a repossession.

> A van called for the goods. One of these men was an ex-boxer, a regular brute. Just the type of 'bruiser' to do the job. Mrs Read, judging what their errand was, did not let them in, but they used force. Mrs Read screamed, and a neighbour came to her aid. The boxer promptly floored him, and the men made off with the goods.[82]

This was not an exceptional case, as Ellen Wilkinson points out. Aylmer Vallance also cites repossession cases involving violence.[83]

As we saw in the Manchester case cited above, repossessions were sometimes resisted by the community itself. The following account shows how this community solidarity operated on Tyneside. Mrs Wrigley was born in Howdon in North Tyneside in 1925. As a child she witnessed a repossession:

I can't remember the furniture coming in, but she must have went to town and got all lovely new furniture. She had one lassie and her man was never out of work, strange to say in them times, but he must have been the lucky one. He was never out of work. She had all these lovely things, and she mustn't have paid for them. And I remember the bailiffs coming, we called them 'the bums.' 'Here's 'the bums' coming.' And they came up, and she was trying to shut the door and keep them out, and they were pushing, the two great big fellas, they were pushing, and she was only little and she was pushing at the other side and she wasn't going to let them in. And finally they got in, and then she fainted, and the fella just picked her up and put her on the bed. And somebody who seen them getting in ran across to the Legion (the Wooden Legion) for her brother, and by the time he came across the stuff was nearly all out. And he says, 'Hey, hey, hey! What's going on?' They said, 'Hey look mate we are just doing a job. We've got to come and collect it. We're sorry that your sister's fainted and that like, but we cannat do nowt about it.' And away the furniture went . . . And I can remember that plain as can be, the two big burly men taking all the furniture away.[84]

It is worth noting that, although we do not know the extent of this particular woman's default, her husband was in regular employment, and Mrs Wrigley was sure that they would not have been far behind with their payments. Obviously, with such things going on in the neighbourhood, this influenced Mrs Wrigley's mother's attitude towards hire-purchase and she became very reluctant to acquire anything on hire-purchase. When she eventually did, in 1939, she was still extremely worried about it and anxious about the repayments. Thus repossessions could activate the solidarity of the community, which sought to resist them, but they were also a source of shame and social embarrassment as another respondent asserted.[85] So what conclusions can we draw from this investigation of neighbourhood sharing and credit on Tyneside?

In his study of Good Neighbour Schemes, Philip Abrams says,

Reciprocity, then, enlists egoistic motives for social purposes. But because that is how it works it can develop only within relationships where each party has something of value to give to the other. On that basis the distinctive nexus of rights and obligations — X and Y both owe benefits to each other and are entitled to receive benefits from each other — that is the essence of reciprocity can develop.[86]

Abrams says that the exchange involved in this type of relationship can be in the form of things that are dissimilar in kind but are perceived to be of equivalent value by the individuals involved. He feels that his research in the community of Sunniside reveals that there is usually a norm of reciprocity (however hidden) behind a lot of neighbourhood sharing. Abrams questions the distinction that Gouldner makes between the norm of reciprocity and the norm of beneficence. What Gouldner means by the latter is the requirement that 'people should help those who need help,' which means that some social relationships are thus exempt from the norm of reciprocity.[87] Abrams found,

> At the level of consciousness there is a structured disjunction; the Good Neighbours help because 'people should help those who need help'; at the same time they get the 'satisfaction' of paying debts incurred long since to other helpers (so often their mothers) or of staking a claim to help themselves in prospective future predicaments — 'well I just hope someone will do the same for me when I need it.'[88]

The evidence presented in this chapter supports Abrams' conclusion that neighbourhood sharing is governed by a norm of reciprocity. This norm of reciprocity can be worked out in various ways. It can involve an exchange of goods or services, which is immediate, or it can be a 'helpful' act for which 'payment' is delayed. This is the type of reciprocity that Mr Lewis was referring to. In this first instance there is an exchange that is perceived as equal by the participants. Another way that the norm of reciprocity can operate is that it can be based upon the idea of helping someone less fortunate (in other words, at one level an individual's action can be motivated by the norm of beneficence) but help is offered in such a way as to also benefit the giver. This is the case with the 'bundle women' or 'runners' who Tebbutt describes, and with the old woman who received payment for running the money club. In both cases the providers of aid are still receiving a service in return for their investment. They are also creating a future support network for themselves in the sense that Abrams' respondent implied.[89] This is one type of reciprocity that develops when there is an imbalance of power between the participants.

The other type of relationship that results from a power imbalance between the participants is best described as an exploitative use of the norm of reciprocity. This type includes illegal moneylending and the illegal trading of shop currency and pawn tickets that took place within working class neighbourhoods (see above). In this type of relationship the limits of neighbourly reciprocity are stretched so that the exchange can no longer be called equal but can be characterised only as exploitative. However, the boundaries between these three types of social action are fluid and it can sometimes be difficult to tell where neighbourly help becomes exploitation. A good example of this is the woman who bought a pawn ticket from her neighbour, described above. It is difficult to tell from this account whether the prime motivation in buying the ticket was to help an elderly neighbour in need, or to scoop a bargain. It is likely, that both motives were present. This is because there is often an instrumental element involved in the solidaristic relationships that exist within the working class. This is due to the interpenetration of different types of rationality. An examination of the use of credit within working class communities shows an interpenetration of the instrumental and affectual spheres of action. (In other words, the overlapping of an element of calculation with emotional ties). This is the basis of the norm of reciprocity that Abrams describes. It is also the central argument of this work, and we shall return to this in later chapters.

Working class communities during the post-war period

To begin with, we should consider an example of the first type of community in this typology: established/'traditional'. A very clear account of this is provided by a retired credit traveller for the Newcastle clothing firm of Locherby's, who started working for the firm in 1947. It should be pointed out, though, that his whole attitude to the colliery villages he traded in is coloured by a wistful nostalgia for a bygone era. It is rooted in the conviction that he was experiencing the life of a community that was preserved unchanged from the pre-war era. In fact, he wrote a Rotary Club Address on the subject of credit trading in which he expresses this opinion — 'The hardship of those days, both physical and financial, produced a quite unique spirit of neighbourliness, compassion, generosity and hospitality.'[90] He goes on to say that the villages he visited managed to retain their old character until the 1970s.

> Unfortunately the 1970s are an entirely different picture. Gone now are the long colliery rows, the roaring fires in black-leaded grates with the stotty bread rising on the hearth. No longer the pit clobber steaming dry in readiness for the next shift.[91]

Despite the obvious romanticisation of the places he visited, this respondent's account does appear to be quite accurate. In some ways the communities he is talking about did remain largely unchanged during the 1950s and 1960s.

He provides us with two concrete examples of older practices that persisted into the post-war era, both of which are also mentioned by Elizabeth Roberts in her study of changing communities in North West England during the period 1940–70.[92] Women continued to 'white-stone' their steps in the way their mothers had done, and laying-out (for funerals) also continued to be performed by a member of the community.

The credit traveller, cited above, felt that this all began to change in the 1970s. He continues with a familiar tale,

> The mining villages gave way to council estates. Our customers now had a front and a back door, and a fence round the garden. And somehow, almost imperceptibly, the old community spirit began to die.[93]

He had a particular reason for being concerned with the death of community (if that is what it was) as it also signalled the death of his business. The younger generation rejected the old credit firms their parents had dealt with, along with the other customs and rituals of the old neighbourhoods.

> The young men and women now handed over 'board money', as they called it, and retained the rest of their wages which they spent in the fast-growing and fashionable boutiques and stores. The older generation still clung to the old ways. They liked to see the traveller and have a crack, but steadily their needs became less and less as retirement and old age took over.[94]

Mrs Blake was the daughter of a miner who grew up in the Blyth area. She says that her parents were eventually rehoused in one of the new council houses purpose-built for miners from the surrounding villages. In fact, the rehousing of the Blyth miners was a gradual process, which began in the 1950s. It was also done with a degree of sensitivity, as whole streets were rehoused together.[95] This is a dimension that is missing from the credit trader's account of the process. Mrs Blake and her husband were married in 1957. They moved into an old terraced house in Cowpen Village, near Blyth, in 1958 and stayed there until 1983. Theirs was an occupationally mixed community, but it was mostly composed of miners and shipbuilders, with a few representatives of other trades. Mrs Blake says that when they first moved into the area it was, 'Like a little village. You had a corner shop, and everybody knew everybody else.'[96]

However, many of her neighbours were much older than her and, as they died, the new residents partly disrupted the old way of life. This happened in various ways, some of which were quite small. For instance, while Mrs Blake's mother used to white-stone her step, Mrs Blake had never done it. If some of the old customs disappeared though, there was still a great deal of socialising among the women in the community. Mrs Blake says they were always 'popping in' to each others houses for tea or coffee during the day when their husbands were at work. This female social network also provided informal aid, just as it did in the earlier period. The main difference was in the form that this aid was likely to take. Aid seems less likely to have been given in the shape of food or money, but Mrs Blake could get a neighbour to look after her children whenever she needed to go shopping. The women in her area would also pass on their children's clothes and toys to their neighbours. During the time Mrs Blake lived in the area, it did not become rougher and more dangerous in the way that some places did. However, even going by Mrs Blake's account alone, there was a degree of change in the community. There is also another aspect to this story which was only uncovered in conversation with Mrs Blake's son, but we should consider her own account first. Mrs Blake said that she was not sure whether changes in the community were due to the fact that the new residents had a slightly more privatised lifestyle, or were simply the result of more women going out to work and, consequently, having less time for socialising.[97] So while the area was not as close-knit as it once was, there was still a sense of community. When Mrs Blake went out to work, in 1975, she still felt comfortable about leaving her youngest child with a neighbour who was not working, and she kept up this arrangement for five years. Although it is now twelve years since she left her old house, Blake has not moved far away, and she is still in touch with her old neighbours.

Mark, Mrs Blake's 29-year-old son, confirmed most of what his mother had said, but he was puzzled by her account of her final years in Cowpen village. Mark said that, although it had remained a fairly close-knit community, and Mrs Blake had got on very well with her original neighbours, during the mid-1970s the area had begun to change. As some of the older residents moved out to live in residential homes, or died, their place has been filled by a new generation of residents. He said, 'It wasn't that you could be mugged or anything, but things were changing.'[98] After the old couple who had lived next door to the Blake family died, a young couple with a child moved in. They had moved from a nearby council estate, and the woman was also the daughter of a local miner. So, like the Blakes, this family also had strong local ties. However, despite this similarity, Mrs Blake did not find her new neighbours altogether easy. Her son remembers much of what he told me next from his childhood, but he had also recently discussed it with his mother, so he was not relying solely on his own memory. The new family next door had begun having violent rows regularly late at night, and which the Blakes could clearly hear next door. The woman was obviously being beaten up quite badly during these rows, and the strain of listening to this began to tell on Mrs Blake. This situation was made worse by the fact that Mr Blake got a job in another part of the country at around the same time. This meant that Mrs Blake was left alone, with her three children, in the house night after night listening to the fighting next door. Understandably, her nerves suffered as a result of this, and her GP eventually put her on tranquillisers. This is the hidden element in her account of why the family moved house. As Mark said to me, 'If it was as great as she made out to you, why didn't they just stay where they were?'[99]

Mrs Blake's experience indicates the ways in which an established/ 'traditional' community can change. It shows how communities continually reconstitute themselves, not least when the inhabitants of old communities are gradually replaced with newcomers. Although this did not completely disrupt the life of the area, it did seem subtly to undermine it. Other people's experiences show how a newly-settled area can regroup over time. It should be pointed out, though, that the boundaries between these areas are often quite fluid. In fact, it is probably misleading to think of an area as representative of only one particular type. So, for example, any individual housing estate may contain parts that are both newly settled and were established. So within any given area there are also micro-communities that have different characteristics from each other. Communities may exist within one of the broad categories I have identified above, but are also continually disrupted and reformed within those categories. This is a complex issue, as some places do not lend themselves to easy categorisation. For example, what about the phenomenon of mass re-settlement (that is, the attempted rehousing of a whole community on a new estate)? Does that create newly settled communities which then have to rebuild social ties, or are residents just able to continue with their lives as before, but with better housing? This was a fairly common project both before and after the Second World War, and we have already seen one example of this in Blyth. Perhaps the most celebrated example in the north-east, though, is Byker. We should now turn to consider the experiences of people in that area.

Byker remained an established/'traditional' community until it began to be demolished, piecemeal, during the 1960s. Malpass and Murie describe the area as it was before redevelopment.

> Byker lies to the east of Newcastle city centre, close to the River Tyne, and was originally developed to provide housing for the industrial working class in the last third of the nineteenth century. The accommodation was overwhelmingly in the form of 'Tyneside Flats' (two-storey houses constructed as flats) at high density and generally lacking one or more of the basic modern amenities of inside w.c., fixed bath and hot-water system.[100]

The area was originally scheduled for redevelopment as part of the 1953 slum clearance programme. However, as so often happens, there was a long delay between scheduling and redevelopment. The Development Plan Review of 1963 proposed to demolish the whole of Byker by 1981 and, between 1963 and 1967, the council rehoused at least 5000 people from the area in other parts of the city.[101] However, at this stage, there were no houses under construction in Byker itself. Malpass and Murie point out that,

> Byker people saw themselves as a cohesive friendly community, and there was good evidence to show that a high proportion of people had lived there all their lives, and that very many of them said they wanted to stay there. Gradually the idea of Byker as a community gathered momentum.[102]

The people of Byker made it known that they wanted to be rehoused together and, after 1968, this became the supposed intention behind the redevelopment of the area. The architect of the new Byker was quoted as saying, '... the redevelopment will be phased so that the people's desire to move from their old worn out house to a new house, down the street, as it were, will be realised.'[103] In the event, the homes of 3000 people were demolished, and many had no choice but to leave the area as their new homes were not built in time; neither were they offered houses in the area at a later date.[104] At the start of the redevelopment, more than 17,000 people lived in Byker. By 1976 fewer than 20 per cent of the original residents were living in the New Byker. The original intention, to retain the community intact, was obviously not realised in practice.[105] So how successful was the redevelopment of Byker in preserving the old community spirit?

The experience of living in Byker today suggests that, if it survives at all, community survives only in pockets or 'micro-communities' within the area itself. I interviewed several members of the Byker Credit Union on this subject. They told me that there was still a limited amount of neighbourhood sharing in the area as well as a degree of sociability amongst neighbours.[106] This conclusion is supported by some of the accounts in Sirkka-Liisa Konttinen's chronicle of Byker. However people today do not feel that Byker is as close a community as it once was.[107] One major indication of continuing mutuality among some Byker residents is the fact that many people trust their neighbours enough to allow them to pay their credit union money for them. Not only that, but the people who do the actual paying are providing a service to their neighbours.[108] Respondents from the Byker area were asked whether there was any informal moneylending going on within their neighbourhood, and they all claimed not. Only one respondent regularly lent money to someone else, and that was to her daughter.[109] There was, however, evidence of neighbours lending money to each other in the Cowgate area, also in Newcastle.

The Cowgate council estate was built between 1920 and 1940.[110] Since then it has acquired the reputation of being a highly deprived area. There is much justification for this, as a recent profile of the area has shown.[111] The area also has a higher than average crime rate. An advice worker claims that the initial response to the idea of forming a credit union in the area was scepticism. '... it was said that the people of Cowgate would steal off their own grannies and how did you expect them to keep accounts?'[112] Such suggestions make it all the more surprising to find evidence of mutuality on the estate, particularly in the form of neighbours lending each other money, yet this does exist.

The manager of Cowgate CAB, Ian Poole, said it was quite common for people on the estate to lend each other money, and that such loans were invariably interest-free. He felt that neighbourhood sharing still took place among small groups of long-standing residents on the estate.

> It'll be pockets of it, and it'll centre around a group of people who may be customers of a catalogue agent living on the estate. So they know that person from time to time will have a pool of money, and we're talking tiny advances. There is no doubt it is about crossing the road and asking for a cup of sugar... That's definitely the case here.

Where the pockets still exist of people who've been here a long time, that's definitely the case, and it's the way they get from one week to the next. If your Giro arrives fortnightly, and your friend's Giro arrives in the interim, then those arrangements are made.[113]

Cowgate was marked by pockets of mutuality, despite an overall breakdown of trust within the community.

The great variety in community is shown by research into the Fenham district, in the west end of Newcastle, where the major/sole evidence was of distrust and suspicion among neighbours. This area provides a contrast to Cowgate, as it is not usually seen as having the same social problems. Fenham is not generally considered to be as deprived an area as many districts in the west end. The council estate in Fenham was built between 1920 and 1940.[114] Fenham was left out of the central and local government initiatives to combat poverty that began in 1973 and were consolidated in the White Paper 'Policy For The Inner Cities' in 1977.[115] Interviews with three women, all members of Fenham Credit Union, about the experience of living in the area provided telling evidence.

When asked if they thought communities had changed since the pre-war period, the respondents replied that they felt that communities were not as close as they once were.[116] Their response was even more emphatic that the Byker respondents. One woman said that she did not consider Fenham to be a community at all.[117] When asked whether, before the credit union had been formed, people in the area lent each other money, the response was general laughter.[118] The group was in total agreement that they could think of no examples of neighbourhood sharing within their area. There was also very little evidence of sociability between neighbours.[119] The women made it clear that they did not feel that they could trust their neighbours either.[120]

Finally, the group was asked about two specific indicators of the existence of trust within the community: help with childcare and with gaining credit. The group felt that childcare should be shared only within families. None of the three women had felt able to trust neighbours with their children.[121] As well, none of the women had ever heard of neighbours obtaining credit for one another in the shape of a Provident order, or a loan of another sort. Neither would they have considered taking out a loan for one of their neighbours. Overall, they did not feel that, apart from through the credit union, people had co-operated with each other over the use of credit in the way that they used to.[122]

It should be pointed out that there was no evidence of co-operation between neighbours over the use of formal types of credit on Tyneside.

Only one of the money-advice workers I interviewed had dealt with a situation where a client had incurred a debt in another person's name. A debt counsellor at Newcastle CAB, said that she had come across clients who had obtained a Provident order in their mother's name, but no cases of neighbours doing this for each other were uncovered.[123] Agents of mail order catalogues do tend to recruit their friends and neighbours as customers but, as they constitute a potential source of profit for the agent, this can hardly be characterised as a form of neighbourhood sharing. How can we make sense of these diverse accounts of working class community in the post-war period?

Working class communities of the first type in the typology, established/'traditional', are characterised by a large degree of internal structural interdependence. So, while they may quite often form a homogenous occupational community in terms of their relationship to the outside world, internally the members of that community perform a diverse series of complementary tasks and services for each other. Malpass makes precisely this point about the old community in Byker.

> There were women noted for their expertise in midwifery or in laying out the dead. The basis of this mutual self-help whether in Byker, Bethnal Green or Barton Hill, was the common class position of the local population. The working class were, and to some extent still are, more dependent upon their neighbours and relatives to help them through the inevitable crises of life because of their restricted access to professional services.[124]

This formed the basis for a form of social cohesion. In the post-war period this social solidarity has been increasingly undermined by the pressure of social change, and it was eventually almost completely eroded in most communities. Again, Malpass has detected this within the Byker area.

> The growth of the social services has tended to redistribute the caring role onto professionals employed by the local authority who come from outside the culture of the working class community and prefer to define problems and solutions in terms of the body of theory which underpins their claim to expertise.[125]

The disappearance of the type of women described above, who perform services such as the laying out of the dead in their communities, is indicative of this change. Practices such as donkey-stoning doorsteps were an indication of the shared norms and values that accompanied this type of social solidarity. However, the decline of the latter type of practice is indicative of a change in shared norms and values, not the complete abandonment of them. This change in values is best characterised as 'modern neighbourhoodism'.

Philip Abrams contrasts the type of traditional neighbourhood social network that we have considered above with what he calls 'modern neighbourhoodism'. He says,

> ...most neighbourhoods today do not constrain their inhabitants into strongly bonded relationships with one another. Those that do are either exceptional or regrettable. Generally the old equation of problems, resources and closure which produced the diffuse trust and reciprocity of the traditional neighbourhood type networks, within which care in 'critical life situations' could effectively be provided for and by local residents, has plainly collapsed in the face of new social patterns.[126]

Here Abrams is discussing the type of change described above, the decline of internal structural interdependence. However, there was also a concomitant change in normative orientation towards neighbours which can be characterised as 'modern neighbourhoodism'. The first point I would wish to make about my conception of this is that it does not mark a complete break with traditional neighbourhood relations. Here I would want to endorse a point that Abrams makes about the continuity between the two periods. He feels that only two features have survived the traditional neighbourhood type: close kinship relations between parents and children, and the practice of gossip. 'Modern neighbourhoodism' is more to do with the feeling that one's neighbours are 'there if you need them', rather than being an active expression of mutuality. This is the conclusion that is suggested by the responses of the Byker residents, in particular.

The two developments outlined above — the decline of internal structural interdependence, and a change in the shared norms and values of a community — are very common occurrences within working class neighbourhoods in the post-war era. They are fundamental trends within social relationships. Of course many factors will influence the development of these trends and the rate with which these changes occur, but they are significant trends in the nature of neighbourhood relations. The third development I want to discuss, a decline in trust, is contingent to an even greater extent. This is a situation that has arisen only in certain communities on Tyneside that have a high degree of social deprivation and a higher than average rate of crime. Two examples of this type of community cited above are Cowgate and Fenham. The Meadow Well estate on North Tyneside provides a further example, and we will consider this area in a later chapter. The main reason this has not been included in this section is that the atmosphere of distrust which exists on the estate makes it more difficult to obtain interviews with residents than was the case with the areas I have included here. Giddens argues that in the modern period the locality is no longer the source of security that it previously was. He makes the point that trust can no longer be anchored in criteria outside the relationship itself.[127] So ties based upon locality (for example) can no longer offer a sufficient basis, in themselves, for trust. This is precisely the phenomenon that we are witnessing today in areas like Cowgate, Fenham and Meadow Well.

Conclusion

This chapter has dealt with social relationships within working class localities. It has also attempted to determine whether they have changed over time. It began with a discussion of working class communities during the interwar period and examined the practical workings of mutuality in particular areas through the use of oral history. An appreciation of this does much to counter the nostalgic vision of communities, while also reasserting the continued importance of the concept of 'community' itself. It is argued that where mutuality was a feature of working class life, there was also an instrumental component. Neighbourhood sharing in working class areas during this period is best seen as a form of credit in itself. This can almost be equated with the latter-day 'LETS' system, in the sense that it was an exchange of goods and services that usually did not involve cash payments. The work of Philip Abrams was employed to explain this, and it was concluded that neighbourhood sharing is governed by a norm of reciprocity. This also applied to the way in which working class neighbourhoods used credit (in the monetary sense). In this case there is often a power imbalance between the participants. This can operate in two ways: it can involve the norm of beneficence, or it can become an exploitative use of the norm of reciprocity. However, the boundaries between these three types of social action are fluid, and it can sometimes be difficult to tell at what point neighbourly help becomes exploitation.

   Three types of community were identified as existing during the post-war period: established/'traditional'; newlysettled; regrouped/partially regrouped; and examples of these types of community on Tyneside have been considered. As we explored the different factors that contributed to change within those communities this opened up a further problem. This led to a consideration of the process through which communities are transformed and a description of the different stages which communities have gone through in becoming regrouped. I argue that working class communities of the first type in the typology, established/ 'traditional', are characterised by a large degree of internal structural interdependence which led to a certain type of social cohesion. In the post-war period, though, this solidarity becomes increasingly undermined. Abrams' notion of 'modern neighbourhoodism' indicates the points of continuity with the older neighbourhoods. It has been argued that there has been a restructuring of the relationship between the individual and the community in very many working class neighbourhoods in the post-war era. However, not all communities necessarily experience the breakdown of trust that has occurred in the most deprived areas.

2

'Taking an Interest in your Neighbours, or just Taking Interest from your Neighbours?' Illegal Moneylending and the Working Class

We can be reasonably sure that moneylending, of some sort, has always been a feature of working class life. Melanie Tebbutt says, 'Various forms of moneylending were practised in most of the less prosperous working-class districts by the end of the nineteenth century, and were perhaps most deeply entrenched in the poorest.'[1] The social investigator Charles Booth found that moneylending was practised extensively among the London poor. He said of one deprived district of London that 'every street has its lender, often a woman.'[2] Although Booth paid scant attention to the issue of moneylending, relegating it to the 'Minor Notes' section of his final volume, he does make two points that are worth noting. Firstly, he implies that while the street moneylenders were usually women there were also male lenders 'in the shape of the man who will "sub" in the public-house'.[3] It would seem that, as far back as the nineteenth century, gender had an effect on the way money-lending was practised. The other point that he makes, and which remains relevant to this study, is, 'There is no legal protection to the lender; terrorism is relied on.'[4]

Of all the types of credit used by the working class, moneylending is, in many ways, the most difficult to investigate. This is not just due to the lack of existing sources, but also to the real difficulty of getting people to talk about the subject. It should be pointed out at the outset that it is for this reason that this chapter is largely based upon documentary evidence (both primary and secondary), and my reliance upon this type of source becomes heavier for the present period. Although a small number of people did consent to be interviewed on the subject, respondents who were willing to discuss other types of credit flatly refused to divulge what they knew about moneylending in either the present or the past. There were several occasions when not only was this line of questioning blocked, but the respondent made it clear that, although he or she has had experience of moneylending, they were not prepared to discuss it. There are several possible reasons for this unwillingness and the researcher cannot make reluctant interviewees discuss issues when they do not want to.

The difficulty of investigating this topic was acknowledged as long ago as 1917 in one of the first major studies of this type of borrowing, conducted by Vesselitsky and Bulkley. They point out that the 'atmosphere of secrecy and gloom which envelopes the subject of loans' was a real impediment to their inquiry.[5] In fact, they found that people were far more willing to discuss their pawning habits (itself a form of credit that was distinctly lacking in respectability) than to talk about moneylending. They go on to say,

> Some doubtless deny the fact of borrowing through fear of prosecution and imprisonment; others resent the imputation as a stain upon their good name; but in many cases reticence was rather due to consideration for their benefactor, 'a poor woman who lets us have money when we needs it,' doing it only to oblige her neighbours, and who, of course, cannot afford the fee for registration without which no one may lawfully practise the business of money-lending.[6]

So all these factors lead to a disinclination to discuss moneylending, and they are all just as valid today, as we shall see later.

Vesselitsky and Bulkley say that there were two systems of moneylending at this time. The first system was available only to more 'respectable' borrowers who could show a clear rent-book or some other form of security. A lump sum was advanced which was then repaid by weekly instalments. Interest was deducted at the outset, at the rate of from 1s. 6d. to 4s. or even 5s. in the pound.[7] Even though there were fines for delay, this system had the advantage of avoiding the excessive compound rates that resulted from the second type of loan where only a few shillings at a time were borrowed. The rate of interest for the second type of loan was almost invariably 1d. in the shilling, and the money was usually borrowed on a Monday and repaid with interest on the following Saturday. As Vesselitsky and Bulkley point out, this works out at 608½ per cent per annum.[8] When a borrower was unable to repay the loan, he or she became trapped in the clutches of the moneylender. This same rate of interest, of a penny in the shilling per week, is also mentioned by Booth and by Maud Pember Reeves in her study of working class families in Lambeth during the early years of the twentieth century.[9]

So who were the moneylenders? Vesselitsky and Bulkley say that there were many different types of lender at this time and, again, evidence from other sources would seem to support this assertion. They say that

> It may be a company formed for the express business of money-lending; or a small shopkeeper who combines money-lending with his other ostensible business...it may be a friend or relative of the publican, who stands by the side of the bar ready to oblige a customer; it may be 'a woman who goes about selling tea'...or it may be 'a woman like myself across the street.'[10]

This description of the variety of moneylenders in London at this time also applied to other parts of the country. Several other observers have offered similar accounts of the period before 1918.

John Benson also identifies several groups of people involved in commercial moneylending. The first were small-scale entrepreneurs (or penny capitalists) active in other spheres. These included street bookmakers, credit drapers, and small shopkeepers, who lent money as an extension of their usual activities. The second group was one of working class people who had managed to accumulate a small amount of capital, through a windfall or by saving. The third group were foremen, who had accumulated the capital from their wages, and the means to pressure borrowers to pay by virtue of their position.[11] As Vesselitsky and Bulkley suggest, another source of funds was the street traders who were so numerous in the early years of the 20th century. One example of this type of lender appears in a Northumberland woman's description of George Bradney, the travelling fish merchant who, '... did well until he became a money lender. Poor George, that was the end of the fish. He got done.'[12]

After the passing of the *Moneylenders' Act*, in 1900, 'getting done' became an occupational hazard for the unlicensed lender. The Act required all moneylenders to register themselves, but the local female moneylenders of the type described above were usually unregistered.[13] We have already seen that Booth noted the widespread existence of local female street moneylenders, and they remained a feature of many of the poorer working class districts, at least up until the Second World War. Several working class autobiographies testify to the truth of this statement. A typical example is given by a Southampton docker's daughter, who remembered, 'Every street had its resident money lender, usually a woman who charged "outrageous rates of interest".'[14]Carl Chinn says that Booth's observation that every street had a moneylender, usually a woman, 'was as true for the slum neighbourhoods of Birmingham in the 1930s as it had been for London in the 1890s...'[15] If we accept that this type of female street moneylender was very common before 1945, then how did they conduct their business? What methods did they use to ensure repayment, given that they could not use the force of the law?

It has been suggested that a successful moneylender needed to be capable of using violence to ensure repayment. It was said that the street moneylenders used threats and abuse and, occasionally, actual physical force to obtain their money. Interestingly enough, though, when the relationship between lender and borrower had no affectual (that is, emotional) basis, the outcome of the transaction became dependent upon who had access to the greatest physical force: 'A powerful friend or relative is often a valuable asset.'[16] In other words, in those cases where the lender resorted to coercion, the outcome was uncertain. Vesselitsky and Bulkley make one final point that remains relevant for today's situation,

> It is, of course, obvious that it would be better to save beforehand against a rainy day, but where the full income is barely adequate to meet the ordinary needs of the household, it is difficult to put away anything...[17]

Tebbut agrees with the distinction that Vesselitsky and Bulkley make between the two types of borrowing but adds, 'It was not uncommon for a woman to be paying for both kinds at the same time and from the self-same moneylender.'[18] She questions whether the alternative chosen was dependent upon status, citing a case of unlicensed moneylending that came before Greenwich police court in 1929. The witnesses in this case referred to sums under £1, for which the customary 1d. in the 1s. 0d. was charged, as 'borrowed' money, while the term 'loans' was used to describe only amounts over a £1, which were subject to a different repayment method.[19] As she points out, Vesselitsky and Bulkley also noticed that the term 'loan' was only used to describe certain types of transaction. The implications of this are quite significant, as it seems to have led to a greater sense of obligation on the part of the borrower to repay 'borrowed' money. Melanie Tebbutt says that working class borrowers placed the greatest importance on honouring small debts. Francie Nichol, who ran a cheap lodging house in South Shields before the First World War, found that her lodgers were so grateful for any financial assistance that they offered her interest 'If regulars couldn't pay, well ye let them go for a bit. Sometimes they'd give ye a penny interest or somethin' when they paid ye back they were so grateful.'[20]

Thus, 'Paying a few pence interest on a small loan also seemed more like recognition of neighbourly help than a business transaction.'[21]

The borrower certainly felt socially obliged to repay certain types of loan. In Birmingham,

> During the 1920s a man from Studley Street remembered that his mother, borrowed 2s. 6d. each week, year after year, from the street's money-lender. The interest charged on this type of loan was exorbitant, at least a penny in the shilling, which worked out at an annual rate of interest of 433.5%. Yet this woman would no more have thought of reneging on her debt than she would have done of leaving the street. To have done either would have meant the loss of her position within the community.[22]

Chinn felt that the urban poor felt a social obligation to pay back debts, particularly those owed to members of their own communities. This pressure must have been increased when the borrower did not look on the transaction as a 'loan' but as money 'borrowed' from a neighbour.

The relationship between moneylender and borrower could take on a different complexion in cases where the borrower began to feel exploited. Tebbutt gives an example of a moneylender who had obviously become excessively exploitative in the eyes of her neighbours. The woman in question was Mathilda Vale, who had been lending small amounts to her neighbours for some time. In 1913 she appeared before Smethwick Police Court and, as a result of the evidence her neighbours gave, was fined. Although her customers were unable to calculate her interest rate, they had begun to feel that they were 'paying through the nose' for loans.[23] The resulting gossip led Vale to send out letters accusing her neighbours of slander. As Tebbutt says, though, the willingness with which these borrowers made their disclosures was unusual.[24] It would seem that in many cases intimidation played a part in maintaining the silence of witnesses. If this was not a factor, the gratitude of the lender to the borrower for providing them with a service would often ensure the continuation of secrecy. Finally, it must be remembered that even if a borrower did not feel grateful to a lender, they may not have had access to an alternative source of credit. So if a borrower assisted in the prosecution of their moneylender, they would be cutting their own financial lifeline. All of these reasons are still relevant today, and make it as difficult as it ever was to prosecute money-lenders. Communities viewed local moneylenders with ambiguity — they were necessary in times of need, but this could lead to resentment as much as gratitude.[25]

The 'street' moneylender on Tyneside

In order to explore the relationship between the moneylender and their community further, we should now turn to consider the evidence gathered for moneylending in Byker in East Newcastle. My research suggests that, in some ways, illegal moneylending was a fairly marginal activity among the Tyneside working class during the interwar period. This was mainly due to the fact that there were other options available which cost the user less. The moneylender was seen as a last resort. In Tom Callaghan's autobiography, which describes Benwell in West Newcastle during the late 1920s and 1930s, he tells us that there was an 'unregistered moneylender' in the street in which he grew up.[26] Moneylending certainly seems to have been quite widespread in Byker during the interwar period. One of my informants described it as an area with a moneylender at the end of every street.[27] She said that these 'street' moneylenders were all female, and she described exactly who they were and where they lived. On the other hand, her knowledge of male moneylenders is somewhat vague: 'There were men moneylenders too. I never knew where they lived. I only saw them knocking on people's doors.'[28] This brings us back to the issue of the difference that gender makes to the way that moneylending is carried out.

A man, whom we shall call Mr Jones, began moneylending as a boy in Byker in 1938, and carried on doing it, illegally, throughout the 1950s. As well as telling of his own activities he also described a female lender, whom we shall call Mrs Black. Although this is fairly scanty evidence upon which to base an argument these two individuals were, in many respects, typical male and female lenders. To begin with, though, let us consider how Mr Jones began moneylending, at the age of twelve. He claimed that he was able to lend money because, as a boy, he had various odd jobs:

> With me being always working in the stables and that, I always seemed to have money, and the lads used to get their pocket money and just spend it. Well when we went to Shipley St Baths here, they couldn't afford to gan, they were skint. So it was a penny to get in. So I used to lend them a penny, didn't I?[29]

We can see that Mr Jones began moneylending quite spontaneously and, moreover, he continues to lend in this ad hoc manner. His motivation for lending money appears not to have been purely instrumental, but he was not acting altruistically either. After a spell in the army, Mr Jones eventually started his own business. Continuing to live in Byker, he was slightly better off economically than his neighbours, who he continued lending money to. His usual interest rate, when he charged interest, was half-a-crown in the pound.[30]

The first point to make about the way that Mr Jones carried out his business is that he offered the same explanation for his high interest rate as any lender operating in a 'high risk' market would offer: 'Some they'd take the money and they wouldn't pay me back. So you gained on one, you lost on the other.'[31] The difference between Mr Jones and a commercial lender operating in this type of market (for example, The Provident) is that Mr Jones did not act in an instrumentally rational way. In other words, he did not conduct his business in a way that would have maximised his profit; instead he acted in accordance with his own feelings at the time. This is not to say that he did not make a profit, as he must have done, but that perhaps in Mr Jones' case there is some truth in the assertion that he gained from one what he lost on another. For instance, it seems that Mr Jones did not charge interest on money that he lent to individuals he knew very well, or had a particular liking for. Mr Jones's rate of interest, though notionally set, was negotiable, because, he reckoned, people would shop around for the best interest rate.

> They'd gan aroond and get the cheapest one. Say they come to me and said, 'Mrs Black's only taking one and six in the pound,' so I'd have to say, 'I'll take one and three.' That's how it went.[32]

Although this seems to indicate that Mr Jones and Mrs Black were in direct competition for customers, for the most part they catered to different sections of the community with only a small degree of overlap. We should now move on to explore the difference between these two lenders.

On the whole Mr Jones lent money to men to spend on drink and cigarettes, and conducted most of his business in public houses, while Mrs Black operated mostly from her own home and her customers were women who wanted money to meet their family's living expenses. Their operations worked like this: there was a moneylender in most pubs in Byker, and some of these were women 'street' moneylenders who simply continued to conduct their business from a table in the lounge. This had two effects: it expanded their potential client group to include men, while at the same time it brought them into direct competition with lenders like Mr Jones. In fact, in the case of Mr Jones and

Mrs Black, if there was any competition between them it was of a fairly amicable nature, as they were apparently on quite good terms with each other. This may have had something to do with the fact that they continued to operate within 'separate spheres' inside the public house itself. As Mr Jones puts it, 'I was in the bar and she was in the lounge.' Finally, Mr Jones would occasionally lend money to women who needed cash to pay for household expenses, if they asked for it, thereby encroaching on the territory of the 'street' lender. However, whenever he did this he always had a great deal of difficulty in obtaining repayment. This seems to suggest that the social mechanism that worked to ensure repayment of loans was gender specific, and did not function outside the male and female networks in which it usually operated.

Mrs Black was older than Mr Jones and had begun moneylending before he had, but he was unable to say precisely when. According to Mr Jones, Mrs Black originally worked as a cleaner and then went to work in various factories. She later became a Provident agent and this, in turn, led her into moneylending and she ended up with a moneylender's licence. Mr Jones describes it like this:

> She worked for her money, and she decided to gan into the Provi, and she says to herself, 'Well I'm getting interest off the firm, I'll lend a couple of bob on me own and get the profit off that.' So she was making both ways. When they came to her house and said 'Ee Mrs Black I duvn't want the Provi 'cause its too dear,' she'd say, 'Well how much are you wanting?'[33]

So Mrs Black used her position as a Provident agent to enable her to select her customers (after all she knew who were the 'good payers' and who were not) and then stopped working for the Provident and set up her own business. Mr Jones says that Mrs Black did not use physical violence in order to obtain repayment of loans, but that she would often embarrass people into paying. She would often do this in the local pub, by making it known to the others present when someone owed her money. This sort of behaviour did not lead to resentment, according to Mr Jones

> She was a straight woman. She hadn't a bad name just because she was a moneylender... She just wanted to make money, and I mean she didn't squander it. She never hurt anybody.[34]

There is an obvious problem here, inasmuch as this is one money-lender's account of another lender. If people did feel exploited by

Mrs Black's moneylending activities they would be hardly likely to tell Mr Jones, who was himself a moneylender. It was not possible to question Mrs Black's old customers, but it was possible to gain some idea of the way Mr Jones was seen by his contemporaries. Mr Jones says that he did not use physical violence in order to obtain repayment, and other old residents of Byker confirmed this. In fact, their overall impression of Mr Jones seemed to be quite favourable. This was a difficult line of questioning, but it is perhaps interesting that although other respondents did not actually condemn Mr Jones, they very clearly disapproved of moneylenders as a group. Typical remarks included, 'There was no difference between them and loansharks today,' and 'What they did was wrong.'[35] Another respondent, Mr Wrigley, whose paternal grandmother was a street moneylender in a colliery village on Tyneside during the 1930s, described the problem that arose when she died:

> She always kept her money in a bag underneath her pillow. I always remember her getting it out and giving me something...When she died there were three sons and a daughter and none of them would go and collect the cash. Even though they were hard up they didn't want to know.[36]

His father used to go scavenging for coal on pit heaps at this time, and his uncles were also very poor. Despite their poverty, though, they felt that it would have been unethical to have taken the profits from their mother's moneylending.

To return to Mr Jones, he remembered,

> A lot of people used to say 'It's wrang for ye to dee that.'[that is, make a profit from lending money]...Well I'd say 'Then it's not right borrowing, because if it wasn't for me they wouldn't survive.'[37]

Mr Jones went about debt collection in a fairly haphazard way, not least because his whole business was organised around his own drinking habits in local bars. This was the reason that Mr Jones ended up writing off a lot of debts. As he puts it,

> If you had twenty clients you might lose two or three. So you used to put them to one side at the end, you know, bad debtors. In fact, some bars you didn't gan in so you never got your money. So it was my fault.[38]

Mr Jones would not go to a particular bar solely to collect money. He would always go wherever he felt like going at the time, and if this resulted in some debts being forgotten then he just accepted that. He says that if a customer did not pay then he simply would not lend them any more money, and this was the only sanction that he admitted to using.

Mr Jones himself acknowledges that his approach was not very businesslike. If we look at what he says about his motivation, though, there is an apparent contradiction. On the one hand he justifies his fairly high interest rate on the same grounds as any other lender lending to low-income consumers (the high risk of bad debt, as well as the fact that they are providing a service that would otherwise be unavailable). On the other hand he feels that his moneylending was part of the everyday mutuality of the community he lived in. He puts it like this,

> Me lending it was just like... to help. To think that I was helping somebody. I mean there's times I'd say as lang as I get my money back I'm happy... Say one of these alang here or in the back lanes [said] 'Eeh Billy I've got me rent to pay, and I owe £5, they're ganna throw as oot.' I'd say, 'Hey, here pay it. Give as it back when you can,' and they did do. There was a lot of people like that.[39]

Mr Jones went on to give examples of the type of neighbourly help that many have seen as being characteristic of the working class during the interwar period and, he said, continued in Byker during the 1950s. When it was put to him that, however altruistic his motives were, his activities were still profitable, his response justified his position:

> It was profitable, but I mean... if you had that money in the bank, you'd be getting interest on it wouldn't you? Well there you are, you're entitled to some interest aren't you?[40]

There was one thing that Mr Jones mentions that is entirely symbolic of the mixture of rationalities that he employed: the use of a pint of beer as interest. Some of the men he lent money to in public bars would simply give him the same amount back with no interest. Instead they would send him down a pint of beer to express their gratitude for the loan. Can we call this 'interest'? How can we explain the apparently contradictory nature of his activities?

If we consider the evidence that Vesselitsky and Bulkley present, then we can see that moneylending could be based purely upon instrumental rationality (that is self-interest) in the earlier period. This is not to say that, even when a moneylender became dependent upon brute force to extract repayment, there may not have been an affectual (that is emotional) component to that relationship in the beginning. It is quite clear from their evidence, and from the other sources cited above, that the relationship between lender and borrower could 'turn nasty', and possibly violent. This was not the case with the relationship between Mr Jones and his lenders, nor, according to Jones, was this true of Mrs Black's relationship with her lenders. Both of these lenders conducted most of their lending within gendered local networks, although there was also a degree of overlap. These networks were based around the street (in the case of Mrs Black) and the pub (in Mr Jones' case). There was, thus, an affectual component to their lending in the first instance and it remained an important part of their practice throughout. We now have to consider the implications of this.

Max Weber said that the instrumental orientation was the dominant one in modern society. However, if individuals are governed by instrumental rationality, how do we account for the way the moneylenders described above conducted their business? It would seem that some further explanation is needed, and this can be found in the work of Richard Munch, who attempted to formulate a new synthesis of sociological theory based upon the work of Weber and Durkheim. He asked how social order could be maintained in a society governed by self-interest. In order to answer this question he makes use of Durkheim's concept of 'interpenetration'. Munch says that social order in an undifferentiated system is not problematic, as everything takes place within the community. However, social order is a problem in more complex societies where the differentiation of various spheres of action has occurred. He feels that there must be some form of 'organic solidarity' for societies to cohere, but that it does not stem naturally from functional interdependence in the division of labour (as Durkheim says), it comes about through the interpenetration of the differentiated spheres of action.[41]

My argument here is that moneylending within working class communities formed just such an interpenetration zone. It is an area where the laws of utilitarian action and the ethics of the working class community interpenetrate. Moneylending took place within gendered affectual networks but was also a very real form of exploitation. However, it was not always experienced as such by the participants for a number of reasons. Making a profit from other members of the community ran counter to the communal ethics of the group, and this is what those individuals who criticised Mr Jones were giving expression to. Yet the practice of moneylending brought into being a new ethic which was censorious of those individuals who did not honour their debts to their lender. A pint of beer is the very symbol of sociability, yet it was used to replace the payment of interest on a loan. In all these ways the utilitarian and the affectual interpenetrate.

So a study of moneylending in working class communities during the period before 1960 shows an 'interpenetration' of the instrumental and affectual spheres of action. It shows that there could be an instrumental element involved in the solidaristic relationships that existed within the working class itself. A further example may reinforce this point. Arthur Harding's autobiography described life in Bethnal Green after the First World War:

> My sister Mighty did very well in the war, when people started buying more expensive things. She was well established down the Gardens as a money-lender and credit clothier, and now that people were getting regular money they came to her more often. All the neighbours came to her and people from the other turnings nearby. After the war she started organising outings for the people she done business with. The people from the Gardens came and people from all over Bethnal Green. They went to Brighton, Southend, Hastings and Eastbourne. Sometimes they had two coaches.[42]

Affectual networks formed the basis for commercial transactions which, in turn, generated new social networks. So we can see that the separation of the communal and instrumental spheres of action can become impossible. This raises a question: is this true of moneylending today?

In the previous chapter it was argued that there were three types of working class community during the immediate post-war period: established/'traditional', newlysettled, regrouped/partially regrouped. During the 1950s, Byker belonged to the first of these categories. The community showed a great deal of continuity, in terms of both the physical and social environment, with the pre-war period. Both Mr Jones and Mrs Black are better seen as examples of the type of money-lender who existed in the earlier period than as examples of the type of lenders created by the changed circumstances of the post-war period. Did the post-war period produce a new type of moneylender? In order to answer this question, then, we will have to look at evidence pertaining to the period after 1960.

From 'street' lenders to loansharks

David Vincent says that during the post-war period,

> ... the local structures of lending centred on the pawnbroker and the corner shop had decayed, partly because of the disappearance of mass unemployment, which began to make poverty more an individual phenomenon, and partly because of the emergence of new forms of debt, which were easier to incur and more difficult to escape. Although street money-lenders could still be found in hard-pressed neighbourhoods, they had to compete with more commercial ventures with better means of ensuring repayment of their high interest rates.[43]

Slum-clearance programmes had been contributing to the decline of pawnbroking, even before the 1930s. The redevelopment of many inner city areas that took place after the Second World War finished off many of the remaining pawnbrokers.[44] The first point to consider about moneylending in the post-war period is that it took place in an entirely different context. Although new types of credit became available during this period, there were no longer as many alternative sources of credit available to very low income consumers. Obviously the entire working class did not belong to this latter category, but a significant section did and, for the most part, no longer had access to a pawnbroker or a local corner shop in an emergency. While this factor may have had the effect of strengthening the power of the moneylender, there were other changes at work that would have served to weaken the position of the moneylender. After the end of the period of austerity, in 1947, Britain entered into the long boom. Increased individual prosperity would have done much to undermine the position of the local moneylender. What happened to street moneylenders during the period of post-war affluence? Does a new type of illegal lender emerge during this period?

In many respects moneylending practices are not susceptible to neat historical divisions. Firstly, with regard to the interest rate there is no significant difference. Contemporary moneylenders do charge extortionate rates of interest (up to a million percent or more in some cases) but, as we saw above, so did 'street' moneylenders in the pre-war period. Secondly, there are widespread reports of the use of violence by contemporary moneylenders but, as we have seen, it could also be used by moneylenders in the earlier period. Indeed, Mr Jones says that many of the other male lenders that he knew used violence, or the threat of it, to ensure repayment. Thirdly, as Vincent suggests, the old 'street' moneylenders do not disappear altogether during the 1960s. They were not totally replaced by a 'new' type of lender, even if they do appear to have become less common. If a 'new' type of lender does gradually become more dominant during the post-war period, what exactly is the difference between them and the 'old' type of lender?

During the post-war period illegal moneylending in working class communities was much less likely to involve an affectual element than it previously was. It is no longer primarily carried out by members of local, gendered, networks. The 'street' moneylender has been partially supplanted by the 'loanshark'. The difference between street lenders and loansharks is not to be found in their rates of interest or in their use of physical violence. A loanshark is an illegal lender who either comes from outside the community in which they operate or, if they live within it, operates solely by the use of terror. In either case there is no affectual element in the relationship between lender and borrower. There were violent street lenders during the earlier period, but most lenders were usually women who were part of a local social network rather than male lenders with a known criminal background.

The difference between lenders in these two periods is reflected in the terminology used in the literature. Virtually all accounts of moneylenders in the earlier period refer to 'street moneylenders', while all contemporary accounts of moneylending refer to 'loansharks'. Peter Reuter offers this definition of loansharking:

1. The true terms of the loan are not legally recorded.
2. Both the borrower and the lender believe that the true transaction is illegal.
3. The use of threats or violence in the event of the failure of a loanshark borrower to make repayment on time, while not necessarily anticipated by the borrower, are certainly understood by him to be a possible consequence of the type of agreement into which he has entered.
4. The interest rate is near or above the legal limit.[45]

Reuter includes the second clause in the definition in acknowledgement of the fact that loansharking transactions are sometimes conducted behind the facade of a legal loan. It should be immediately apparent that this definition could also apply to illegal moneylending in the earlier period. So we cannot make a hard and fast distinction between lenders in the period before 1960 and those in the later period purely on the basis of Reuter's definition alone. According to this definition they are both 'loansharks'. If we look at the literature, though, it seems as if the dominant type of illegal lender begins to change after the Second World War. The stereotypical lenders of the earlier period are those described by Booth (the woman down the street, and the man in the pub). In the period after 1960, though, the typical illegal money-lender is someone who comes from outside the local community. Or, if they do live in the locality, they are also much more likely to be part of a criminal fraternity after 1960.

The crucial development in the post-war period which has enabled the growth of loansharking has been the use of benefit books as collateral. This is vitally important because, as soon as this element is introduced into the relationship, the individuals involved no longer need to have any trust in each other. The lender was guaranteed a return on their investment regardless of the borrower's feelings about them. This is one of the factors which has enabled more individuals from outside communities to lend money illegally. This is not to say that there were not individual moneylenders who did not belong to the communities in which they operated during the earlier period, or that all exploitative lenders today come from outside their host communities. The point is that, before the 1960s, most lending in working class communities was carried out by local lenders based within affectual networks, and that this type of lender has become less common since the 1960s. To substantiate this claim it is necessary to look at some of the literature about loansharking in the current period.

The first point to make is that there is extensive evidence to show that the practice of loansharking is widespread in Britain today. With the increase in the number of people on benefit in recent years, loan-sharking has become a problem in many parts of the country. The introduction of the Social Fund, in April 1988, seems to have done little to alleviate this situation, as it would appear to be unable to cater for claimants' needs.[46] Credit unions are often created as a response to the activities of loansharks in an area, so this is one indicator of the extent of this type of activity. A typical example was the Rhydelefin Credit Union set on the deprived Glyntaff Farm Estate in Wales. This is an estate where 80 per cent of households claim housing benefit and 38 per cent of the families are single parents. Mrs Jean Williams, a community co-ordinator who had lived on the estate for 12 years, told *The Times* in 1989:

> We are trying to find a way to cut out the loansharks who prey on our people. They don't come from the estate, they just drive in and

cause misery. Many of the families have desperately low incomes and can't get credit anywhere else. But many have to take out a second loan to pay the first loan and have to pay interest on both loans — it gets frightening. One unemployed man with six children was having to pay £30 a week. One family I know were going without food to keep up the payments.[47]

Unfortunately it is all too easy to find examples of this type of unscrupulous lending elsewhere in the country.

Investigators from Strathclyde Regional Council spent a lot of time gathering evidence of loanshark activity, to be used to obtain a warrant for their arrest:

> . . . loansharks flourish in areas suffering from a high level of general poverty where they often prey on the most financially disadvantaged members of our society. In the course of our investigations we found that many of those who used the loansharks were one-parent families, families whose sole income was DHSS benefits and even homeless persons.[48]

The Strathclyde team goes on to discuss the type of people that are involved in illegal moneylending,

> The individuals who act as loansharks, lending money at usurious interest rates and using violence and other illegal practices to recover debts, are often small time gangsters and the practice is frequently associated with other criminal activities such as extortion and drug peddling. The moneylenders cannot show themselves to be fit and proper persons to be engaged in a credit business and are not licensed by the Office of Fair Trading under the Consumer Credit Act.[49]

Both Tyne and Wear County Council and Newcastle City Council have also carried out investigations into illegal moneylending.[50]

Under the *Consumer Credit Act* of 1974 it is illegal for anyone to lend any amount of money for interest if they do not have a consumer credit licence.[51] Loansharks have no legal right to demand repayment, and this is why they often use violence, or the threat of it. It is obvious from the Welsh example that the loansharks in that area were not part of the community they preyed upon. It is apparent from the Strathclyde report that the loansharks in that area are not of the type that Booth describes, and do not live in the communities that they exploit. One of the moneylenders they describe lived in the Castlemilk area of Glasgow, nearly 15 miles from the area in which he operated, which was Paisley. Another lived in the Bridgeton area of Glasgow and worked primarily in hostels.[52] They also point to cases where gangs are involved. One of these gangs operated from a shopping centre, which is fairly common among contemporary loansharks. In none of the above cases did loansharks belong to or make use of gendered local networks in the manner that lenders in the earlier period did. Was this also true of money-lending on Tyneside?

Loansharks on Tyneside

There is some evidence to suggest that female 'street' lenders still existed in Tyneside in the 1960s, 1970s, 1980s and 1990s. In 1969, the *Evening Chronicle* published an article entitled 'Victims of the misery makers', describing women who lent money to their female neighbours allegedly in the name of 'neighbourliness': 'Under the guise of generosity, the good neighbour down the street can bring untold misery to many women who cannot handle cash.'[53] The article went on to say that social workers felt that this practice was quite widespread in the North East. It also implied that it was an old practice that had been revived 'in poorer areas of the city', rather than one that had gone on continuously since the interwar period. This could be true but we cannot assume that, before 1969, all parts of Tyneside benefited enough from post-war prosperity to completely eliminate street moneylending. It seems more likely that the practice went into decline during the 1960s. The amounts involved would seem to be quite small, according to the article, ranging from 2s. to a few pounds. However, the interest rates charged were very high, with 400 per cent quoted in one case. This, then, was roughly the same rate as that charged by the more unscrupulous lenders in the pre-war period, and by some contemporary loansharks.

The 1969 *Evening Chronicle* article also quoted an example of an illegal moneylender that conforms more to the stereotype of the modern loanshark (although this term is not used by the writer). The person in question was a man 'who was running a full-time business in illegal lending in several streets', with more than 100 customers.[54] The women he dealt with handed over their family-allowance books as security for a loan. He obtained payment, not through threats of violence, but by threatening 'court action' to those of his customers who did not pay. The article suggested that the old 'street' moneylenders coexisted with the new type of loanshark at this time and, as we shall see below, this was true even more recently.

The first reference to 'loansharks' in the Tyneside district appeared in the *Sunday Sun* of the 12 June 1977: 'High priced loansharks preying on hard-up North-East families are taking State cash set aside for children.'[55] The article stated that illegal moneylending was taking place in Byker, Killingworth, Longbenton and Wallsend. These moneylenders also took family-allowance books as security for loans. The pattern of this type of lending is clearly communicated in the findings of Tyne and Wear County Council's investigation of illegal moneylending:

> This disreputable (and wholly illegal) scheme works this way — the moneylender, through his network of contacts, quickly gets to know when a potential borrower is in financial trouble. He then approaches the potential customer — often a woman, frequently a single parent — and offers a comparatively small loan of money against the security of their DHSS book. The borrower, often desperate for ready money, is in no position to argue. She hands over her payment book to the money lender, first signing a number of payment vouchers, and then receives the loan. Loans are commonly from £30 to £200 and usually go to paying fuel and housing debts.[56]

Once in possession of the payment book, these moneylenders could then use any one of several methods to cash the vouchers at the Post Office as the weekly repayment on the loan. It is perhaps significant that the warning that appears in Tyne and Wear County Council's consumer magazine, *Shop Around*, against illegal moneylending was accompanied by a photograph of a male lender taking a benefit book from a female borrower in exchange for cash. The article was headed by the message: ' ... Don't worry you're not in trouble — he is!'[57] Tyne and Wear County Council's investigations clearly indicated that loansharks were usually men and their victims were usually women, a conclusion supported by an examination of the sources cited above. So what has happened to street moneylenders during the period of the expansion of loansharking?

There is a great deal of variation in the type of localised, informal borrowing that takes place in working class areas on Tyneside today. In the previous chapter we saw that there appeared to be very little moneylending of any sort between neighbours in either Byker or Fenham. In the Cowgate area of Newcastle, on the other hand, there would seem to have been a certain amount of borrowing between neighbours on a non-profit basis. It should be made clear that, whatever the real extent of this type of informal borrowing, it was not great enough to prevent loanshark activity on the estate. The then manager of Cowgate CAB, Ian Poole, said that loansharks operated in Cowgate but people did not complain to the CAB about them through fear of violent reprisals. He said,

> Loansharks have been seen at the queue at the Post Office, which is three doors away, handing child-benefit books through car windows. Those of us in the know, know exactly what they're doing, because the child benefit book is then returned to the car window a few minutes later once they've drawn their money from the Post Office.[58]

Although there was no evidence to suggest that there were street moneylenders in any of the above areas, there was evidence that locally based female moneylenders were still operating in other parts of Tyneside in the 1990s. Advice workers at the Money Matters Project in Newcastle stated that this was the case. They said that the street moneylender was often 'the old woman at the end of the street who lends money for things for the children'.[59] The advice workers felt that this type of moneylender was usually seen as benign, despite the fact that they could charge interest upwards of 100 per cent. This also fitted in with an account of a street moneylender on the Meadow Well estate in North Tyneside whom we shall call Marge the Moneylender.

A female respondent, who had been a community worker on the Meadow Well between 1987 and 1990 (whom we shall call Mrs Flannery), worked closely with a lot of families on the estate, and discovered that many of the mothers she came into contact with were borrowing from Marge the Moneylender. Marge the Moneylender charged interest of 100–200 per cent but was still perceived as benign by her customers.[60] Like the female moneylenders of the earlier period, she lent mainly to women, who would borrow comparatively small amounts of money for various purposes. Mrs Flannery said that one of the main reasons people borrowed from Marge the Moneylender was to repay other creditors. Women sometimes went to her when they were unable to meet their HP instalments or Provident payments. In such cases, the women could later find that they had paid off the original debt but were still repaying Marge a year later! Borrowing often took place for special events such as Christmas or birthdays, or to replace items that had been damaged or stolen. The latter was important, because many people on the estate were uninsured.[61]

Marge the Moneylender fits the stereotype of a street moneylender. She lived on the estate itself, and did not use violence in order to ensure repayment. Mrs Flannery said that her approach to her customers was to make them feel that she was helping them out. She would say, 'I'm just a friend lending you this.'[62] Mrs Flannery felt that Marge manipulated her customers by playing upon their loyalty to her, and that this was a very effective way of doing business. In other words, she was able to manipulate skilfully the affectual element in the relationship for instrumental purposes. Whole families could borrow from her, and this gave her the opportunity to play family members off against each other in various ways. For one thing, it meant that she had the threat of telling other family members if someone did not pay on time. Marge would also use latent sibling rivalry as well. For example she would say, 'Your sister's going to buy X, aren't you?'[63] She was also adept at making her customers borrow more money. Mrs Flannery felt that she could appear to be very sympathetic towards her customers, and it was precisely because she appeared friendly that they took on more debt. She was a street moneylender who was particularly skilled in exploiting the norm of reciprocity. Yet an exploitative use of the norm of reciprocity involves stretching the limits of neighbourly reciprocity so that the exchange can no longer be seen as equal.

An important point to consider here is that the activities of women like Marge the Moneylender were likely to be very limited in terms of their coverage of a specific geographical area. The presence of street moneylenders on an estate does not mean that there will not be any loanshark activity in that particular area. This is true of the Meadow Well estate. The Meadow Well estate saw a Credit Union created to protect the residents from loansharks. In an article in the *Evening Chronicle* (1992), 'Fear: the twilight world of the vicious loansharks', a community helper on the Meadow Well estate said, 'Young mothers here talk about the moneylenders taking their benefit books, then meeting them outside the post office to take half the money they've just drawn out.'[64] It was this type of lender, not the likes of Marge the Moneylender, which seem to be the dominant type on the estate.

When interviewed in 1993 Margaret Nolan from Meadow Well Credit Union she knew of only one female lender actually living on the Meadow Well estate at that time, but that a few years previously there had been more. The reason that there were so few locally based lenders was that those women who were a bit better off than their neighbours had all moved away. Hence the old 'street' moneylender has all but disappeared on the Meadow Well and, it could be argued, had become increasingly rare elsewhere too. Margaret Nolan felt that it was the new type of loanshark, from outside the area, that was the dominant type of lender on the estate today. There is one further dimension to this picture: many people may have become increasingly reliant upon help from members of their own families. Margaret Nolan claimed that while 'street' moneylenders may have become less common in recent years, people were more reliant upon help from particular individuals within their own families, often a father or a grandfather, who has access to a comparatively large amount of capital, typically a redundancy payment.[65] This suggests that the provision of credit may have become increasingly internalised within families (where this was possible) and that there is some truth in David Vincent's notion that poverty has become more of an individual rather than a community phenomenon.

The main difference between illegal moneylending in the pre- and post-war periods is the erosion of the importance of social ties in the later period. Obviously this is a generalisation and street lenders, such as Marge the Moneylender, still operate through social pressure. However such lenders do appear to be less common now than the new type of loanshark, who employs coercion of some description (rather than social pressure) as a means of ensuring repayment. Graham Dixon, the manager of the CAB in Newcastle, said that he had dealt with clients who had debts to loansharks. He found that the problem was that the only way to deal with loansharks was to have them arrested, but this was incredibly difficult to accomplish as arrests were usually followed by reprisals. As he put it,

> If a loanshark is arrested, or whatever, then obviously someone will have to be 'paid off.' The clients are aware that this is a risk and that, if they take it, they may end up with broken arms or whatever else may happen.[66]

The advice workers intimated that their clients had indicated that some loansharks were also members of the local criminal fraternity, thus increasing the potential for violence. Such individuals were likely to live in the area they lent in; in this sense they may be considered as part of the 'community'. They are certainly more likely to be known to their customers than the loanshark who appears only on benefit day. However the mere fact of living in the area does not make this type of lender benign, or imply any trust in the relationship.

Conclusion

There has been a gradual change in the dominant type of illegal money-lender (or loanshark) operating in working class communities. Before the 1960s, most moneylending took place within local, gendered, affectual networks. This did not mean that the relationship between lender and borrower was not based upon exploitation during this period, or that the relationship between the two could not become acrimonious, or even violent, in some cases. It meant that moneylending was an area where the communal ethics of the working class interpenetrated with the laws of utilitarian action in a number of ways. Affectual networks formed the basis for commercial transactions which, in turn, created new social networks. Although this conception of social action is taken from Munch's work on the nature of modernity, it is not adopted in order to reject Marx's analysis of capitalism, but rather as an attempt at refining it. The argument here is that an examination of the social relationships involved in moneylending within working class com-munities shows that there was often an instrumental element involved in the solidaristic relationships within the working class itself, and this is often overlooked in historical accounts of the 'traditional' working class. So the social relationships involved in moneylending cannot be explained purely in terms of the cash nexus.

The dominant type of illegal moneylender begins to alter during the 1960s. The female 'street' lender becomes increasingly rare, while the male 'loanshark' from outside the community became more common. This did not occur because the old affectual networks disappeared, but because many working class areas have become increasingly homo-genous and were thus less likely to contain people who are 'a bit better off' than their neighbours. There is some evidence to suggest that (non-commercial) lending within families may have become more common, thus supporting Vincent's assertion that poverty has become more of an individual rather than a community phenomenon. However, the growth of credit unions in recent years, as a communal response to loansharking, warns against the wholesale adoption of this argument. Finally, although illegal moneylending may have become more heavily governed by pure instrumental rationality during the post-war period, there are also still instances of street moneylending in which an inter-penetration of instrumental and affectual rationality predominated.

3

'The Changing Fortunes of a Petit Bourgeois Chameleon' the Relationship between Small Shopkeepers and Working Class Communities

While we know that the working class has always used some form of retail credit, our knowledge is limited by the lack of available sources. David A. Kent points out,

> Although historians of retailing in the eighteenth and nineteenth centuries agree on the ubiquity of customer credit, the literature, reflecting the paucity of evidence, contains few illustrations of its nature and extent.[1]

He used the documents generated by the workings of the Insolvency Debtors' Courts in order to investigate the issue, concluding, 'Well into the 1840s and beyond, publicans and small shopkeepers were routinely obliged to provide short-term credit to their working-class customers.'[2] This was a potential cause of insolvency for those traders who extended too much credit to their customers. Kent notes,

> Publicans and shopkeepers were especially prominent among insolvents with numerous debtors; they made up 60 per cent of those with more than 21 debtors and over 80 per cent of those with more than 100.[3]

Kent found that 22 per cent of the insolvents in his sample were owed a greater amount of money than the sum they had been jailed for.[4]

The other side of this story was the experience that customers had in dealing with small retailers. In 1845, Engels noted that the poor often became victims of the small shopkeeper. He says,

They must deal with the small retailers, must buy perhaps on credit, and these small retail dealers who cannot sell even the same quality of goods so cheaply as the largest retailers, because of their small capital and the large proportional expenses of their business, must knowingly or unknowingly buy adulterated goods in order to sell at the lower prices required, and to meet the competition of the others.[5]

Engels shows that these small dealers were also notorious users of false weights and measures. In *The Communist Manifesto*, Marx and Engels say that shopkeepers and pawnbrokers both belong to the bourgeoisie, as they exploit the poverty of the workers.[6]

Is this the true class position of this group of people? Although the relationship between small shopkeepers and their customers was based upon exploitation, was it just that? In other words, can we see another dynamic at work in this relationship other than naked self-interest. Or, to use Marx's phrase, is it purely governed by the cash nexus?

The shopkeeper and the community

Robert Roberts had parents who kept a corner shop in Salford during the first quarter of this century. He describes the relationship that existed between the small shopkeeper and their customers in a working class area at that time. He remembers his mother saying, 'In the hardest times, it was often for me to decide who ate and who didn't.'[7] The decision to grant credit was crucial for both the shopkeeper and the customer. For a customer it meant status and security. Roberts says that, 'A tick book, honoured each week, became an emblem of integrity and a bulwark against hard times. The family had arrived.'[8] The shopkeeper, on the other hand, depended upon the right choice of customers for their survival. Roberts describes a nearby shop, very like his own family's, that '...was continually changing hands as one little dealer after another slid into near-bankruptcy and left.'[9] This was the result of granting credit too freely. Assessing the potential credit worthiness of a customer meant taking into account all the factors that might indicate an inability to pay. These included the size of the family, its general health, whether the husband had a problem with drink, their use of the pawnshop, and their previous credit record.[10] If it was granted, though, such a credit facility could become a 'lifeline' for families struggling to survive.[11]

The relationship between the small shopkeeper and the customer could remain amicable as long as both parties satisfied each other's expectations. Basically, the shopkeeper expected to be paid on time, and the customer expected the shopkeeper to meet their need for credit. It was, however, very easy for this balance to be upset if the shopkeeper felt he or she was being taken advantage of, or the customer's expectations of the shopkeeper proved to be too high. One customer who asked Roberts' father for money for the gas meter was met with a curt refusal. His father later complained, 'Damn it all! We lend 'em food, now we gotter loan 'em the light to eat it by! It's not a shop, this, it's a bloody benevolent society!'[12] There would appear to have been an expectation among customers that local shopkeepers would lend them money. Kent found that, in the nineteenth century, many publicans and shopkeepers lent money to their customers. He concludes,

> The frequency with which these tradesmen listed such debts suggests moneylending was a service expected by their customers; indeed it may even have been necessary to ensure continued custom.[13]

While shopkeepers did not take kindly to being asked for what they felt was excessive credit, customers must also have resented having their purchases chosen for them, on occasion, by the shopkeeper. Roberts' father refused to sell 'fancy relishes to them as can hardly buy bread and scran [margarine]'.[14]

Roberts brings out the interdependence of shopkeepers and customers in working class areas. Roberts noted the degree of social stratification within the working class itself:

> Division in our own society ranged from an elite at the peak, composed of the leading families, through recognized strata to a social base whose members one damned as the 'lowest of the low,' or simply 'no class.' Shopkeepers, publicans and skilled tradesmen occupied the premier positions, each family having its own sphere of influence.[15]

He clearly felt that shopkeepers belonged to the upper strata of the working class. They shared the culture of the working class but, on occasion, also tried to ape the manners of the middle class in an attempt at 'betterment'. Roberts' father, however, was a skilled engineer and an active trade unionist. While Roberts' mother was not only a shopkeeper, she performed several services for the people in the area. Roberts says that his mother acted as ' . . . village scribe, communicating on behalf of the unlettered with magistrates, county courts, boards of guardians, charitable societies, hospitals, sanatoria, or soldiers serving away from home.'[16] As well as this, she also offered her services as an unpaid doctor to her neighbours.[17] In this way, small shopkeepers put back some of what they took from communities.

The fact that small shopkeepers were an integral part of their communities can be seen more clearly by looking at parlour stores. Bill Williamson's account of the mining village of Throckley, at roughly the same time, cites examples of small-scale attempts at retailing by the residents themselves on an informal basis. These parlour shops were important in small, isolated, village communities which may not have possessed an official shop. In Throckley, however, they were in competition with the Co-op, where they obtained most of their goods. Williamson's mother stated:

> I remember also in Mount Pleasant and other colliery rows, little shops. Some were huts in a garden; some were in an outhouse in the yard. One was owned by Mrs Barry, one by Cecil March, one by Mrs Donnison, one by Mrs Liddle. These shops were useful for small items. They sold haberdashery, sweets, also food. Most of these people bought stuff from the Co-op, put on coppers, but they did get the dividend from the Co-op for their purchases... [18]

This seems to have been the usual way that parlour stores obtained their goods.

Some of those interviewed for this work said that there had been parlour stores in the villages around the area now known as the Leam Lane Estate in Felling, which were demolished in the slum clearance programmes of the 1930s. One of these shops was in the village of Jonadab. This shop was run by a local woman who purchased all her goods from a nearby Co-operative store. This practice had the advantage of allowing the 'shopkeeper' to make a profit while charging the customer very little above the purchase price.[19] Bill Williamson's mother says that the shops in Mount Pleasant did not offer credit. However the shop in Jonadab ran on 'tick'. So, although some parlour stores offered credit, others did not. Like Robert Roberts' mother, the women who ran the parlour shops also offered a number of services to their communities. They could also act as moneylenders, unpaid midwives, and a community police force, intervening in any disputes. It is difficult to class the relationship between this type of small shopkeeper and their customers as purely exploitative. The granddaughter of the woman who kept the parlour shop in Jonadab said of her grandmother:

> She left a lot of money when she died, but she was a hard-working woman for the community. She did everything. You see in them days, well everybody relied on somebody with a bit of know-how.[20]

The local corner shops helped many people to survive during the 1930s Depression of the interwar years, as the testimonies collected in *Memoirs of the Unemployed* show.[21] Most of the people interviewed obtained their groceries on credit from small stores. This could leave families with debts that would take them years to clear. Shopkeepers may have often offered 'unpaid' services to their communities, they were also capable of unscrupulously exploiting the poverty of those around them, as Engels has suggested. A London house painter, quoted in *Memoirs of the Unemployed*, said small grocery stores in poor working class districts that ran on credit charged approximately 25 per cent more for their goods than did cash stores.[22] On the other hand, though, if their customers fell upon hard times, then small shopkeepers often suffered too.

The interdependence of small shopkeepers and their customers is explored in Melanie Tebbutt's history of pawnbroking and working class credit. She points out that the owners of small shops were usually women. It was also women who applied for credit, and did the shopping. So, like other forms of working class credit, corner-shop credit was predominantly female. Tebbutt is mainly concerned with pawnbroking, but she does make a number of points about back-street pawnbrokers also applicable to small shopkeepers. She says, ' . . . the pledge shop was firmly rooted in the community and trusted in a way which external organizations were not.'[23] This point is brought out in a description of a pawnshop in Liverpool that she quotes,

> The proprietors of this establishment are well known to their customers, they having been born and brought up in the locality, and of course there is a familiarity existing between the proprietors and their customers which is not to be found everywhere.[24]

Like small pawnshops, corner shops were also rooted in the community through local ties, as the experience of Robert Roberts shows. Tebbut feels that, in middle-class areas, there was a different relationship between the shopkeeper and their customers. In such areas the relationship was more servile, as ' . . . the retailer had to ingratiate himself into the customer's favour.'[25] Finally, she feels that the working class viewed pawnbrokers in a different light to shopkeepers. She says that, a sense of mutual obligation often characterised relationships at the corner shop, while the pawnbroker's position was more ambiguous, so their customers had fewer qualms about cheating them.

The gradual decline of the corner shop

Pawnbroking went into decline in the interwar years, but not small shops. Using contemporary estimates, Paul Johnson calculated,

> In 1931, despite the interwar development of department stores and multiples which by then accounted for about 25 per cent of retail trade, something between one-half and two-thirds of the 750,000 retail outlets in Great Britain were family shops, employing no assistants.[26]

However, the proportion of trade done by small, local retailers has gradually declined. Sydney Pollard says that the proportion of trade carried out by independent outlets was: 100 per cent in 1800, 65 per cent in 1939 and 31 per cent in 1980–81. Although small, independent shops still enjoyed considerable success during the interwar period, Pollard shows that by the early 1980s small shops were eclipsed by larger outlets.[27] In his account of consumer society in Britain, John Benson points out that the century between 1880 and 1980 saw the rise of co-operative stores, department stores, chain stores, supermarkets, hypermarkets and mail order houses.[28] Given the multiplicity of new retail outlets developed over this period, it is perhaps surprising that small retailers have not been even more marginalised.

There are several reasons for the continued success of small shops. Most obviously, there is the proximity to the consumer. It is always more convenient to buy things locally, and if this means paying a bit more for them, then this can be offset by the cost of the journey to a bigger shop. Levy points out,

> ...poverty may play a part in preventing people from buying in distant places with their larger shops. Jarrow, for instance, is in a sense an industrial suburb of Newcastle-on-Tyne, it is certainly not a self-contained distributing centre. Yet the poverty of the inhabitants is such that very few of them before the war could, afford even the moderate expense of a journey to Newcastle to do their, shopping.[29]

He also makes the point that the urgency of a purchase can mean that a nearby shop has to be visited in order to obtain it. Charles Booth noted that it was the poorest families who made the most journeys to the shop. He describes one family who not only bought everything on credit from one shop, but only bought items as they were needed. So, as he puts it, 'They go to their shop as an ordinary housewife to her canister . . .'[30] In his study of the lives of the women of the urban poor before 1939, Carl Chinn says,

> Another advantage of the corner shop was that although prices might be a little higher than in shops along main thoroughfares, it was possible to purchase from the proprietor the tiniest amounts of food, from a single rasher of bacon to a halfpenny worth of milk.[31]

The corner shop has always had the advantage of offering small amounts to those who cannot afford to buy in bulk. Finally, as Levy points out, 'There can be no doubt that the giving of credit sustains the popularity of many small retailers. It is an old tradition of the small shop.'[32]

Although they have by no means disappeared, as we have seen, a number of factors have contributed towards the decline of small shops. Peter Scott explains,

> In Britain the early housing estates built under the *Addison Act* of 1919 excluded, the corner shop, thereby favouring nearby centres and string-street developments as well as the mobile shop and the hawker.[33]

He says there are more corner shops 'in old industrial towns containing large tracts of low-income housing' than in non-industrial towns and dormitory suburbs.[34] Corner shops are a feature of old working class areas, even if that is not the only place they are found. It would certainly seem that the newly built interwar housing estates were not supportive of small shops. Ann Hughes and Karen Hunt give the following account of Wythenshawe, a Manchester council estate built during the 1930s.

> Shops were built after the houses and were often left untenanted: rents were high because no subsidies were possible, and profits uncertain because customers were scattered over a fair distance. So the first women to come to Wythenshawe had to rely on expensive deliveries and travelling shops, or walk over a mile, sometimes along unmade roads, to Northenden.[35]

Another contributory factor was the number of shops put out of business by the depression of the interwar years. Tebbutt points out that a number of small shopkeepers ran into financial difficulties or bankruptcy during this period. Shopkeepers were particularly vulnerable during a trade dispute, when they had to balance their customers' demand for credit with their own ability to provide it.[36] Finally, there has been a fundamental change in consumers' shopping habits, with more people shopping in larger stores, particularly after the Second World War. In Lancashire:

> By the end of the 1960s many women had all but deserted the corner shop in favour of the new and cheaper supermarkets usually situated in the town centre and visited perhaps only once or twice a week.[37]

Despite the decline in the numbers of small shops, the tradition of corner-shop credit has survived into the present, even if it is not as widespread as it used to be. Sandra Wallman's 1984 study of eight households in South London showed that the practice continued during the 1980s.[38] It has also been found that Asian families often obtained credit from the local Asian community shops.[39] Evidence gleaned from this and other studies suggests that while this type of credit has not gone away, it has become increasingly rare. In the Policy Studies Institute's 1994 study of how low-income families make ends meet, only 5 out of the 74 families interviewed reported that they ever put things 'on the slate' at their local shop.[40] As we will see, most corner shops on Tyneside no longer extend credit to their customers. That Money advice workers in both Byker and Cowgate had no clients with experience of corner-shop credit is a good indication that corner-shop credit is not widely used in those areas. We will consider the local situation in more detail later.

There are several reasons the corner shop continues to be used as a source of credit by sections of the working class. Firstly, there is the persistence of absolute poverty which requires the use of some form of credit to bridge the gap between income and basic needs. The local shop is an obvious place to begin seeking such assistance, even though it may not always be granted. It may also be preferable to some of the alternatives, such as the Provident or loansharks, which present themselves to those on low incomes today. One informant suggested that older people might use it because it is a form of credit they have grown accustomed to:

My mother-in-law died about two years ago, and up until then she would continuously go and get credit from the corner shop. She would run up a bill of say £40–£50 and then she would pay about £20–£30 back out of her pension, and then she would get the food back again up to that level. She was brought up with it all the time... She never reneged on her credit, but she always got that back again midweek... This goes on in various areas of Jarrow and Hebburn today.[41]

Moreover, as a National Consumer Council report pointed out, 'The consumer can and does programme his/her purchasing behaviour and in the process simplifies decision-making by relying on habit.'[42]

The interviewee felt that, on Tyneside generally, although some people still used this type of credit it was not as widely used as it once was: 'It was very heavy during the 50s and in the early 60s, but when the supermarkets came in it declined, but it was always there for the people who didn't have the cash.'[43] Although supermarkets undoubtedly did contribute to the decline of corner shops, as we have seen, they were not always accessible to the very poorest. One recent nationwide development which has undoubtedly further undermined corner shops, though, is the opening of branches of the supermarket chains Aldi and Netto in deprived areas. As a recent article in the *Guardian* pointed out, both of these companies offer goods that are cheaper than their nearest rival (Kwik Save) as they concentrate on unbranded goods, or goods which were previously unknown in this country.[44] Netto specifically targets low-income consumers, not only by offering a selection of (mainly) lesser-known goods at very low prices, but also by the strategic location of their stores. There are branches of Netto in Newcastle in Kenton, Cowgate, Benwell and Byker.[45] All of these stores are in deprived areas, and two of these areas (Byker and Cowgate) have been studied as part of this research. The manager of Cowgate CAB, Ian Poole, felt that local people had benefited from having a local branch of Netto. He described the shops available to local people,

You'll probably be aware that there just aren't shops here. I mean this is laughingly called 'Cowgate Shopping Centre,' but the only real shop is Safeways across the traffic island. Now you'll probably be aware that Safeways really isn't accessible, generally speaking, to people on income support, although some people from the estate do use it. The real boost has been Nettos here. What I do see there, when I go in and get milk for the bureau, is people who I know are on benefit with a trolley full of stuff that they feel they can afford. So if anyone has been a social service, Netto has.[46]

Small shopkeeping has been gradually declining over the period we are concerned with here, and this decline has been hastened by the rise of supermarkets and discount stores. This process is still continuing today, as Ian Katz says,

> Between 1979 and 1992 the number of shopping centres in Britain almost doubled from 395 to 686. Superstores, almost unheard of two decades ago, now number almost 1,000. In 1980 only 12 per cent of grocery sales were through out- of- town sites now the proportion is about half.[47]

The effect of these developments on the small retailer is spelt out by Derrick Eastwood, assistant national secretary of the British Independent Grocers Association, as quoted by Katz: Put it this way ... '20 years ago there were 70 000 grocers; now there are 30 000.'[48]

Having looked at the changing fortunes of small shopkeepers over the period we are concerned with, we should now turn to consider their class position.

The class position of the small shopkeeper

Rowntree's second social survey of York, conducted in 1936, described the situation of the small shopkeepers in that city:

> Some of these shops were once relatively prosperous, but have lost much of their trade through the removal of the resident population by slum clearance, or through the competition of chain stores or other low-priced shops in the city. Others have never provided a reasonable living; they were taken as a last resort by men who had lost their jobs and could not find regular employment. Again, some of them were originally kept by women to make a small addition to the earnings of their husbands, who were in regular work. But now the men, through illness, old age, or other causes, have fallen out of employment and the shop has become the sole source of the family income.[49]

This depiction of the hardship suffered by some small shopkeepers hardly fits in with the stereotypical image of the prosperous trader. The shopkeepers Rowntree describes are not only proletarian in origin, but their material circumstances have not been significantly altered by their new occupation. This conclusion is borne out by Levy, who points out that the economic and social condition of many small shopkeepers is not always good and they ' . . . frequently cannot earn more than the highly paid industrial worker'.[50] Income is not, however, the factor that determines an individual's position within the class structure, so we should consider how class is to be defined.

The particular conceptual framework adopted here is Wright's neo-Marxist approach to social class. Wright's goal is the development of an adequate Marxist 'class map', which he admits he has not yet achieved.[51] However, Wright's class scheme has been through a number of transformations in the process. He begins by distinguishing between 'class' and 'occupation' before locating individual jobs within his class scheme. Wright's second class map will be explored here, as this is most appropriate to the purpose of explaining the class position of small shopkeepers. It should be pointed out, however, that Wright developed the central concept used here, that of 'contradictory class locations', in his first class map, to explain the position of the 'new middle class' in advanced capitalist societies. This term refers to occupations he felt were 'torn between the basic class relations of capitalist society'.[52]

Wright's second class map reflects relations of exploitation rather than domination. Wright defines exploitation as 'an economically oppressive appropriation of the fruits of the labour of one class by another'.[53] He points out that it is not only capitalists who are able to exploit workers but that 'certain non-owners are able to exploit other non-owners on the basis of their organisational assets and/or their skill/credential assets.'[54] I would argue that this is often the way that working class credit operates. We have already seen one example of this with regard to the parlour stores which existed in more remote villages during the interwar period. This is an example of the way that an informal use of credit by the working class (through shops which had no legal basis) can lead to intra-class exploitation. Another example of this is illegal moneylending within working class communities, which we considered in the previous chapter. Both of these activities give rise to contradictory class locations.

Wright says,

> Within capitalism, the central contradictory location within exploit-
> ation relations is constituted by managers and bureaucrats. They

embody a principle of class organization which is quite distinct from capitalism and which potentially poses an alternative to capitalist relations.[55]

This should make it clear that we are using Wright's concept in a quite different context to the one in which he uses it. This is not done to cast doubts on his original usage of the concept. Instead we are attempting to highlight the complexities that can arise when an exploitation-centred approach is deployed in an entirely different context: not only to relations of consumption rather than production, but also to the informal (rather than merely the formal) economy.

Shopkeepers do not stand in the same relationship to the mode of production as the working class does. It has been suggested that they are not involved in the production of surplus value, but can only convert surplus value created elsewhere.[56] It is probably more accurate to say that they add exchange value, as opposed to use value, to the products they sell. However, small shopkeepers in working class communities are very often proletarian in origin, and they may continue to work in their previous job after they acquire a shop or they may ultimately return to it. This means that, as individuals, their class position is ambiguous and, in the case of those who continue in their former occupation, their class cannot easily be determined by looking at their relationship to the means of production. Even if shopkeepers cease to work outside the shop they may still have strong ties with the working class. So is it more appropriate to view such shopkeepers as part of the working class than as part of the petite bourgeoisie?

Marx saw the petite bourgeoisie as a 'transitional' class comprising the self-employed who employ little or no wage-labour.[57] Wright's definition is consistent with this:

> The only thing which defines the petty bourgeois is ownership of certain kinds of assets — land, tools, a few machines, perhaps in some cases 'skills' or credentials, and self-employment, but not work autonomy. [58]

If we accept this definition, then small shopkeepers do belong to the petite bourgeoisie. However, as is suggested here, it is not so simple. Wright sees the petite bourgeoisie as potentially being neither exploiter nor exploited within capitalist relations, although they can also be either. In fact, Wright does not deal with this group in any detail, as he does not see it as forming the principal contradictory location within contemporary capitalism. This is probably true, but as Wright asserts: '...they will typically hold contradictory interests with respect to the primary forms of class struggle in capitalist society, the struggle between labour and capital'.[59] The argument here is that, although small shopkeepers must be seen as part of the petite bourgeoisie, they form a contradictory location within exploitation relations in a way that other members of the petite bourgeoisie do not. This is because, as Marx and Engels point out, they exploit the poverty of the workers. However, their objective material interests and their cultural predisposition can also lead them to side with the working class in a struggle between labour and capital.

It may be useful, at this point, to give a specific contemporary example of this. One concrete way in which small shopkeepers often side with the working class is to support their struggles against workplace closures. As we saw above, the fortunes of small shopkeepers and the communities they serve are so interdependent that it is in the interests of small shopkeepers to support such struggles. This tendency was seen with particular clarity during the miners' strike of 1984–5. In *The Enemy Within* Raphael Samuel *et al* looked at the effects of this strike on mining communities. Their informants describe the reactions of several local shopkeepers to the strike. We now consider some of these accounts.

The first is of what sounds like a straightforward act of solidarity.

> The majority of shopkeepers have been great. For example, there's a guy over the road who sells bread, and every day he sends over four or five dozen bread cakes for pickets. He never takes money for them. We've been over and tried to pay him, 'cos we know what's happening to his business, but he will not take the money.'[60]

Here is a similar account of the relationship between the miners and the shopkeepers.

> Most of the shops in the village are pretty good with you if you're a miner. There's a video shop round the corner from us. It gives videos for half price to try to help us any way they can.[61]

This miner went on to say that there was also another dimension to this solidarity, as those shops which served policemen have subsequently lost business. Due to the role of the police in the dispute, the attitude of local shopkeepers towards them became a major issue. A shopworker also pointed out that shops serving police from outside the area had had their windows broken.[62] Despite the presence of some coercion, though, the fact remains that it was in the interests of shops in those communities to support the strike. This identification with the working class does not occur only in times of struggle. As Willmott and Young note of East London, shopkeepers and publicans in that area were '...in many ways more akin to the working class people they serve than to the professional men and administrators with whom they are classified'.[63]

It is not going to be argued here that all shopkeepers will feel such empathy with the working class. The owners of larger retail outlets can be located in the bourgeoisie proper, due to their status as large employers (and thus exploiters of labour power). This point is made by Vigne and Howkins in their discussion of the role of the small shopkeeper in Salford, Bolton and Liverpool before 1918. They say,

> Shopkeepers do not in any sense represent a unified stratum or class but are rather to be seen in the very specific context of the area in which they work and particularly in the spread of their trade.[64]

Vigne and Howkins go on to discuss the variations in their circumstances, 'For some were owners of property and capital and employed staff while others had assets which were scarcely more and sometimes less than a working man.'[65] Having established the historical context and discussed the class position of the small shopkeeper, we should now go on to consider the implications of the contradictory class location of small shopkeepers for social relationships in working class communities in more detail. In order to do this, we should first review the literature that deals specifically with the social position of small shopkeepers.

The Petit Bourgeois Chameleon

The difference in circumstances that Vigne and Howkins identify meant that some small shopkeepers felt uncertain about their class position, while others were able to identify firmly with either the middle-class or the working class. Vigne and Howkins felt that there were several reasons for the variety of class attitudes held by small shopkeepers. The first is the fact that shopkeeping was not usually a job they performed all their lives. Shopkeepers tended to have had experience in another area of work, at an earlier or a later stage, or even at the same time as working in their shop. Vigne and Howkins found that, in at least 41 per cent of the shopkeeping families they interviewed, wives and mothers took an equal or greater share in shopkeeping than their husbands. They make the point,

> As class membership is customarily and officially designated by the occupation of the male parent, the effect on class consciousness of female parents holding jobs of equal or superior status to their husbands' must have been significant.[66]

Vigne and Howkins conclude that small shopkeepers were more convinced of their status within the community than of their class position.

They then examine the social position of small shopkeepers as their neighbours perceived it, suggesting there are two main factors affecting their respondents' placing of shopkeepers:

1. Their own individual social class and standing in the working class and community.
2. The type of community in which they lived, whether socially diverse or homogeneous.[67]

Salford has been taken as the archetype of a self-contained community with an insularity that shaped the residents' perception of class.[68] Their respondents stressed the economic power that the Salford shopkeepers had through the granting or withholding of credit, and the fact that they were a bit better off than the rest of the community. The Salford respondents tended to see shopkeepers as an elite, while Bolton people did not feel that they ranked very high socially. This is partly due to the fact that all except one of the Bolton sample lived in close proximity to the local bourgeoisie, and they were aware of who the 'real' elite were in their town. Liverpool respondents, by contrast, displayed a more diverse set of attitudes to shopkeepers. One Liverpudlian again stressed the influence of those who gave credit,

> They provided the tick whereby you lived. This is the kind of thing you see ... I mean even the clothes you wore were on tick — they were on credit, nothing bought for cash.[69]

As in Bolton, though, the shopkeeper was not seen as being of any great social importance, due to the simple fact that richer people lived nearby.

The evidence presented about Salford does not contradict Robert Roberts' opinion that, in that particular district, small shopkeepers were perceived as belonging to the upper strata of the working class. In fact, it suggests that shopkeepers occupied a position equivalent to that of the skilled working class in their communities, who would seem to have regarded shopkeepers as their social equals. In his discussion of the Oldham working class during the nineteenth century, John Foster draws a similar conclusion:

> The small shopkeepers held a key position in the working community and seem to have been fairly closely associated with the 'labour aristocracy.' Many were themselves retired spinners and engineers (or members of their families) and judging by marriage patterns close links were maintained.[70]

It seems that in many ways small shopkeepers were social chameleons. They took on the character of the neighbourhood they inhabited. This is the point that Christopher P. Hosgood makes in his study of small shopkeepers during the period 1870–1914. He says, 'It seems that they had the ability to assume the class identity of the community which they served.'[71] Hosgood argues that small shopkeepers should be seen as integral members of working class communities, even though their position within these communities was ambiguous. This ambiguity centred around the provision of credit to the community.

> Economically, by acting as the 'bankers of the poor', shopkeepers were able to exert much influence over the neighbourhood. However, they also recognized that in times of hardship they had a certain obligation to provide either a credit lifeline or preferential treatment to regular customers.[72]

Hosgood points to the contradictory nature of the outlook of the small shopkeeper: on the one hand they had a desire for personal independence; on the other they seem to be motivated by a sense of social duty. Hosgood seeks to counteract the view, expressed by Geoffrey Crossick and others, that small shopkeepers were embattled little men and women who did not interact with their community.[73]

Small shopkeepers became particularly important to the life of the community during times of economic hardship, whether this was the result of economic depression or of industrial conflict. Hosgood makes the point made above, about the ambiguity involved in provision of credit during times of hardship. Some shopkeepers' motives for providing credit in such circumstances may not have been humanitarian or solidaristic but instrumental, as they may have done so only to retain customers. He goes on to give an example of the type of help that shop-keepers offered their neighbours in times of distress: the Leicester shoe industry lock-out of 1895 which put 23,000 shoehands out of work. Hosgood shows how the hardship that the strikers were experiencing soon spread to the shopkeepers who depended on their custom. Some shopkeepers even attributed their bankruptcy to the dispute. He says,

> To combat the distress affecting both shopkeepers and customers, domestic shopkeepers formed a number of ways and means' com-mittees, which had the power to confer upon out-of-work families the right to a special tariff of prices. Shopkeepers and union leaders met to ensure that workers' strike pay could go as far as possible.[74]

Neither was this an isolated example of this type of action. In 1904, during a time of recession, a number of bakers in Leicester distributed loaves to the unemployed. Vigne and Howkins also point to examples of shopkeepers who took part in the common charitable effort of the district to feed poor neighbours. Historically, then, small shopkeepers have offered material support to their customers in times of economic hardship. Hosgood goes on to point out a further way in which shop-keepers played an important role in their communities, by acting as treasurers of the poor.[75] They did this through the provision of food clubs and Christmas or 'Goose' clubs. As he says, though, contemporary views of these clubs varied considerably.

Hosgood begins his analysis of shopkeepers' place within working class culture by acknowledging the importance of Ellen Ross's claim that working class culture was a compound of male and female cultures, as husbands and wives inhabited separate worlds. Hosgood argues that local shops should be seen as a 'social as well as economic nexus' that operated within the female world.[76] As female leisure was integrated into their workplace, that is the domestic world, the local shop was an important site of sociability. This function of the corner shop was facilitated by poor families' habit of making small, frequent purchases. Hosgood points to evidence, from the autobiographies of Robert Roberts and others, of the way that shops could become an important centre of local gossip. He also makes the point that shopkeepers were not passive onlookers in their communities, as this quote from the daughter of a Chatham greengrocer shows.

We enjoyed the company. We enjoyed seeing people, and we learned to mix with everybody . . . and you were never lonely, not when you could talk to anybody.[77]

However, while shopkeepers were integrated into the female side of working class culture, they were largely absent from the male cultural world of friendly societies and working men's clubs.

Shopkeeping was seen by many workers as a means of escaping waged labour, but this escape was not always permanent, as Hosgood makes clear.

By the end of the nineteenth century, the turnover rates of small traders were quite phenomenal. Of all general shopkeepers and greengrocers in business in 1882, only 28 per cent and 14 per cent respectively remained a decade later. Clearly, the majority of workers who embarked on a career in retailing were not permanently escaping their former occupations. Failure in business returned them to the world dominated by the workshop and the factory, if indeed they had ever entirely left this world.[78]

Many small shopkeepers had a rather precarious foothold in the petite bourgeoisie. Nevertheless there were always those who were attracted by the ideal of independence shopkeeping offered them, so the trade was never short of new recruits. Hosgood points out that, on occasion, shopkeepers actively defended the lifestyle of the working class, with regard to their drinking and shopping habits for example. He argues that it was because shopkeepers were an integral part of working class communities that they defended working class values. Hosgood sets this view of small shopkeepers against John Benson's claim that shopkeeping was a divisive force in the working class because it engendered a spirit of individualism.[79] We should now turn to consider a contemporary study of small shopkeepers.

The most significant piece of sociological research into the social position of small shopkeepers in recent years has been conducted by Frank Bechhofer and others. This research has appeared in various forms. What follows is a summary of the team's findings and their ongoing reflections on the subject, rather than a consideration of each piece individually. The first point to consider is that their findings and conclusions bear a remarkable similarity to Hosgood's. Their starting point is that small shopkeepers are neither bourgeois nor proletarian but are members of the petite bourgeoisie. Bechhofer and Elliott also argue,

> The petite bourgeoisie is like a chameleon, taking its colour from its environment. Thus, the precise nature of relationships with manual workers, with peasants, with factory owners, capitalist farmers, with migrant labour or foreign employers varies widely.[80]

They see small shopkeepers as a social anachronism in many respects, as their values and attitudes seem to belong to an earlier age. Finally, like Hosgood, they found that the idea of independence was centrally important to small shopkeepers.

The Bechhofer study of small shopkeepers was conducted between 1967 and 1972, with a sample drawn entirely from Edinburgh: 398 shopkeepers and their spouses were interviewed between August 1969 and July 1970.[81] They feel that small shopkeepers are governed by what Max Weber termed 'economic traditionalism' in all aspects of their business. The shopkeepers in their sample were resistant to new ideas about how to run their business and did not want to build up their business in any major way. In other words, their attitude was not that of the determined entrepreneur, and their outlook was distinct from that of the capitalist class. Bechhofer *et al* argue that their outlook is also quite distinct from that of the working and the middle class. I would agree with this, and would add that this flows from their contradictory location within the class structure. Part of the reason for the distinctiveness of this group is that they come to rely heavily on their own resources and those of their family, as the whole family is usually involved in running a small shop.[82]

The similarities between the findings of the Bechhofer study and those of Hosgood suggest that there is a great deal of historical continuity in the social position of the small shopkeeper. There are two further points of continuity to be drawn out. The first is quite simply that the occupation is still characterised by relatively high 'economic mortality' rates. Bechhofer *et al* estimated that '...approximately 20 per cent of Edinburgh's shops were 'failures', and closed or changed hands at least once every six to twelve months.'[83] This suggests that small shopkeeping still provides a fairly precarious foothold in the petite bourgeoisie, and may still often return many workers to the workplace they originally escaped from.

Secondly, Bechhofer *et al* see the relationship between the small shopkeeper and the working class community in very similar terms to Hosgood. They point out,

The nature of the occupation and especially its work situation is such that it offers occupational mobility without social mobility and herein lies one of its most intriguing aspects for the student of social stratification.[84]

This means that a manual worker could acquire a shop and retain his/her old social network. This is further facilitated by the isolation of the small shopkeepers from their peers, and the lack of associational life within that occupation. This leads them to say,

There is certainly a small group (approximately 10 per cent of the sample) who come from manual backgrounds, who run shops in working class districts, and who live in those same areas. It is entirely possible that some of them will share working-class culture in a great many respects.[85]

The above quote comes from a 1974 paper, when the team's analysis of their findings had not been completed. In a later piece they point out that although social origin has little effect on voting behaviour the location of the shop does make some difference. This means that 'those whose shops are in clearly working class areas are rather more than twice as likely to say they will vote Labour'.[86] This returns us to our original point: as a result of their contradictory class location, small shopkeepers are petit bourgeois social chameleons. Having explored the secondary literature, we should now turn back to consider the implications of their social position for small shopkeepers before the Second World War.

Class and contradiction

So far we have established that small shopkeepers in working class areas were quite often of working class origin even though, in the act of becoming shopkeepers, they joined the petite bourgeoisie. They were part of the communities that they served, and they enjoyed a position within their community similar to that of the labour aristocracy. However the ambiguity over their social position meant that small shopkeepers did not necessarily identify themselves with the working class. As Bechhofer *et al* point out, small shopkeeping offers occupational mobility without social mobility. This seems to have given rise to two types of outlook: those shopkeepers who were happy to be an integral part of the local community, and those who sought to remove themselves from it.

Examples of the first type of shopkeeper were to be found all over Tyneside during the interwar period. How were these small shopkeepers perceived by the local working class? If we take the case of one such family in Byker that several respondents mentioned, the Cowans, it would appear that they were not seen to be significantly different from their neighbours. As one woman put it,

> He was just like us, but he was a bit better off on account of he had his Business . . . They were very nice people. In fact, when I had my last baby they bought the dress for the bairn.[87]

The author of the CDP's history of shopkeeping in Benwell in the west of Newcastle says,

> The typical Benwell small shopkeeper of the early 19th century was locally-oriented, relating not to the wealthy middle classes of Old Benwell but to the local working class community. One of the most active founder members of the Cochrane Street Working Men's Club, for example, was Charlie Thompson who ran a barber's shop on Adelaide Terrace.[88]

There were also shopkeepers who seemed to be doing their best to distance themselves from the local community. The Bramble family were a notable example of this type of shopkeeper in Benwell. They set up business in Adelaide Terrace in the 1880s as boot and shoe manufacturers and general dealers. William Bramble was also an important landlord in Benwell. One resident said, 'He owned nearly half of the Terrace. He used to come along in his frock coat, gaiters and top hat, collecting the rent.'[89] After their fortunes improved, the Brambles moved from Adelaide Terrace into Benwell Hall, a large house with its own grounds. This move was symbolic of the family's intended upward social mobility. However, the author of the study felt that although the Brambles distanced themselves from small shopkeepers in the area, they never quite made it into the bourgeoisie proper.[90]

It would seem that there were shopkeepers who actively sought upward social mobility as well as shopkeepers who were relatively content to remain within their communities. Yet, we cannot necessarily draw a hard and fast distinction between them. Some shopkeepers may have remained within working class communities, and even played an active part in the life of those communities, but still yearned for social betterment. Robert Roberts' mother would seem to be a case in point here as, although she did become an integral part of her local community, she had strongly objected to moving to the district in the first place. In fact, she agreed to move into the Salford shop only on condition that the family move on after two years.[91] This suggests that, even the most 'integrated' small shopkeeper may feel a degree of ambivalence towards their community.

Let us now turn to the other question raised at the beginning of this discussion. What exactly is the relationship between small shopkeepers and their customers. And, how is this relationship conditioned by the contradictory class location of small shopkeepers? The contradictory class location of small shopkeepers would appear to result in contradictory attitudes towards their working class customers. There are those shopkeepers who would appear to have no empathy at all with their customers, and also to take every opportunity they get to cheat them. There are shopkeepers who appear to take part in the life of the local community and deal sympathetically and honestly with their customers.

Paul Johnson gives an example of each of these types of shopkeeper in his description of corner-shop credit before 1939 and, taken together, they provide a further illustration of the type of attitudes described above. The first was written by Miss Llewelyn Davies in 1899 as part of a survey of life in a poor district.

> The kind of shops you notice are first of all small general shops, where the trade is almost entirely a 'booking' one. The terrible debt burden is round the necks of most of the people, and the object of the small shopkeeper is to fasten it securely there. Not only are high prices (that is, compared to the quality) charged, as is natural and inevitable, but the accounts are often falsified — the 1d. slipping into the 1s. column — and the customers are often so ignorant and helpless that such things escape notice.[92]

The second comes from Francie Nichol's description of the general dealer's shop that she ran in South Shields, on Tyneside, from 1935 until the war.

> ... poor people make good customers. They can't always pay on the dot, but they're honest if you trust them. And they can never be bothered to shop around. If they know where they can get all they want handy then that's where they'll go. They like a place where they can come in drunk and know you'll give them the stuff they want even if they've forgotten what they came in for ... They want

a place they can come in with their curlers or in their slippers and dressin' gowns. They know you aren't goin' to diddle them by Bamboozlin' their little bairns if they send them in with a message.[93]

We have already seen how shopkeepers can display either of these attitudes towards their customers. Some shopkeepers did 'bamboozle' their customers; others, like Robert Roberts' family and Francie Nichol, appear to have dealt honestly with their customers. So, is there a clear distinction between these two types of shopkeeper, or can both of these attitudes be held simultaneously?

Engels points to some of the ways that certain small shopkeepers cheated their customers, and it is easy to find other nineteenth century accounts that do the same. Janet Blackman points out that local Co-operative societies '...were set up primarily to serve the workers' families who had suffered at the hands of local well-established shop-keepers'.[94] She gives the example of Stocksbridge, near Sheffield, where people had

...complained of discriminatory pricing, of inferior stock sold as the best quality, for example tub-butter sold to the workers as fresh butter, and insults from the shopkeeper if comments were made about such trade practices.[95]

It seems likely that this disdain for the industrial working class was the result of two things. Firstly, up until the middle of the nineteenth century many grocers had not had to deal with the labouring poor. As J.A. Rees points out, 'the grocer had been up to 1846 at any rate ... a minister of luxuries to the rich.'[96] So they may have resented the extension of their trade to embrace the growing urban proletariat. As well as this, not all the grocers of the mid-nineteenth century were, like the small shopkeepers of Benwell, of working class origin. As a result, they would not necessarily feel any empathy with their working class customers. It is not, perhaps, until later in the century that men like Robert Roberts' father began to dominate this type of trade.

It has been suggested, then, that the character of the small shop-keeper may have undergone a change during the nineteenth century, and that this may have resulted in a more sympathetic attitude towards their working class customers. Thus, while they profited from the community they also served it in other ways, as Robert Roberts' mother did. Such involvement in the life of the neighbourhood was not uncommon, though it was by no means universal. Even if there was a change in the social background of small shopkeepers, with more shopkeepers originating from the working class, this did not always mean that they were content to remain an integral part of the communities they came from, as the Benwell evidence shows. The exact nature of the relationship between the shopkeeper and the community was dependent upon the personal characteristics, and possibly the social background of, the shopkeeper. Despite their objective position as exploiters of their communities, local shopkeepers could be perceived as either friends or foes by their neighbours. In other words, the relationship that existed between shopkeeper and customers was contingent upon a number of factors, and this was a result of the ambiguity of their class position. However, I would argue that this should not lead us to make a simple distinction between 'good' and 'bad' shopkeepers, as the way that individual shopkeepers were perceived by their communities is not necessarily a good indication of the way that they conducted their business. This is because there are a number of difficulties involved in examining the behaviour of small shopkeepers towards their customers.

The first of these is suggested by Engels when he says that small shopkeepers may 'knowingly or unknowingly buy adulterated goods'.[97] In other words, it is difficult to tell whether some of the abuses of their position are intentional or not. In contrast to Robert Roberts' mother, Francie Nichol 'yearned' for the small shop that she eventually became the owner of and, as we saw above, she certainly displayed a sympathetic attitude towards her customers. However, after the outbreak of the Second World War, she was prosecuted for selling bags of flour that were underweight. She says that this was not intentional, and offers a perfectly credible explanation of how the goods came to be underweight in the first place.[98] She says, 'It was wrong for anybody to cheat poor people and my customers were certainly poor.'[99] The problem with this type of evidence is that, although her depiction of herself as an innocent victim is plausible, ultimately we only have her word for it. The second problem is that customers' perceptions are not necessarily reliable. This is because, as we shall see below, it may well be coloured by their feelings for a particular shopkeeper. A further consideration is the difference which the location of a shop made to the power relationship between shopkeepers and customers. For example, it would have mattered whether an area was 'rough' or 'respectable'. Some shopkeepers in poorer working class areas continued to overcharge their customers for credit during the Depression of the interwar years, even though their customers may have been dependent upon them for their survival. However, shops in more affluent working class areas may not have offered credit to their customers, even at this time.

It would seem that during the interwar years small shops in areas that housed the skilled working class did not usually offer credit. If we compare accounts of Byker and Heaton during this period, we can see that there was certainly a difference between these two areas. One of the respondents of this survey lived in the Heaton area of Newcastle during the 1930s, an area that, as David Byrne says, housed the 'respectable' working class during this period.[100] In fact, it was one of the strongholds of the 'labour aristocracy'. My informant told me that the local food shops did not give credit, and they usually displayed a sign informing their customers that credit would not be granted.[101] She felt that it did not fit in with the ethos of the respectable working class to obtain groceries on 'tick'. In fact, she knew of only one woman who did manage to obtain credit from a local shop, and this led to a great deal of marital conflict when her husband found out.[102] However, this type of credit was freely available in Byker (an area of Newcastle that housed less skilled members of the working class) during the same period. The point here is that in those areas where no credit transactions took place, small shopkeepers were in a less powerful position within the community. In other areas, working class customers were largely dependent upon the honesty of the local shopkeeper.

There were a number of ways in which small shopkeepers could abuse their economic power within the neighbourhood. Some of these, such as the selling of adulterated goods and the use of false weights and measures, are described by Engels. However, as we have seen, it may not always be clear whether such practices were deliberate or not. Even if we concentrate our attention only on credit transactions, the evidence is ambiguous.

Obviously the first question that we need to answer is: did small shops charge interest? Paul Johnson makes the point that it can be difficult to calculate the cost of shop credit to the consumer as, '...interest was often charged indirectly by selling inferior goods at inflated prices to customers tied by their tick book to a particular shop.'[103] Some of my interviewees claimed that corner shops never charged interest, while others cited specific cases where they did. One respondent described a small general dealers on Bensham Road in the Bensham area that her mother worked in:

> The goods were top prices. When they bought goods it was itemised in the book and totalled up when they came to settle. Often it was more than they could afford, so it was carried forward to next week.

Their books were never clear. My mother was told to add two shillings to their bill each day.[104]

What is not always clear in such accounts is whether the customer knew they were being charged interest. If we return to the shop in Byker mentioned above (Cowans') respondents offered two conflicting accounts of the shop's trading practices. One interviewee said,

> We all shopped there because we didn't bother going very far for shopping. Well we didn't have money to go on the trams. Things were a wee bit dearer there, but we were glad of it, because we got tick all the week until pay-day.[105]

This woman said that Cowans charged about a ha'penny more than other shops for the goods themselves, but that they did not charge interest. She did not feel exploited by the shop, even though it was a bit more expensive, as she felt 'he knew we couldn't pay exorbitant prices.'[106]

A male respondent painted an entirely different picture of the shop:

> They sold everything...owt you wanted, put it on the tick bill, and she'd put her extras on y' see...Say it was two shilling for a pound of bacon, y' know just a rough idea, well it would be three shilling if you got it on tick.[107]

So this man felt that they had two different prices: one for cash customers, and one for those who bought on credit. How can we explain this discrepancy between the two accounts?

In this particular instance it could be due to the fact that the woman interviewee knew the family better than the man, and her attachment to them may have coloured her memory of the past. Alternatively, she may not have been aware of just how much extra she was being charged as a 'tick' customer. Of course, the male respondent's account could be wrong; but it is, perhaps, more likely that the woman was unaware of how much extra she was being charged. It is also more characteristic of people to idealise the past, even in such a small way, than it is for them to imagine that they were being charged for something that they weren't. Another interviewee gave this account of corner-shop credit during the interwar period in Gateshead:

> My children were all well fed (for the period) and this was probably due to the fact that the corner shops would extend credit on a week

to week basis, but the prices were above those charged in the larger stores such as Liptons, Walter Willson's, Kemps etc.[108]

This man also said that corner shops did not charge interest to 'tick' customers, although he concedes that they were more expensive than other shops. So it is impossible to generalise about this question. All we can say for certain is that some corner shops did charge interest, but it is not apparent whether their customers always knew this. Then, as now, corner shops were more expensive than larger stores but the amount that the shopkeeper added on for credit customers (if any) probably varied greatly from shop to shop.

Another of my respondents offers a deeper insight into the ways that shopkeepers could covertly charge for 'extras'. This is a practice that I shall call: 'creative pricing'. This woman, whom we shall call Mrs Wrigley, worked in a corner shop in a working class area on the banks of the Tyne during the Second World War. Most of the customers of this shop obtained their groceries on 'tick'. She says that all the customers (cash or credit) were actually being charged more than they realised.

> When the customers came in and they wanted cheese it was one and tuppence a pound but, when you looked on the chart at the back, he charged one and four. That allowed for your wastage, you know when you cut bits of cheese and you have spare. So the customer paid for the wastage, and the same with the bacon ... [109]

One particular incident that Mrs Wrigley described says a lot about the way that small shopkeepers used 'creative pricing' to maintain good relations with their customers.

> This lady come in and swore blind she had paid her bill. Well when you paid your bill it was written in the book. Of course it wasn't marked off in the book, and she was adamant she had paid it. It wasn't a lot. Anyway [the owner] said, 'Who did you pay?' and she says, 'Well I'm not sure now but I know I paid it.' So he says, 'Right o.k. we're not going to argue about it.' He said to me, 'When that lady comes back in I'll serve her.' So what he did was he put a ha'penny or a penny or tuppence a week onto her bill ... So he got his money back by putting the odd coppers on.[110]

When we consider incidents like the ones described above, we have to view some of the more benign practices of small shopkeepers in a different light. Mrs Wrigley's family were customers of this particular shop before she worked in it. She told me,

> My mother would give me a note and I would go round and get what she wanted, you know. That was put in the book and then you went at the weekend and paid it and they had all these rows of Tyne Mints, Black Bullets, Humbugs and what have-you. You see when you paid your bill he always gave you, I should imagine it would be about a half-pound of, these boiled sweets. Like a token of goodwill. So everybody who paid their bill got the sweets from him.[111]

So this practice literally sweetened the pill of payment. However, when it is seen in the context of the deceptions I have described above, it seems very likely that the customer would unwittingly have paid for the sweets through some form of 'creative pricing'.

Whatever the degree of exploitation actually involved, though, this system of credit was founded upon the illusion of mutual trust between the shopkeeper and the customer. It does also seem as if some shops conducted their business more honestly than others. One woman described working in a corner shop in Byker during the 20s and 30s like this.

> We had a large book called the 'tick' book. The customer's name was on the top of the page, there was no address though, as the boss always knew everybody and trusted them. They ticked all week, ¼ 1b butter, ¼ lb margarine, ¼ lb tea, all of this went on the tick page. On Friday night or Saturday night they came to pay, and pay one shilling off the back debt, then they got a lot more groceries back.[112]

We have already seen that the shopkeeper could abuse this trust by covertly charging interest, just as the customer could by leaving an unpaid bill. On the whole, though, this system worked. Customers did not feel as if they were being taken advantage of, and shopkeepers usually got paid regularly. In fact, customers usually felt an obligation to pay their debts, even if a shop was no longer there. One elderly resident of Hebburn told this story of when he was a boy in the 1920s,

> The man in the corner shop had to close his shop, as it was going to get knocked down. He called every Monday for money owing. After a few weeks he saw the look in my eyes, handed me the two pence back, and said 'I won't be coming back, you've been a good customer, always speak when you see me.'[113]

Both the extent to which shopkeepers were viewed as part of the community, and the extent to which they saw themselves as part of the community would seem to have varied. As we saw above, many shop-keepers were of working class origin and this facilitated an identification with their customers. Mr Lewis, who was born in South Shields in 1928, described the owners of a corner shop in the street he grew up in as 'a very ordinary couple'. I then asked him what exactly he meant by that, and whether he would describe them as working class?

> I think their outlook and their aspirations were still very much working class, even though they had a business as it were. I think he worked in the shipyards originally, and I think he'd had an accident, got some compensation, and they'd been saving. So they got the shop. I think they just rented it, what they bought was the goods and the goodwill from the [previous owners].[114]

Mr Lewis points out that not only did this particular shop sell virtually everything that local people needed, but it was literally 'open all hours'.

> They sold everything. So you could get firewood, butter, shoelaces, candles, you name it, you could get it there. They were open from early morning till late at, night. Even when they were shut they were open. If you rattled the sneck, you, know, they were there. Really it was our store-cupboard, we didn't keep, anything at home because you could just pop in there.[115]

This is what Booth meant when he said that poor people 'go to their shop as an ordinary housewife to her canisters . . . '[116] Such a facility, although profitable, must also have been quite troublesome to the shopkeeper and so was also, in a sense, a service to the community.

Mr Lewis certainly viewed the owners of this particular shop as part of the local community. Although he and his friends did sometimes steal things, He said, 'We wouldn't nick from him because he was part of the group. Part of the community. There was no thieving within the community.'[117] So, as Hosgood says, small shopkeepers were integral members of working class communities, even though their position within those communities was ambiguous. Mr Lewis was quite certain that the owners of the shop he describes did not charge interest on goods bought on credit. However he says that the goods they sold were a bit more expensive than they would have been in larger shops.[118] Although Mr Lewis's account of this shop is quite favourable, we still have to bear in mind the possibility that the owners were practising some form of 'creative pricing' that he was not aware of. So we should now try to make some kind of assessment of the difficulties and contradictions involved in the relationship between the small shopkeeper and the community.

Our starting point must be that the relationship between small shopkeepers and their customers is based upon exploitation. However, when we consider some of the evidence presented above, it becomes difficult to explain this relationship purely in terms of naked self-interest, or, as Marx would have it, in terms of the cash nexus. There are other attachments at work here. So how can they be adequately theorised? I would argue that it can best be explained in the way in which we explained illegal moneylending in the previous chapter: in terms of the interpenetration of the instrumental and affectual spheres of action. We can certainly see evidence of some sort of affectual attachment on both sides of the counter. However, we can also see evidence of a certain amount of mistrust, particularly in the attitude shopkeepers had towards their customers. So we also have to consider the implications of the consistent use of deceit on the part of shopkeepers, most notably in the field of 'creative pricing'.

Hosgood's assertion that small shopkeepers were an integral part of their communities is correct; small shopkeepers and their customers were members of the same community. However, Hosgood notes the contradictory nature of the small shopkeepers' outlook, and this is echoed in the research of Bechhofer *et al.* The latter found that small shopkeepers have an attitude that is distinct from that of the working and the middle class. It is argued that this distinctive attitude flows from their contradictory class location, and that this is the reason for the ambiguity in their behaviour towards their customers. This is why small shopkeepers can, almost at the same time, be both supporters and defrauders of the working class. So in explaining the particular version of the interpenetration of rationalities that this gives rise to, we need to introduce another concept, that of emotional labour. This term was originally used by Hochschild, who pointed out that it was most important when trying to make a sale.[119] It can be defined as the deliberate promotion of affectual attachment as part of a business transaction through the management of appearances. As we shall see later, this is a feature of various types of working class credit. However, there is a paradox at the heart of relationships that involve such an exploitation of emotions. The paradox is that quite often some sort of genuine affectual attachment coexists alongside the deliberate promotion or manipulation of such an attachment for 'business' reasons. This can be explained in terms of Hochschild's distinction between 'surface' and 'deep' acting. In the case of small shopkeepers, as we have seen, it can be quite difficult to actually distinguish the motives for any particular action. However, there are also cases where it is quite clear what is going on. For instance, one obvious example of emotional exploitation is the case of the woman who claimed she had not paid her bill and was subsequently made to repay it unwittingly. On the other hand, the actions of the shopkeeper who had his shop demolished and then wrote off the remainder of the money he was owed would seem to be the result of a genuine affectual tie.

It may be helpful at this point to locate the type of exploitation of emotion that I have described above within a more general theoretical framework. To be more specific, I feel that it can be usefully located within the work of Erving Goffman on the way individuals manage appearances during social encounters. We should think of the actions of the small shopkeepers we have considered above as what Goffman calls 'performances'.[120] Goffman distinguishes between sincere performances (in which the individual concerned believes in his own act) and cynical performances (in which the individual concerned is not taken in by their own act). Cynical performers may delude their audiences for their own personal gain or for what they consider to be their own good.[121]

The argument here is that the majority of credit-givers who deal with the working class are involved in a type of performance that is, in some way, 'cynical'. As we have seen, this is a complex issue as it can often be difficult to determine the extent to which the 'performance' of small shopkeepers is cynical or sincere. Goffman says that performers tend to give an idealised impression of themselves. The behaviour of small shopkeepers should be seen as a somewhat idealised performance in which, as petit bourgeois chameleons, they attempt to make their behaviour acceptable to the community in which they live. This could take a number of forms, from the use of 'creative pricing' to the open expression of cultural values held by the community as a whole. This could be as much the result of a desire to 'fit in' as of a desire to increase profits. This is further complicated by the fact that many shopkeepers were themselves of proletarian origin, and thus may be more 'sincere' in their performance. As well as this, Goffman makes the point that an individual can come to believe in a performance that was originally cynical and vice versa. So there is a 'natural movement back and forth between cynicism and sincerity'.[122] I would argue that this is particularly true of small shopkeepers, due to their contradictory class location, and which makes them both exploiters and supporters of the working class. We can now turn to consider small shopkeeping in the period after 1945.

Small shopkeepers and the community after 1945

The first point to consider in an analysis of the relationship between small shopkeepers and the community in the post-war period is that the old pattern of receiving groceries on 'tick' continued into the 1950s and beyond in certain areas. The authors of *Coal is Our Life* said that many of the women in Ashton continued to buy their groceries on 'tick' from the local shops.[123] One of my respondents, a miner's daughter born in 1956, also told me that her parents continued to receive credit from various local shops, including the butcher's, until the early 1970s.[124] This is consistent with the argument that I have presented elsewhere, that there is a great deal of continuity between the interwar years and the immediate post-war period. However, it would seem that alongside the gradual decline of corner shops as such in the post war period there has also been a decline in the number of such shops that offer credit, as I indicated above.

The argument pursued below is that the changing nature of working class communities has been a significant factor in the decline of the number of corner shops offering credit. The provision of small-scale credit in local shops is very much part of the informal economy. Debts incurred in this manner would seem to have dubious legal status, even if they were to be pursued through the law courts. For example, the *Consumer Credit Act* of 1974 did not apply to most credit transactions of less than £30. When we also take into account the fact that, as the NCC claims, the complexity of the Act has made it difficult for creditors to ensure that they complied with its provisions, it does seem highly unlikely that many small shopkeepers would have felt confident of the legality of pursuing such debts.[125] In practice, though, this type of debt can often be so small as not to be worthwhile for small shopkeepers to pursue in this manner. I would argue that, unlike some of the other types of credit we will consider here, corner-shop credit has to be based upon some type of mutual trust or understanding between the shopkeeper and the community. So I see it as an indicator of the amount of trust that exists within a given community. This type of credit should be viewed in the same way as we would view neighbours obtaining credit for each other, an issue I explored in an earlier chapter.

In addition to questioning money-advice workers about corner-shop credit, I also asked several shopkeepers in Newcastle's east end if they offered 'tick' to their customers. One shopkeeper I interviewed, from Heaton, rarely granted credit and, when he had, the debts were often not repaid. He said that he had not pursued any of his debtors through the small claims court, and had no intention of ever doing so. He gave two main reasons for this. The first was that some of these debts were based only upon a verbal agreement, so he had no proof of the transaction actually occurring, and second was that, as a small trader, the demands on his time were already very great and he felt he did not have the time to pursue small sums through the legal system. He reasoned that, if he ever was to pursue one of his debtors through the courts, he would have had to spend time in court but, if a court was to rule in his favour, then he would also then have to spend time collecting the money owed to him.[126]

The Heaton shop described above displays a notice requesting customers not to ask for credit, as refusal may offend. This was also true of a grocer's shop in the Byker Wall I visited, and of a shop in the Walker area of Newcastle. According to Ian Poole, shops in the Cowgate area also display such notices.[127] Most corner shops seem to be doing their best to actively discourage customers from seeking credit in the first place. This does not mean that it is impossible to obtain credit from these shops, as the testimony of the Heaton shopkeeper indicates, but that credit is granted very rarely, and only to customers who the shopkeeper has a 'special' relationship with. The Heaton shopkeeper currently allows two of his customers to have an 'account' with him, but he said that he had known them for 16 years.[128] The owners of the corner shop in Walker said they 'only gave credit occasionally, not as a regular thing'.[129] Finally, the Byker shopkeeper said that, despite the notice, people often asked for credit, which they still would not grant. In this case, the shop was run by an Asian family, and one of the women in the family said that they had offered credit to only one person who had been a personal friend.[130] So, even in the case of shops displaying notices discouraging customers from asking for credit, they will grant credit in exceptional circumstances. It is fairly obvious that these 'exceptional circumstances' are conditions whereby the shop-keeper feels he or she can trust the individuals concerned. This was particularly true of the family that ran the Byker shop. They said that on the occasions when they had granted credit for newspapers, the individuals concerned had run up a large bill and then disappeared. They were quite explicit about the fact that they did not know the people in the area well enough to trust them.[131] Although he did not trust his customers, as a group, enough to extend credit to them the Heaton shopkeeper seemed to have made more 'exceptions'. However he said that this amounted to only ten individuals in his 16 years of trading in the area.[132] The Walker shopkeeper, on the other hand, was less forthcoming on this subject.

There are also other factors that seem to have contributed towards the decline of corner-shop credit. Some of these are suggested in the PSI's 1994 study of how low-income consumers make ends meet. As we saw above, only five out of the 74 families interviewed reported that they had ever put things 'on the slate' at their local shop.[133] If we consider the accounts of the individuals in this study who handled this type of credit, though, we can gain some idea of why it is so rare today. Firstly, we should note that 'trust' is again emphasised in the account of one of their respondents:

> I can go across to Joe and I can say to Joe, 'Can I have a few things to go on?' and he'll say 'Go ahead.' He lets me run up £10. The amount varies from person to person — he'll know who he can trust.[134]

However, there is also another element present in these descriptions of contemporary corner-shop credit that is largely absent in pre-war accounts: the element of embarrassment. The authors of the report go on to say that the woman quoted above was ' ... embarrassed at having to resort to doing this and would only do so if there was no-one else in the shop at the time'.[135] The other respondents in the PSI study also seem to use corner-shop credit as a last resort and, when they do, an element of shame or embarrassment always seems to be present. This is because this type of credit has largely fallen into a state of disuse, and so it is no longer the norm (in any type of working class area) to use it. Corner-shop credit may also have particularly negative associations, with the Depression of the interwar years for example, that people wish to avoid. The authors of the PSI study say,

> In many ways putting things on the 'slate' was seen as an old-fashioned way of borrowing, with a stigma attached to it. It was clear evidence to your neighbours that you were unable to manage your money.[136]

The perception of corner-shop credit as an 'old-fashioned' form of credit also leads to the belief that it is no longer available. The authors of the PSI study say,

Jacqui 'thought that had gone years ago' and was surprised to hear that some still used it as a credit facility. One or two merely assumed it was not available where they lived.[137]

It has been suggested earlier, by North-East informants, that this type of credit may have been sustained by some members of the pre-war generation accustomed to it. As that generation gradually died out, it seems, so did the custom of obtaining groceries on 'tick'. The other factor that has eroded this type of credit has also been discussed above: the demolition or closure of older shops. In such cases there is a physical discontinuity with the earlier period, that is, the old shops are just quite simply no longer there! If we take Byker, for example, it is hard to see how any of the old shops could have survived the redevelopment of that area. However, even those shops which have survived physically into the post-war period will, almost inevitably, be under new ownership. The post-war period has seen many small shops come under Asian ownership, and this has also had an effect upon the relationship between the small shopkeeper and the community. We should now try to make some assessment of the impact that ethnicity has had upon this relationship.

The impact of ethnicity

Racial harassment is a constant feature of the lives of many black and Asian people living in Britain today. Nationally, the number of racially motivated incidents has been steadily increasing since 1988.[138] Racial harassment is also part of the everyday experience of many black and Asian people living on Tyneside, where the number of incidents has also increased in the 1980s.[139] The 1990 Newcastle City Council Action Plan for Racial Equality stated,

Racial harassment is experienced by many members of the minority ethnic communities in their daily life in Newcastle. It takes many forms: attacks on the person range from verbal abuse, serious physical attack endangering life; attacks on property ranging from depositing rubbish in gardens to lighted rags through letter boxes; and persistent interferences with daily life.[140]

This is the context in which we should consider the experience of Asian shopkeepers living in the area. This is not to say that Asian shop keepers in the region live in a state of constant siege, or that they never enjoy good relations with their white neighbours but that, particularly in certain areas, there is a climate of racism. A Newcastle City Council report on racial harassment found, 'Perceived racial incidents were more likely in the Elswick, Wingrove and West City wards than elsewhere in the City.'[141] All of these areas are in the west end of Newcastle, and that part of the city has become notorious for racially motivated incidents. Although it is not clear from the published information what proportion of incidents involved shopkeepers, the chair of the Racial Equality Sub-Committee at the time of this report, Mo O'Toole, confirmed that some of the reported incidents did.[142]

Although racial intolerance often goes unreported, it has been high-lighted by certain dramatic, and often tragic, events. One of these was the murder of the Asian pensioner Khoaz Miah in Newcastle's west end in 1993. This prompted the *Evening Chronicle* to mount an investigation into racism in the west end in general. The resultant article gives some indication of the nature of this problem. We shall now briefly consider this. The article quotes the sub-divisional commander of Newcastle's west end police force, Superintendent David Swift, as saying:

> My contacts with people of ethnic minority in the area say at some time they have all suffered racial abuse and harassment. Sadly it is a fact of life that there is an awful lot of ignorance in the community.[143]

The paper's own investigations reveal the same sorry tale, 'Victims have told the *Evening Chronicle* they are abused daily by white bullies. They suffer name calling, assaults, stone throwing and attacks on their homes.'[144] It may be true that this racial harassment is perpetrated by a minority of the people living in the area, as several people assert in the article, but this does not diminish its consequences for the victims.

The Tyneside riots of 1991 was another event which highlighted the problem of racism in the area. Beatrix Campbell has been instrumental in bringing out this aspect of the riots, so let us now turn to her account of them. She begins her account of the disturbances with a description of the events in Ely, in Wales, where the 'riot season' began. Campbell shows that, despite public protestations to the contrary from the residents and the police, there was a very definite racial element in the disturbance in that area.[145] In fact, the riot had been sparked by a series of incidents with distinct racial overtones centred around a local Asian grocer's shop. This was not an isolated incident. Campbell points out, 'Asian traders in the city were the regular victims of attacks that went way beyond the normal aggravation they would expect as shopkeepers providing services late at night.'[146]

There was also a strong element of racism in the riots on Tyneside, most notably on the Meadow Well estate in North Tyneside. The outcome of the disturbances in that area was that the Asian traders were quite literally driven off the estate, never to return. Campbell pointed out that this was not simply an attack upon property as such, although the riot did provide some with an opportunity for looting, but a racially motivated attack. She describes how one resident had to plead with the rioters to allow her to get an Asian family out of a shop before they firebombed it![147] She was greeted with the reply 'They're all the same! You've got two minutes to get out!'[148] During the looting of the shops one of the rioters was heard to shout, 'Don't do that one, it's a white man's shop.'[149] This is obviously an extreme example of hostility towards Asian traders but, nevertheless, it is also indicative of what appears to be a fairly widely felt resentment towards this group. It was hardly an isolated incident. Equally, several visits were made to a shop in Heaton, where there was every indication of a good relationship between the local community and the Asian shopkeeper. To investigate the impact of ethnicity upon the relationship between small shopkeepers and the local community properly a separate study would be needed. However, it is an issue that we do need to take account of in considering the relationship between the small shopkeeper and the working class community.

The breakdown of trust

Although the Asian traders were specifically targeted during the riot, white shopkeepers on the Meadow Well estate have also been attacked. A 1994 *Evening Chronicle* describes how a white shopkeeper was also forced to leave the estate. It says that,

> Veteran butcher Emily Hoult was driven out of business by a series of raids after more than 40 years. Thieves have forced 79-year-old Mrs Hoult to quit the shop she started back in 1953. 'It's the saddest day of my life,' said Mrs Hoult as she shut up for the final time.[150]

Mrs Hoult closed her shop because her takings went down as a result of families moving away in the aftermath of the riots, and because of the number of robberies she had experienced. Her shop was on Avon Avenue, the street where all the Asian traders had been forced to leave, and was one of the few shops remaining in the area after the riots. It became an increasingly vulnerable target. Mrs Hoult said, 'Things just got too bad. No one's living around here any more and that makes it all the easier for the villains.'[151] The significance of this incident is that it illustrates just how altered the relationship between the shopkeeper and the community has become in recent years. Taken together with the rest of the evidence from the post-war period, it shows us that, regardless of their colour, shopkeepers do not generally have the close relationship with their communities that they once enjoyed. It seems that, in some respects, the racial element only exacerbates the tensions that may already exist in the relationship between the small shopkeeper and the community. The key element in this changed relationship is the breakdown of trust.

This decline of trust within communities was discussed in an earlier chapter, where Anthony Giddens' work was employed to argue that it is one of the ways in which the consequences of modernity have become more radicalised. The change in the relationship between the shopkeeper and the community is a further instance of the erosion of locality as a source of ontological security, to borrow a phrase from Giddens.[152] As he says, trust can no longer be anchored in criteria outside the relationship itself.[153] So ties based upon locality (for example) no longer offer a sufficient basis, in themselves, for trust.

The other theme that emerges from our consideration of the post-war period as a whole is the increasing domination of instrumental rationality in the actions of individuals, as Max Weber pointed out. This does not replace a purely affectual orientation to action, but leads to less of an interpenetration between the instrumental and the affectual spheres in the later post-war period. Again, this is something that is also true of the relationship between small shopkeepers and working class communities. As pointed out in the Introduction, the basic direction of the change in social relations discerned here can be described in terms of the movement from Gemeinschaft to Gesellschaft. This movement from Gemeinschaft-like relations to Gesellschaft-like relations is the basic, underlying, movement in modern society. What we have seen so far is that this tendency is present in the development of relationships within working class communities, and between those communities and small shopkeepers.

Conclusion

This chapter has dealt with the relationship between the small shopkeeper and the working class community, and the way in which this has altered over time. We have seen that the working class has always made use of informal credit from corner shops. Working class customers also expected their local shopkeepers to lend them money in times of hardship. There was an interdependent relationship between shopkeepers and customers in working class areas before the Second World War. Shopkeepers were an integral part of their communities in this period, and they often offered unpaid services to those communities. However, this did not prevent them from unscrupulously exploiting their neighbours when the opportunity arose.

The ambiguous, and sometimes contradictory, behaviour of small shopkeepers towards their customers flows from their contradictory class location. Wright's second class map, which reflects relations of exploitation rather than domination, has been useful in explaining the class position of small shopkeepers. We saw that small shopkeepers belonged to the petite bourgeoisie. Wright does not see this group as forming the principal contradictory location within contemporary capitalism, and this should not be disputed. Small shopkeepers form a contradictory location within exploitation relations in a way that other members of the petite bourgeoisie do not. This is because, as Marx and Engels pointed out, they exploit the poverty of the workers. However, their objective material interests and their cultural predisposition can also lead them to side with the working class in a struggle between labour and capital.

We then moved on to consider substantive studies of small shopkeepers, finding that, in many ways, small shopkeepers were social chameleons taking on the character of the area they inhabit. This is the point that Hosgood makes in his study of small shopkeepers during the period 1870–1914. It is also the view expressed by Bechhofer and his colleagues in the most significant contemporary study of small shopkeepers. They found that independence was centrally important to small shopkeepers and that their behaviour was governed by 'economic traditionalism'. This led them to conclude that their outlook is distinct from that of the capitalist class, the middle class and the working class. This is a result of their contradictory class location.

The contradictory class location of small shopkeepers gives rise to contradictory attitudes towards their working class customers. Some small shopkeepers were content to be an integral part of their community, others sought to remove themselves from it. In practice, they often held both of these attitudes simultaneously. In fact, most small shopkeepers seem to have displayed a degree of ambivalence towards their community. This ambivalence can also be seen in the way that they conducted their business. While some small shopkeepers took every opportunity they could to cheat their customers, others seem to have dealt honestly with their customers and taken part in the life of the local community. However, once again, we found that it was difficult to draw a hard and fast distinction between these two types of shopkeeper. We also saw that the way that individual shopkeepers were perceived by their communities was not necessarily a good indication of the way they actually dealt with their customers.

Although the relationship between small shopkeepers and their customers was based upon exploitation, it cannot be explained purely in terms of instrumental rationality. It is best explained in terms of the interpenetration of the instrumental and affectual spheres of action. I argue that the particular form of the interpenetration of rationalities involved in this relationship is partly the result of what Hochschild calls 'emotional labour'. This type of behaviour can be located within the work of Goffman on the way that individuals manage appearances during social encounters. I argue that the majority of credit-givers who deal with the working class are involved in a type of 'performance' that is, in some way, 'cynical'. However, it is usually difficult to determine the extent to which the 'performance' of small shopkeepers is, in Goffman's terms, 'cynical' or 'sincere'.

Finally, the old pattern of obtaining groceries on 'tick' continued into the 1950s and beyond in certain areas. It was not until considerably later that this practice began to decline. The changing nature of working class communities has been a significant factor in the decline of the number of corner shops offering credit. This is because corner-shop credit has to be based upon some type of mutual trust or understanding between the shopkeeper and the community.

4

'Just Like One of the Family' the Agent, the Established Firm and Working Class Credit before 1945

Introduction

The relationship between 'agents' or collectors and their customers is central to the whole edifice of the weekly-collected credit system used by the working class. The agent, as intermediary between the creditor and the debtor, has a central role in this study. In the discussion that follows, the term agent refers to any individual acting on behalf of any organisation that offers 'doorstep' credit to individual consumers. 'Doorstep' credit is usually described as 'weekly-collected credit' by the industry itself.[1] This is because loans are usually paid in weekly instalments and, 'The instalments are usually collected personally by someone who calls on the customer each week or month.'[2] So the agent acts as the interface between the consumer and the organisation. As the agents of mail order companies fulfil the same function, if there is an agent involved in a transaction, mail order credit can also be seen as a type of 'doorstep' credit. It should be pointed out that this definition has been made deliberately wide in order to encompass all the different types of credit 'agents' who deal with the working class. As well as looking at agents of mail order companies and check trading companies, we will also consider those credit drapers who dealt with the working class directly. The reason for this is that the relationship between the customer and the person offering them credit is of crucial importance in any type of credit collected by agents who regularly visit customers in their own homes.

Collectors are often from working class communities themselves, if not from the areas in which they operate. Most agents begin by offering their services to their immediate circle of family and friends and, if they do not already know a customer, then they will usually develop a close relationship with them over time. This process is facilitated by the fact that agents, or collectors, are often women, employed by a company on a part-time basis, selling to other women. So, a close personal relationship exists, or will usually develop, between agent and customer. This can be beneficial to the company involved, as such close personal ties can create custom in the first instance, and ensure regular payment once a transaction has been entered into. On the other hand, the loyalties of the agent can often be divided between the company and the customer. The situation can be less ambiguous when an agent is a full-time employee for that firm, but this still does not ensure the agent will side with their employer. Nevertheless, those companies which offered credit to the working class in the past used a network of local agents, and the same system continues to be used, often by many of the same firms, today. Some of the companies which traded in this way before the Second World War are still doing so today. A discussion of the history of these firms, then, will enable us to see how this method of trading originated, and how it works in practice.

A durable form of credit-trading

It has been suggested that, in the years following the First World War, club or check trading provided an impetus to the growth of certain small-scale retailers:

> This movement, which was more widespread in the North than in the South of England, flourished in the periods of heavy unemployment and for many families provided the only method of affording new clothes. Some multiple shop firms were prominent in this form of trading, for example the Provident Clothing and Supply Company Ltd., and other large firms, for example Great Universal Stores Ltd., operated the system by means of agents or collectors and mail order delivery rather than through fixed shops; but the majority of the retailers taking part in such schemes were small-scale retailers.[3]

After 1945, however, many of the small-scale retailers trading on the club or check system began to go into decline and have now become relatively scarce. This has not been the case with the two major firms cited above: the Provident Clothing and Supply Company and Great Universal Stores Ltd.

Great Universal Stores was founded in 1900 as Universal Stores.[4] Today it is a large, successful company which includes several subsidiary mail order firms, the most notable of which is Kays.[5] The other large mail order company which operated during the interwar period, and is still successful today, is Empire Stores Ltd. This company is considerably older than Great Universal Stores. Empire Stores, and the Provident, were created during the nineteenth century and they are good examples of the old, established, family firm. As well as being of a comparable age, though, reasonably coherent company histories exist for both of these firms, which is not the case with Great Universal.

The continued success of these two firms is quite apparent. Most of their customers are drawn from working class communities, where they continue to operate by utilising a number of 'agents'. A number of studies have found that mail order and check trading are forms of credit that are particularly associated with low-income consumers. Janet Ford points out,

> Research in the early 1980s showed that there were some forms of credit used predominantly or exclusively by those living in or on the margins of poverty — for example, tallymen, money-lenders and check-traders. In 1980, the NCC survey showed that 21 per cent of semi- and unskilled manual workers were using or had used check trading, compared to 8 per cent of routine (non-professional/managerial) clerical workers.[6]

The NCC report also called mail order a 'key source' of credit for those on low incomes.[7] A 1989 Social Security Advisory Committee report pointed out that there are considerable differences in the types of credit used by people at different levels of income:

> Credit cards, 'loans' (from banks or finance houses) and store credit all tend to be used more by richer than poorer people, who tend to use mail order companies. Check traders and so on do most of their business with low income customers, but supply only a small proportion of the credit available to that group.[8]

It goes on to say that a survey of benefit claimants conducted in 1982 showed that mail order catalogues were their main source of credit.[9]

The most recent major survey of credit use in Great Britain, the 1992 PSI Report, found that, although all income groups bought by mail order to about the same extent, 'mail-order catalogues formed a high proportion of revolving credit in low-income households'.[10] The PSI report also found that it was mainly those on low incomes who made use of check traders. Some of these reports do not actually name the companies involved, but the phrase 'check trader' is often used to denote the Provident Clothing and Supply Company, although there are also smaller companies which trade by this method. In the case of mail-order companies, there are several that operate in this market. Empire Stores is only one, but it would seem to be the longest standing firm of this type. This is the reason for considering the two firms together as indicative of the phenomenon of an 'established firm' operating within working class communities. As well as this, both of these companies are still trading on Tyneside today.

A 1989 study of families on benefit in Tyne and Wear found that the Provident Clothing and Supply Company was by far the largest check trading organisation in the area.[11] Twenty-six families in the sample had applied for a single payment from the DHSS for a household item and been refused. Sixteen of these families had then acquired the item through mail order catalogue credit. The other families did without the item. Two thirds of the families in the sample owed money to mail order companies.

Both Empire Stores and the Provident have a number of common elements: they are established firms, and thus could be seen as 'traditional' forms of credit by the working class, and they both use a system of local agents. Gillian Parker has spelt out the implications of this latter fact:

> The weekly 'callers' from shopping check companies and small-scale moneylenders are often from well-established 'family' firms and this influences the way in which they are regarded by their customers. Women do business with the company that their mothers, and even grandmothers used and the callers come to be seen as family friends.[12]

The personal relationships involved in this type of business transaction can mean that women feel an obligation to pay, even when this will lead to severe financial difficulties. Parker points out that another reason that women are reluctant to miss payments is that it would cut them off from a source of credit that may be the only legal option available, the alternative being to go to an illegal moneylender. So is this personalisation of a business transaction the reason for the continued success of the two companies cited above? There are other possible reasons, not least the fact that these companies have a captive market, as they are prepared to offer credit where other companies would refuse it. We also need to ask, though, what explanations do the companies themselves offer for their success? It is possible to answer this question by a survey of the literature the companies have produced about themselves. This involves a detour into the company history of both firms, but it is a necessary detour.

We can now look at each of the two companies in turn, beginning with the older, Empire Stores.

The story of Empire Stores

Empire Stores was founded in 1831 by an Italian immigrant, Antonio Fattorini, when he opened a small jewellery and fancy goods shop in Leeds. The official company history, by Patrick Beaver, says that Antonio Fattorini began as a travelling packman, or pedlar. Beaver spends considerable time contrasting the humble origins of the firm with the large, modern business it later became. One feature of the company's development of interest, is the 'Watch Club'. By the mid-nineteenth century there were three Fattorini jeweller's shops. These were providing interest-free credit 'to customers of standing', which excluded the working class. The Fattorinis' aim was ' ... to introduce a system of credit which would enable working people with little or no credit worthiness to buy watches and clocks without risk of bad debt to the firm'.[13] This would enable the firm to reach the more affluent, skilled working class. The method they devised to achieve this was a system of clubs that agreed to meet every week at a public house, to pay 6d.a head into a common fund for 50 weeks. When the club had accumulated £1.5s it was sent to one of the Fattorini shops to pay for a silver pocket watch. The shop gave a discount on the watch, which was put into the club's social fund. The watch was then raffled to the club members, and this went on until all the members had received their watches. Beaver says,

> These watch clubs with their easily available interest-free credit were a success from the beginning, and as the paying of the weekly subscription became an occasion for meeting friends and neighbours and having a glass of beer, they developed into valued social institutions.[14]

The clubs were self-policing. They had a committee that excluded bad payers, and they imposed fines on any members late with their subscription. All this was good for the firm. It enabled them to greatly expand their clientele with only minimal risk to profits. By the end of the nineteenth century, there were about 1000 Fattorini clubs spread throughout the country, attesting the popularity of this system of purchasing.[15]

The watch clubs are interesting in that they employed the same method of credit control as the contemporary mail order catalogue agent: social pressure. The only real difference would seem to be that watch clubs existed for men, and their activities were carried out in public in a male environment (the pub) while catalogue selling is now primarily directed at women, and takes place in the home. The Fattorinis would seem to have been the first company to develop the idea of customers policing themselves. This method has subsequently been employed by every firm trading in this way. When all the members of a watch club had received watches, the club would then go on to purchase a watch chain, or a set of cutlery in the same manner. Many clubs were some distance from the organising shops, and this led to the introduction of club catalogues. The watch clubs began in the 1850s and by the 1890s they had become 'Watch, Clock & Jewellery Clubs', and this was the beginning of the Fattorini mail-order business.

The next phase in the company's development was the detachment of the mail order side of the business from the retail shops. This occurred in 1907 with the creation of the Northern Trading Company in Bradford. Beaver says,

Northern Trading agents were not only active in Bradford but all over the north of England, for in addition to advertising the firm had representatives to recruit new agents at pitheads, public houses and factory gates. In those days a husband was responsible for his wife's debts and the firm only accepted men as agents, although in practice it was usually the wives who did the work.[16]

With the establishment of Northern Trading the company greatly increased the number of potential customers it would appeal to. The club system had reached only the labour aristocracy, but Northern Trading offered the whole of the working class (skilled and unskilled) the chance to purchase household goods on credit. Beaver refers to *Round about a Pound a Week*, by Maud Pember Reeves, to indicate the type of customer they sought. As Beaver says, the appeal of the 'weekly' system to families on about a pound a week was that they needed to know exactly what their weekly expenditure would be. So, the use of a system of weekly payments allowed women to budget more carefully, and the fact that an agent called to collect the payment meant that the money was paid on time.

The company changed its name to Empire Stores Limited on 28th June 1910, when it was registered under this name with a nominal share capital of £100. The company continued to grow in the following years, despite the First World War, and the Depression. Beaver points out that the mail order industry tends to flourish during an economic recession,

> ...for the newly unemployed were forced to resort to the 'weekly' to obtain many necessities such as clothes, bedding and other domestic items. In the 1920s and 1930s mail order demand rose to record heights...[17]

Empire Stores took responsibility for bad debts, warning agents to be careful not to give too much credit to new customers to begin with. Beaver says that bad debts amounted to only six per cent of the company's transactions during the Depression.[18]

After the Second World War Joseph Fattorini became the head of the company and, with a marketing executive called Mick Wells, he set about remodelling the company. They sought to win over the 'new affluent working class' to mail order shopping. This entailed a reorganisation of the firm to 'put it on a modern, efficient footing'.[19] A similar post-war restructuring took place within the Provident Clothing & Supply Company, as we shall see. For both firms it was as much about changing the image of the company as it was about increased organisational efficiency. Beaver points out that as workers became more affluent, mail-order companies had to face up to the fact that their industry had a reputation for selling poor quality goods. This was because, in the past, they had 'catered mainly to a class of custom that was attracted by the cheapness and availability of credit'.[20] Mail order catalogues had to compete with High Street shops in the post-war period, and this forced them to begin to trade in branded goods. The result of this move, says Beaver, was that, by 1960, there were virtually no nationally advertised goods that could not be obtained through a catalogue.

The company histories of both Empire Stores, and the Provident make much out of their move into 'the computer age'. The installation of computer systems would appear to be a source of great pride to both firms. In the case of Empire Stores, an IBM computer was installed in 1968 to take over the majority of the firm's clerical work. All the organisational improvements that the company introduced, though, still did not tackle the ongoing problem of the company's image. Despite all its efforts, the company found it hard to shake off its association with the dark days of the Depression. So they still needed an improved public image, and they turned to market research to provide it for them. As a result, they changed the way that they recruited agents.

Up until this point, the company had used its full-time representatives to recruit agents by 'cold canvassing'. By the early 70s though, every other mail order company was using postage-paid coupons to advertise for agents. In 1975, Empire Stores also adopted this approach. This posed the problem of how were creditworthy agents to be identified? In the past, the expertise of the full-time representative was relied upon to assess credit risk, literally on the doorstep. Beaver says that this did not turn out to be a problem as 'advertising produces perfectly satisfactory agents and does not increase the number of bad debts'. The company subsequently adopted 'a system of judging creditworthiness on a statistical evaluation of prospective agents'.[21] This was found to be more reliable than the personal evaluation of the sales representative. The company still continues to 'cold canvas' for agents, but more than half of its agents are now recruited through advertising. This means that the type of people who can become agents can now be more strictly controlled, as it is no longer left up to an individual to make the decision because the process has become bureaucratised. The company switched from the use of personal judgement to evaluation through a points-scoring system in 1978. This might be cast as a move towards what Weber called bureaucratic 'management'. Weber said, 'The reduction of modern office management to rules is deeply embedded in its very nature'.[22] This means that transactions are no longer decided upon individually, but by the use of a set of fixed principles. We need to note, however, that the use of personal evaluation and personal contact was still maintained along with this rationalisation of recruitment procedures.

The reason for the continued success of the company, according to Beaver, is '... the consistent following of a policy of making goods available to working people at a low profit and maintaining a high turnover by so doing'.[23] How exactly was this achieved? Firstly, by the use of mail order, which the company history defines as:

> ... a commercial retail enterprise carried on mainly by means of the mail, whereby customers order, from illustrated catalogues sent to them twice a year by post, general merchandise of every description and receive their orders by parcel post, rail or road. All goods are sent to the customer on an 'approval' basis and on a system of extended credit.[24]

The advantage of this system, according to Beaver, is that it eliminates the middleman, as catalogues buy direct from the factory. This allows them to buy in vast quantities, or even take over the entire output of a manufacturer. Also, as they buy for a whole season, they can combat inflation by forward purchasing. The mail order system also lessens operating costs, as there are 'no idle shop assistants waiting for customers'. Beaver says that these are the reasons for the growing popularity of mail order and that, in 1981, 20 million people used the system and they made an estimated half million purchases daily.[25]

The company history also openly acknowledges the importance of 'the agent' to their continued success. It is worth noting here that the company appears to see all of its potential customers, and agents, as female. For example, if a customer becomes an agent ' . . . she will receive 10 per cent of the total sum of her business'.[26] The central importance of the agent for the company is spelt out. 'As far as Empire Stores is concerned she will also be acting as a highly efficient means of credit control, for it takes a tough customer to bilk her neighbour.'[27] Beaver goes on to say,

> Today Empire Stores deals with some 400,000 part-time agents, each of whom serves an average of five customers and handles a turnover of £350 a year. Between them they send to the Bradford head office a total of over six million orders a year which altogether consist of more than 16 million items.[28]

Catalogue selling, then, has successfully combined modern, bureaucratic procedures with the more personal techniques traditionally employed in the field. We have also seen that mail order continues to be widely used among those on low incomes and benefits. Before accepting Beaver's explanation for the continued success of companies like Empire Stores (that is, it provides high quality goods at an affordable price) we should also consider an alternative view. There is not a great deal of secondary literature on mail-order companies, but Sally Baldwin offers us a quite different view to Beaver's:

> In Scotland, door-to-door tallymen are not all that common, their place being usurped, perhaps, by mail order shopping . . . Mail order firms do not charge an identifiable interest rate, but obviously the notional price is inflated to include a financial charge. Their prices tend to be expensive, brand names are conspicuously absent and a number of firms sell clothes that are of a degree of shoddiness.[29]

Baldwin also makes the point that catalogue companies, as well as using an agent, can also deal directly with the customer. This is undoubtedly true and, for some, this method may have its advantages, and indeed mail order generally may be very helpful to some people, such as those unable to travel to shops.

However, this still does not really explain the success of mail order companies in the post-war period. This seems to have been due to several factors which we will discuss in detail later. However, for the moment, it is worth making two points about the continued success of mail order in recent years. Firstly, this form of trading has expanded so as to encompass more upmarket merchandise. So the mail order market has become more segmented. Secondly, it is the single most accessible form of commercial credit, as we shall see below. Those without the wherewithal to secure mortgages, personal loans, and High Street credit, are the most frequent users of catalogue credit. As the 1992 PSI Report found, 'A quarter of catalogues (24 per cent) were used by people with no other source of credit. They therefore formed a sector of the market distinct from other forms of credit.'[30]

We can now turn to examine the history of the Provident in order to bring out the similarities between it and Empire Stores which have been already mentioned in passing.

The story of 'The Provi'

The Provident Clothing & Supply Company was founded in Bradford in 1880, by a former Methodist insurance collector, Joshua Waddilove.[31] Waddilove had seen poverty first-hand while collecting insurance, prompting him to begin supplying checks to the poor of Bradford, as a charitable gesture. He used checks that could be redeemed at local shops, rather than money, to prevent the recipient spending it on drink. Word of Joshua's charitable deeds spread and he found that he was inundated with requests for checks from women who were willing to pay for them in weekly instalments. Joshua was then compelled to hire helpers to collect the weekly payments. He then arranged for the shops he dealt with to give him a discount as payment for the extra business that he brought to them, and thus created the trading system that Provident still uses today.

The company history, as we might expect, documents the rise of the company in some detail pointing out,

By 1910 there were more than 3000 Agents of what had become to be known as 'the good old Provident' or 'the poor man's banker.'

There were 85 offices from Aberdeen to Llanelly and turnover was near £1 000 000.[32]

It goes on to describe the firm in 1980. 'Today, firmly integrated in a society which has accepted the necessity for credit, Provident has some 15 000 Agents working out of 519 branch offices and a turnover of £80 000 000.'[33] The figures speak for themselves. The exploitation of poverty can be a lucrative business. The Provident, like Empire Stores, has grown from 'humble beginnings' to become a successful, modern company. What explanation does the firm itself offer for this?

The Provident describes its own post-war history as a period 'when the giant awoke'.[34] What is meant by this is that the company had been a 'sleeping giant' until 1962, when the company changed hands and, somewhat later than Empire Stores, began its post-war facelift. In 1962, the company was bought by Ralph Yablon, a former Bradford solicitor. Gordon Waddilove (the grandson of the company's founder) remained as chairman.

Up until this point, checks had had to be paid off within 20 weeks. The company now abolished the 20-week limit, and introduced vouchers on a 50 or 100 week basis in order to cope with the increased demand for consumer durables. There was also a drive to extend and increase the range of shops in which Provident checks could be used. The company consciously set out to change its public image. The new management wanted Provident to have a contemporary image. 'But customers, and, especially many potential customers, still retained an impression of Provident as a firm through which you just bought coal or shoes.'[35] Again, like Empire Stores, Provident was a firm bound up with its past. Both firms had enjoyed considerable success during the Depression, but after the war they wanted to shake off the coal dust and ditch the 'cloth cap' image, to appeal to a new generation of workers, most of whom were more affluent than their parents had been.

The company brought in (the inevitable) marketing consultant to prepare a report, and then acted upon the recommendations. This led to the creation of a newspaper, marketing magazine and television advertising campaign. The Provident also began to expand into new areas. In 1967 foreign holidays became available on credit through Key Tours and, in the same year, the company began to offer its customers a motor-insurance scheme. As the company history puts it 'The giant had got himself a new suit of clothes.'[36] Like Empire Stores, Provident also improved its administrative machinery. They installed a new 'super-efficient' computer centre at Bradford Head Office, which increased the amount of control the central office could have over the localities. There was a similar process of bureaucratisation in the Provident to that which took place in Empire Stores, with the Collection Book changing to meet the needs of the computer. As with Empire Stores, though, the tightening up of the central-administrative machinery did not mean the abandonment of a system of local agents using personal evaluation as a means of credit control. Restricted access to mainstream credit has been one of the factors that has sustained the types of credit we are concerned with here. The role of the agent in 'cultivating' customers would seem be the other factor that has helped to keep them alive.

We can now move on to consider in more detail the role the agent played during the interwar period.

The role of the agent

The importance of the close personal relationships that usually developed between the agent of a credit company and their customers has been acknowledged by various commentators. It was also a feature of the way that the working class used other financial institutions. Paul Johnson points out that while the weekly call of the insurance agent imposed a discipline for saving upon working class housewives, it also had a social function.[37] The weekly call of the tallyman, or Scotch draper, had the same dual purpose, as an ex-tallyman explained:

> In my days as a traveller the key used to be under the mat or in the potted plant. And I used to let myself in with the key and open the sideboard drawer, and there was the money. This is the way it is done . . . it is complete confidence.[38]

As we will see, this sort of trust between the customer and the collector was not at all uncommon. Melanie Tebbutt points to the commercial advantages of such a 'friendly' relationship for the credit trader.[39] She also describes the negative aspects of this relationship, as tallymen had a reputation for sharp practices, and for making customers buy more than they could afford.[40] Tebbut says that the growth of new housing estates, which lacked the extensive social networks of the old districts, made women even more vulnerable to unscrupulous traders, with 'dumping' particularly prevalent in the suburbs.

'Dumping' seems to have been quite common during the interwar period, as one of the leading house journals of the credit trade pointed out in 1928:

Let us first take the method of forcing goods in houses on approval, in the hope that the occupant will be weak enough to keep the goods, and to commence paying for them when the trader concerned practically refuses to remove the goods.[41]

The author of this article then goes on to bemoan the fact that some firms allow anyone (even working class people) to become their part-time agent in a district.

Generally speaking, they are people of the worst type, often living in slum districts of our great cities and towns, men and women devoid of prestige, personality or dignity, and destitute of any kind of business ability.[42]

This article triggered a reply from Wilfred Lawson of Newcastle upon Tyne. He titles his article rather unambiguously: 'The 'Part-Time Agent' System. Not an unfair method in our trade.' Mr Lawson says that he himself uses this method of trading, and then goes on to make the case for it.

Every credit trader has amongst his own customers numerous potential agents, and as he can make the choice himself — good agents. Why look further? Your customers may have occasionally introduced a friend to your traveller, but could and would do much more, with a definite promise of reward. [43]

However, even he adds a note of caution, advising that new agents should be given limited responsibilities to start with. This alerts us to an important distinction, which we will explore further below — the difference between a full and part-time agent.

For the credit agent, their customers were indeed a valuable source of information. In a contemporary manual for credit traders, Edward C. Warren, a teacher of economics and commercial practice, is explicit about the advantages that a would-be credit trader could gain from exploiting this source properly. He says,

Full investigation into the financial standing of the family of each new customer is readily made by personal inquiry, on the spot, from existing customers. These, again, seem always able to provide tracing information about the removal and new address of any customers leaving the district. Collectors, by reason of their frequent calls, learn the life-history and habits of their customers and gain advance knowledge of impending marriages, births, and suchlike, so that potential orders for goods are quickly booked.[44]

The importance of this type of information-gathering is also stressed in an article that appeared in *The Credit World* in 1930 entitled: 'Hints by a collector-supervisor for collectors.'

Keep your ears open for gossip regarding impending marriages and make a note of the dates. There are usually some nice orders to be picked up at these times. Similarly, regarding funerals: if you hear of a death in the family, go along and tactfully suggest that in the event of any mourning being required etc. etc.[45]

As we will see below, collectors did make a point of gathering this type of personal information about their customers. After all, for the credit trader, both birth and death can lead to 'some nice orders'.

In the days before credit referencing, other credit traders were another source of information about potential customers. In 1929 *The Credit World* published a speech given to the Newcastle Upon Tyne Credit Traders Association by Mr Forgie which traced the history of the Association.

Just seventy-six years ago today ten travelling drapers met and founded this society. They were better known as Scotch Drapers in those days ... The first meeting was held in the Cordwainers' Hall at the corner of Nelson Street and Clayton Street.[46]

Apparently the members passed a motion, ' ... which required members to send in a list of bad payers so that they could be listed and issued in printed form for the guidance of the society'.[47] The Newcastle association was undoubtedly very successful. In 1931 this list, known as The Newcastle Protection Register, was receiving 500–600 names per week, ' ... and the total at present was 46 414!'[48]

In addition to co-operation between credit traders engaged in the same type of business, there was also co-operation between traders involved in different types of credit. A 1929 article in *The Credit World* describes, 'How Credit Traders and Hire-Purchase Traders Can Help One Another.' It claims,

A considerable number of co-operative arrangements already exist between credit traders and hire-purchase traders, and one of the best-known hire-purchase houses in the furniture trade is associated with one of the largest credit trading concerns. Very little has been said about these connections by the parties concerned . . . [49]

The author then goes on to explain how this co-operation worked.

The credit trader introduces customers to the hire-purchase trader in return for a commission on the business done with them. The 'introduction' is sometimes made without the customer's knowledge. The credit trader and the hire-purchase trader also exchange information regarding unsatisfactory customers, to their mutual advantage. [50]

It is also worth noting that hire-purchase traders would also use local insurance agents in the same manner. Warren says,

One method of eliciting this pre-business information is to enlist the help of local insurance company collectors, whose business is so intimately associated with the lives of people in their district. They are supplied with questionnaires to be completed to give the number and ages of the members of a family and their history, the amount of rent paid weekly, the income and employment of those at work and the period of residence at their present address. All such knowledge comes easily to the insurance collector on his weekly round and is imparted to the dealer for a nominal sum. [51]

Warren does not stop there. He goes on to suggest that enterprising dealers carry this a stage further,

. . . by suggesting that the insurance official obtains early information about forthcoming marriages and anticipated domestic events, so that they may be the first on the scene at the appropriate time with the right goods and the knowledge of how far it is safe to offer terms of payment. [52]

As we will see, there was a final link in this chain which enabled insurance agents to exchange information with agents of 'doorstep' credit companies. There was a free flow of information, not only between different credit companies but between all commercial concerns that dealt with the working class upon a regular basis.

Once credit agents had found a 'good' customer, their next concern was to keep them on their books in order to prevent them from straying to rival companies. One way of doing this was to make sure an account was constantly kept open. On the whole, although collectors wanted to be paid regularly they did not necessarily want a customer to 'settle up' completely, as an article in *The Retail Credit World* (1928) asks, 'Are paid-up customers a problem?' The author is concerned that credit traders may lose custom to shops as a result of improvements in the public-transport system. The collector must, therefore, keep in touch with customers when their accounts are getting low. As one trader puts it, 'It is better to deal with the devil you know than with the devil you don't.'[53] So the article advises 'The vital time for re-selling is when the account is getting low.'[54] It describes the collector as the 'vital link' between the credit-trader and his customers. They quote a credit-trader who says 'Train your collectors to look upon paid-up accounts as a financial loss to themselves.'[55] He suggests that, if a collector is paid commission, they might also be fined for every settled account.

Mail order companies also recognised the importance of a good agent. A BBC2 programme from the mid-1990s on mail order pointed out,

> Good agents were vital to the mail order industry, and finding women who were reliable was crucial to the success of any company...There was often fierce competition within the industry and it was quite common for one company to poach another's top agent.[56]

Agents of mail order companies worked part-time. They were usually women, and they usually sold to their own communities. This meant that their relationship to their customers had a different character to that of the full-time collector. As we have seen, a number of credit firms, including the Provident, employed part-time agents. As well as part-time and full-time agents, though, there was a third type of collector who dealt with the working class: owner-collectors. These were dealers who owned a locally-based credit firm which had very few employees or none. This resulted in the owners of the business being compelled to personally collect payments. So, in terms of their class position, these owner-collectors were in a similar situation to that of the small shopkeepers we considered in the previous chapter (that is they were petit bourgeois). They also held a similarly ambiguous evaluation of the working class to small shopkeepers.

The comments of two owner-collectors, interviewed as part of the 1994 PSI study of doorstep lenders by Karen Rowlingson, are equally applicable to the interwar years:

> People became owners of small moneylending businesses because they were entrepreneurs who were interested in the credit industry

or in sales. The owner-collectors were the least like their customers in terms of social class but this difference did not cause much friction as there was some acceptance and respect between them and their customers.[57]

Like small shopkeepers, they dealt with the working class as consumers rather than producers. So they also occupied a contradictory class location. The significance of this was that they had the potential to side with the working class in struggles to protect working class living standards, as it was in their interests to defend them.

For example, the annual general meeting of the Check Traders Association held in Liverpool on 26 February 1931 noted the effects of the slump on their trade. The President

> . . . referred to the bad trade and general depression which had characterised 1930. Check traders, in common with others throughout the country, but more especially in the Midlands and the North, had had to contend with difficulty upon difficulty, and the utmost care had to be exercised in the conduct of their business.[58]

The President of the Check Traders Association is obviously more concerned with the effects of the Depression upon the credit trade than the hardships inflicted upon the working class, but an article in *The Credit World* (1931) comes close to an expression of sympathy, if not solidarity.

> In the industrial areas there are many credit men who are already feeling acutely the cut in the 'dole'. The difference between what the unemployed were receiving in the past and that which they are now being paid was the amount that they could afford to pay the traveller after providing for their daily necessities. As innumerable credit men know to their cost that narrow margin has entirely disappeared.[59]

A note of caution is necessary here. It is not being argued that credit traders would invariably support working class struggles, or that they would always be sympathetic to the working class. What is being asserted here is that, in a similar way to small shopkeepers, the attitude of some credit traders towards their customers was highly ambiguous. This was largely a result of their frequent contact with them, which could lead to a certain amount of empathy and understanding of working class lives. As well as this, in the case of doorstep credit traders, the issue of the contradictory class location of the traders is less significant than with small shopkeepers. This is because, of all the types of credit agent that offer this type of credit, only owner-collectors can be said to belong to the petite bourgeoisie. These owner-collectors constitute only a minority of the doorstep credit agents who deal with the working class. Many agents (particularly part-time agents) are themselves from the working class. So class fractionalisation is a more important issue than contradictory class location in doorstep credit. Having established the basic contours of the relationship between the agent and the customer, we are now in a position to consider the workings of this relationship on Tyneside.

The role of the agent on Tyneside before 1945

During the interwar period on Tyneside there were a number of credit businesses that employed agents. As well as representatives of mail order catalogues and credit drapers, there were also 'ticket' agents. 'Ticket' agents acted for credit firms which had an arrangement with a particular shop (or a number of shops) that would accept their vouchers. Lady Florence Bell describes this system in her study of working class life in Middlesbrough at the turn of the century: *At The Works.*

> The difficulty of paying for anything for which more than a very small sum of ready-money is needed explains the eagerness with which the housewives of this town embrace any system by which they are able to buy in small instalments. Most of the women buy their clothes ready made, and pay for them and for their boots on the £1 ticket system. I do not know whether this obtains in other parts of the country. These £1 tickets are sold by men who buy them for cash down at certain shops in the town, getting the tickets for 18 s. or even less; and the women, who buy these from them in their turn, pay 21 s., payable in instalments of not less than 1s. weekly, and usually 2 s. 6 d. for the first week. These tickets are available either for one shop or two, sometimes 10 s. goes to a boot-shop and 1 0s. to a draper. The advantage of this system over that of buying from the 'tallymen' or hawkers, is that, although in each case the woman has to make a weekly payment, in the case of the £1 ticket she goes to the shop in the town and can get the goods that she sees at the prices marked in the windows, whereas by the other system she is at the mercy of the tallyman, who may palm off on her at a given price something which is usually sold far below it. She has, besides, to buy the thing unseen from a sample shown her.[60]

Bell's description of the operation of the ticket system in Middles-brough is also relevant to Tyneside. This system was common through-out the north of England before the Second World War. This is apparent from an article that appeared in *The Drapers' Record* in 1906, a year before the publication of *At The Works*. The article, entitled 'Growth of the Ticket System', expressed concern over the growth of 'this unhealthy method of business' in the north of the country. The author points out that the system had certain disadvantages for retailers, who may not always have been as willing to sell goods at the marked prices as Bell suggests. Drapers complained,

> ... customers purchasing goods on the ticket system are growing more astute and are exercising great caution in their purchases in order to secure goods at cash prices. In a large number of cases customers succeed in buying goods from the assistants at the lowest charge and then produce their ticket, when it is obvious that the price cannot be altered. It is also thought that the 'ticket man,' in order to secure customers, puts them up to various moves for the purpose of taking advantage of the retailers. Many drapers regard the whole system as a pernicious one that is calculated to interfere with the successful pursuit of the trade.[61]

Tebbut describes the general development of this type of credit during the period. However, she distinguishes only between shop-run schemes 'and those of large financial organisations such as the Prov-ident'.[62] We need a more detailed explanation in order to appreciate the types of credit used by the Tyneside working class during the period. There were three distinct types of ticket agent on Tyneside by the end of the interwar period. Firstly, there was the private agent who had set up business with a small amount of capital.[63] Secondly, there were the small agencies in the centre of Newcastle which dealt with the city-centre shops. Thirdly, there were the agents of the Provident. Each of these ticket agents had agreements with particular shops which would accept their vouchers.

All over Tyneside there were shops which would accept tickets of one sort or another. The biggest and most important of these were Shephard's and Parrish's. Parrish's, of Byker, and Shephard's of Gateshead, were large department stores, both in working class areas, which operated largely on credit. Shephard's was founded by Mr Emerson Shephard, a cobbler. He came into some capital and opened his first shop in Swinburne Street, Gateshead, in 1906, selling shoes. Then, in 1924, he moved to West Street, Gateshead, and began selling drapery as well.[64] The store closed in 1980.[65] J.T. Parrish's was established in 1879, at 10 Oswald Terrace, Byker,[66] moved to 116 Shields Road in 1881,[67] and closed in 1984.[68] The importance of these stores was that they offered the facility to buy a variety of goods on credit locally. Both had their own currency, which was obtained by taking out a ticket with an agent of that particular shop. The tickets were sold in multiples of a pound, and the interest charged on them was a shilling to the pound. Shephard's and Parrish's began by using the first type of agents (that is self-employed), and these smaller agents may initially have had dealings with only one of these stores. More often, though, they had agreements with several shops. The disadvantage for the customer of dealing with a small ticket agent was that when they purchased a ticket they had to have it made out to only one of the shops which that particular agent dealt with.

Shephard's and Parrish's mainly served the local communities of Gateshead and Byker respectively, but they also attracted customers from other parts of Tyneside, as the respondents who used it testified. People from the West End of Newcastle, though, tended to use shops in the centre of the city, particularly those in the Westgate Road area, which in many ways were similar to Shephard's and Parrish's. Trams from the West End of Newcastle stopped at the bottom of Westgate Road, and the shops that would accept 'tickets' tended to be in this area.[69] These shops included: Wenger's, 101 Westgate Road (est. 1934); J. McAdam & Sons, at 212A Westgate Road (est. 1925); and, Woolf's nearby at 57 Westmorland Road (est. 1911).[70] There were also shops such as Blaylock's (est. 1923) on New Bridge Street that served the same clientele.[71] All these shops sold clothing. Some sold other goods as well and they seem to have run mainly on credit. The shops in the Westgate Road area depended on ticket agents to bring in customers. There were several small companies, in Newcastle city centre which dealt with these shops.[72] An example of this type of agency was T. Archer Lee in Worswick Chambers (est. 1937).[73]

The largest credit agency on Tyneside was The Provident Clothing & Supply Company Limited. As we have seen, the Provident system was, and is, extensively used on Tyneside. The Provident first began trading in Newcastle as The Provident Clothing Club at 362½ Westgate Road in 1893, but it does not seem to have had very much impact until much later.[74] One informant told me that the Provident did not appear in Byker until 1937, long after Parrish's money was already an established part of life.[75] When the 'Provi' (as it was commonly known) became established on Tyneside, it meant that customers of both Shephard's and Parrish's had an alternative way to pay that also offered them more choice, as both shops would accept Provident orders. The Provident system had two major advantages over dealing with a private agent or a smaller company. A Provident order could be used in more shops and in a more flexible manner than 'tickets' from other companies. All the shops described above accepted Provident orders, and a single Provident order could be spent in several different shops.

All the respondents who had used the Provident at this time agreed that it was the best form of credit available to them. As one woman put it,

> You paid the same to Provident as you did to these little agents, but when Provident came onto the scene it was ideal. That's how I brought my family up, with the help of Provident . . . I relied on Provident.[76]

Another respondent described the advantages of Provident orders for her: 'The glory of them was that you could take them to 20, 30, 40 or even more shops, and they had collectors.'[77] So the Provident provided a more flexible form of credit than other firms, but at the same rate of interest: a shilling in the pound. The advantage of the Provident order was that it enabled a customer to shop around, rather than be tied to one store, which meant they could find the most competitive prices. As one of my respondents put it, 'You could use it just like as if you had money in your purse.'[78] The crucial difference was, of course, that money was less expensive.

We also need to consider again the relationship of tallymen, or Scotch drapers, to the working class. There were several firms of credit drapers trading on Tyneside during this period. However, as I was able to conduct interviews with only two retired credit drapers, we will confine ourselves to a brief history of their firms. We have already met one of these, Mr Burton, in an earlier chapter. Mr Burton was employed by the Newcastle clothing firm of Locherby's. We will consider his account of his own experiences as a credit traveller in a later section, as he did not begin working for Locherby's until 1947. However, a further extract from his Rotary Club Address provides us with a brief history of the firm.

> Earliest recollections go back to the early 1800 s, when the business originated with a Mr Teesdale, an uncle of the four Locherby brothers. They began trading as Locherby Bros. and had their business in Blackett Street, Newcastle on Tyne. In 1902 Mr William J. Locherby

purchased the property at 25 Ridley Place, and the business has been conducted there ever since. The colliery villages of south-east Northumberland and Blyth valley were the main source of the business, although journeys were also established in County Durham. The brothers and their staff travelled door-to-door, and such business was commonly known as Scotch drapery.[79]

The other credit draper I interviewed, Jim Macrae, eventually took over a business which his father had set up in 1914. This firm was W.D. Macrae's, and was originally run from a warehouse at 65A Blackett Street in Newcastle.[80] Macrae's was operating in direct competition with Locherby's. Jim Macrae was born in 1916 and joined his father's firm in 1932. Mr Macrae says,

At the age of 16 I started work for my father. Until I was 20, I was father's assistant on his credit rounds, but then took over the Tyneside connection which included Jarrow, Hebburn, South Shields etc. This was a scattered area which I had to travel by bus and train. We were general drapers selling clothing for the whole family as well as household goods.[81]

According to Mr Macrae, when his father began trading he sold suits and other items of clothing, bedding and work clothing, such as pit boots and socks. This was the same trade that Locherby's were engaged in. Mr Burton says that his firm sold 'carpets, blankets, sheets, curtains, clothing, underwear, socks, you name it we sold it!'[82] These firms offered such a wide range of goods because much of their business was conducted in fairly remote villages. They had a captive market, particularly before the development of regular public transport. Both firms also covered quite a wide geographical area. Locherby's tended to concentrate their attentions on the Blyth valley area, but they also did some trading in County Durham, as Mr Burton points out. As well as the South Tyneside route, which Mr Macrae describes, Macrae's also traded in County Durham, and the firm eventually moved to Durham city. The majority of the trade of both firms came from supplying made-to-measure suits for miners.

Mr Macrae described his method of trading in colliery districts.

We used to try to get recommendations for new customers, and we always could find out from the insurance men what sort of payers they were, because we all worked together. We all collected in the same houses. In the colliery villages you went on a Friday night to collect the money, and we were all following each other in and out. There was ourselves and the insurance man and the grocer and all this sort of thing. And the woman of the house she used to sit there with the money that the men had brought in, dishing it out.[83]

The credit drapery trade involved weekly collection, just as the 'ticket' trade did. However, there was no identifiable interest charge in the case of credit drapery. The trader charged inflated prices to begin with. Mr Macrae said,

We didn't used to charge any interest. We incorporated that in the price. But people like Shephard's and Bevan's and that sort of thing they used to put a shilling to the pound on, you see, and so do the Provident.[84]

As we have seen, this was the standard rate of interest such firms charged at the time. However it is interesting to note that, despite Mr Macrae's apparent pride in not charging interest, when I asked him how much he added onto the price he became somewhat vague and said something to the effect of it being 'around' a shilling in the pound! We should now turn to consider the relationship between the credit draper and their customers.

Another passage from Mr Burton's Rotary Club Address gives us an insight into how the travellers perceived this relationship. 'This method of trading took the traveller into the very heart of the mining family. He was a trusted and respected friend indeed.'[85] The importance of the bond between the customer and the agent for the firm is illustrated by the following incident, which was related to me by Mr Burton. He said that one of the firm's travellers, who was known as 'Old John' by the time Mr Burton had joined the firm, had established a round in the colliery village of Cambois (in the Blyth area). When 'Old John' went off to war, in 1914, he was not expected to return. So his 'journeys' were sold off. Mr Burton then went on to describe what happened when 'Old John' did, in fact, come home from the First World War.

So he returned to Ridley Place, went to see old man Locherby, and he said, 'I want me job back.' He said, 'John, I haven't got any work for you.' 'Leave that to me,' John said, 'Give me a few patterns.' And off he went to Cambois. He got into the club at Cambois, the working man's club there, and he measured something like eighteen suits the first day he was out there. And that Cambois journey was one of our biggest journeys . . . He recreated that, simply on his friendship and standing.[86]

Mr Macrae told me that he often received gifts from his customers:

Of course the miners were great people in their gardens, you know. They were great leek growers and onion growers and that sort of thing. We often would get a leek given to us, and when the coal was short we used to often get a lump of coal put in the back of the car . . . There was that real friendly relationship. It was grand, and you were always welcome for a cup of tea with all of these people.[87]

He was then invited to explore this theme further by considering whether he got on well with all of his customers.

Oh yes, we did particularly. In fact I think all credit traders had to because they depended upon them. And you were hoping, when the family got married, you were going to get them as customers also, you see. And it did happen, there's no doubt about it. We had great family connections.[88]

So his reply reveals the instrumental motivation behind the 'real friendly relationship' that he created with his customers. This prompted a further question. He was then asked to what extent his relationship with his customers was calculated? He continued:

You see, there weren't as many motor cars in those days and people depended upon us going to them. Nowadays they would get in their car and go to a main centre, wouldn't they? We promoted it more than most.[89]

At first it might seem from his reply that he has simply changed the subject. However an alternative interpretation is that, he is offering a rationalisation for his behaviour. This is a very similar explanation to that offered by other lenders of this type and it can be summarised as follows: alright, I might be exploiting the people I dealt with, both financially and emotionally, but I was also providing them with a vital service, so it was justified.

This is not to argue that Mr Macrae's actions were totally instrumentally motivated. It is apparent from some of his remarks I quote above that he enjoyed the 'friendly relationship' he had with his customers. He seems to have held a number of contradictory attitudes towards his customers simultaneously. The affectual component of his feelings towards his customers is apparent from certain unprompted remarks that he made during the course of the interview. For example, here is his view of the miners that he dealt with. 'They were nice people. They were great people. They were...rough and honest, but we liked them.'[90] So how can we best characterise such an attitude?

Karen Rowlingson's description of owner-collectors, in the PSI report on weekly-collected credit, comes close to describing the attitude of both Mr Macrae and Mr Burton towards their customers. She distinguishes between two types of owner-collectors: entrepreneurs and paternalists. She says that paternalists

> ...came from a higher social class. The social distance between bor-rower and lender led to a form of detached mutual respect. For the lender this respect bordered on paternalism and, for the borrower, this respect bordered on deference.[91]

As well as this mutual respect, though, there is another element also present in the relationship. As was argued in the previous chapter, the majority of credit-givers that deal with the working class are involved in a type of performance that is, in some way, 'cynical'. We also saw that this was a complex issue, as it could often be difficult to determine the extent to which a 'performance' is cynical or sincere. The actions of Mr Macrae and Mr Burton can be seen as forms of what Hochschild has called emotional labour. This raises the question: how can we square attitudes of mutual respect with the use of emotional manipulation? At this point I would also like to add a further dimension to the discussion. The distinction between practical and discursive consciousness can provide a key to understanding the attitude of collectors to their customers. It is the operation of this distinction that accounts for this discrepancy.

Here we can draw upon Giddens' assertion that the distinction between practical and discursive consciousness is central to structuration theory. He points out that this distinction is not a rigid and impermeable one. He says,

> What agents know about what they do, and why they do it — their knowledgeability as agents — is largely carried in practical conscious-ness. Practical consciousness consists of all the things which actors

know tacitly about how to 'go on' in the contexts of social life without being able to give them discursive expression.[92]

He relates practical consciousness to routinisation. He stresses the importance of activities that are carried out habitually in creating a sense of ontological security in the individual.

> The repetitiveness of activities which are undertaken in like manner day after day is the material grounding of what I call the recursive nature of social life. (By its recursive nature I mean that the structured properties of social activity — via the duality of structure—are constantly recreated out of the very resources which constitute them.) Routinization is vital to the psychological mechanisms whereby a sense of trust or ontological security is sustained in the daily activities of social life.[93]

Routinisation is enacted through the medium of practical consciousness.

It is argued here that the actions of both customers and agents can be understood as manifestations of practical consciousness. In terms of the customers of doorstep agencies, the element of routinisation is very important. They become accustomed to the same collectors calling at the same time every week. So they feel that they are dealing with someone they can 'rely on'. When the particular collector an individual has become accustomed to dealing with leaves the firm (for whatever reason) and a new collector takes over, there is still a link with the firm itself. The particular type of credit used by an individual becomes a means of sustaining that individual's sense of ontological security. For, as Giddens says, 'Routine is psychologically relaxing...'[94] It must be remembered that this is part of the experience of doorstep credit for both customer and collector. For the collector, though, there is another aspect to the routin-isation of their activities through the medium of practical consciousness. It places them at a distance from the consequences of their actions.

Giddens says,

> Human agents always know what they are doing on the level of discursive consciousness under some description. However, what they do may be quite unfamiliar under other descriptions, and they may know little of the ramified consequences of the activities in which they engage.[95]

Both Mr Burton and Mr Macrae explicitly said, 'we didn't used to charge any interest.'[96] In the case of Mr Macrae, as we saw, he was quite proud of the fact that this was what differentiated him from other firms trading with the working class. Mr Burton's answer was a bit more complicated, and it took me longer to establish that he also charged an inflated price ' . . . in order to take care of the customer who was a slow payer'.[97] This euphemistic explanation of his action is quite revealing. By incorporating the interest into the price they charged, these two traders were able to change the meaning that their actions had in their own minds at the level of discursive consciousness. This facilitated the creation of a particular self-image, that of service-providers. In other words, through a degree of self-deception, they were able to redefine their actions as socially beneficial to the communities they served.

In terms of the customer, as has been argued, familiarity with the collector and the firm can become a source of ontological security. It was not possible to interview any of these two traders' ex-customers. However, the same principle applies to all types of doorstep credit. If we now turn to consider other doorstep-credit firms during the interwar period, this should become apparent. One of the features of this type of credit is the fact that it can become a 'family tradition'. This is the point that Rowlingson makes in her study of this type of credit. A fifth of the customers in her study had begun using doorstep credit because they had seen others in their families use it.[98] So this meant that they had a personal link with a particular firm, as they were known by the individual agents of that firm. As we will see from looking at the following account, this pattern of use was already established by the interwar period.

Mrs Wrigley was born in Howdon in 1925. She told me that her mother dealt with Walker's of North Shields, credit drapers, largely due to a family connection.

> Me mother dealt there from being married, through me grandmother, like me father's mother, 'cause she had dealt there all her life. And, as the sons got married, all their wives dealt there. And sometimes it was a man came, and sometimes it was a woman came, and sometimes it was Mr Walker himself who came![99]

The fact that the owner and his sons used to take part in the actual collection of money, and visit customers' homes seems to have created a favourable impression of the firm among some of its customers. Mrs Wrigley describes the owner's son who used to collect from her as having 'no airs and graces at all'.[100] This perceived friendliness on the part of the owners was one of the reasons Mrs Wrigley continued to use the shop. She also felt that the goods, although expensive, were of good quality. This indicates the type of effect that personal contact with the owners of a firm can have upon the customers (Of course, if the personal characteristics of the owners were different, it could have had a detrimental effect upon the firm.). As Mrs Wrigley is describing a similar type of firm to the two credit drapers discussed above, it seems likely that meeting the owners of those firms had a similar impression on their customers. So the lesson here is clear: good agent/customer relationships can boost business and this effect can sometimes be heightened by the involvement of an owner with 'no airs and graces'.

Her mother also used a part-time ticket agent who dealt with other shops. Mrs Wrigley said,

> A lady used to come to the house, more of a friend really than a . . . The majority of them were, weren't they? It was just like an ordinary woman who got these clubs and you paid her . . . She was an agent for Bell Marsh's in Wallsend, Bell Bros. in North Shields and Howard's Stores in North Shields, and you could get a ticket for whatever one you asked for.[101]

So there was usually an affectual element present in the relationship between the customer and the agent, as we have seen. For the agent, this could be a useful means of creating and sustaining business. For the customer this tended to mean loyalty to particular firms but, of course, customers were not purely guided by personal loyalty. Mrs Wrigley pointed out that, as her mother had had two sources of credit, Walker's and the part-time ticket agent, she had been able to use them to the best advantage for herself. If she wanted curtains, for example, she would get them through the ticket agent as she was not overly concerned about the quality. She was more likely to go to Walker's, on the other hand, for items of clothing which she felt needed to be good quality.

As pointed out above, Parrish's, of Byker, and Shephard's of Gateshead, were important sources of credit for the Tyneside working class during this period. If we consider two respondents' accounts of using the latter store at this time, we can see how customers' attitudes are shaped by a combination of economic necessity and the personal characteristics of the agents they deal with.

Mrs Rowntree was born in 1917. She was the daughter of a time-served engineer who worked in the shipyards, and she strongly asserted that her father was skilled and 'respectable'. As we might expect, her father did not, on the whole, approve of credit. However the family did get credit from her uncle, who was an agent for Shephard's. The fact that there was a family connection with the firm made it an acceptable form of credit to her father. She said, 'I don't think that he would have allowed my mother to seek credit from an outside agency any more than he would have allowed her to go to the pawnshop.'[102] In this case, the fact that the agent was a relative helped to make the use of this type of credit acceptable in the first place.

In the case of Mrs Samuel, the other respondent whose parents used Shephard's, the personal characteristics of their agent did not influence their decision to become customers, as they had known nothing about him beforehand. However the religious and cultural affinity between them seems to have helped in cementing the relationship. Mrs Samuel's father had a skilled job. He was a winding engineer in various mines in the Northumberland and Durham area. He was also a Methodist, a teetotaller, and a union treasurer. He epitomised the 'respectable' working class. Between 1925 and 1930, he worked at Wardley colliery in County Durham. He was there during the General Strike of 1926. It was the hardship caused by this strike that led to the family becoming involved with Shephard's. As Mrs Samuel told me,

> So there was something that she must have wanted and there was another lady in another street who said, 'Well, get a ticket for Shephard's.' Me mother didn't know what a ticket was. So Mrs Diamond [the neighbour] said I'll send Mr Carr [the agent] round. So she got a ticket for 30s. You paid so much a week, and we were good payers. If the ticket was paid he'd say, 'Mrs White will you have another one?' 'No, I'll not bother,' she'd say. 'Oh yes, you must have one,' he'd say. And she had nothing in mind, but he would write her a ticket for 30s. And she'd think of something to buy with it. But he came for years, Mr Carr. He was a very nice man.[103]

As well as being 'a very nice man', Mr Carr was also a Methodist, something Mrs Samuel asserted several times. As we can see from the above quote, he also seemed to know how to keep his foot firmly wedged in any door he wished to keep open. From what Mrs Samuel told me, it was the combination of his 'niceness' and Methodism that ensured the family's continued relationship with Mr Carr.

The interpenetration of personal attachment and economic motivation in the mind of the customer can be clearly seen in the next phase of the family's credit history. In 1938, the family was living in Pelaw, a colliery village in Gateshead. They went to Chapel with a woman who owned a small drapers' shop and credit business in that village. Mrs Samuel said that they then had begun trading with this woman, 'Because we knew her and she was just starting up.'[104] So the family took out a ticket with her. However, as she did not carry much stock in her own shop, she was also an agent for Ralph Robson's, a larger draper in High Bridge, Newcastle. The family began going to Ralph Robson's to buy clothing. In 1939, they moved to Stanley in County Durham. The remainder of their debt to Ralph Robson's of Newcastle was then transferred to that shop's agent in Stanley, who Mrs Samuel's mother was also friendly with. By this time, Mrs Samuel's father was earning enough for the family not to need credit to purchase items of clothing. However, they made some further purchases from Ralph Robson's, to help this woman to build up her business.

For collectors, too, part-time work as an agent for a credit firm can become a 'family tradition'. In the case of one family interviewed, the women had been part-time credit agents for three generations. Mrs Thompson began trading as a part-time ticket agent in Benwell and Scotswood in the west end of Newcastle in 1933. Then, in 1937, her daughter, Mrs Hill, took over from her. Mrs Hill's daughter, Mrs Joll, was a collector for the Provident from 1972 to 1991. I was able to interview Mrs Hill and Mrs Joll about both their own and Mrs Thompson's experiences. Mrs Thompson's husband was a skilled worker in Vickers in the west end of Newcastle. She began the ticket business to earn some extra money for the family. Running a ticket agency also gave the agent the opportunity to buy clothes from the businesses they dealt with at a discount. This was one of the attractions it held for Mrs Thompson. She dealt with a number of shops, most of which were in Newcastle city centre. These included Roland Blaylock's on New Bridge Street, Woolf's on Westmorland Road and Goldsberg's on Clayton Street. She was also an agent for Shephard's of Gateshead.[105]

There do seem to have been a lot of drawbacks to being a part-time ticket agent at this time, the main one being that the agent was responsible to the shops they dealt with for their customers' debts. So the agent would receive a bill for the goods that their customers had purchased at the end of the month even when the customer had not paid the agent. Mrs Hill said,

> Me mother used to get very worried about people who were just playing on her and getting these things from her. She was really worried to death about it, in case she didn't have the money to pay her bills. And I said it wasn't worth carrying on like that, because

some of them don't care whether they pay or not you know. I've met these sort of people.[106]

It is worth noting that her daughter (Mrs Joll) agreed with her on this point. So she also felt that some of her customers had no intention of paying. Mrs Hill's account of being a ticket agent emphasises the difficulties involved. She felt that the main advantage of being an agent was that the whole family could obtain discount on the clothing they bought from the shops they dealt with.

However it seems that customers often saw ticket agents in quite a different light. Agents for Shephard's or Parrish's kept the shilling in the pound interest that the shop charged the customer, and also received 9½ per cent interest on top of that. So they stood to make 14½ per cent profit on every pound.[107] It was obviously a potentially profitable business if they had the right customers. As Mrs Rowntree told me, 'People were decked with jewellery, gold, furs and all the rest of it if they were running an agency.'[108] This may have been something of an exaggeration, and we would also need to know what other sources of income such agents may have had. On the other hand, this would appear to be a fairly common perception of this type of ticket agent, as we can see from looking at some evidence from local autobiographies.

Joe Hind was born in 1923 in Battlefield, just south of the parish of Shieldfield, not far from Newcastle city centre. In his autobiography, *A Shieldfield Childhood*, he describes the regular visit of the ticket man to the family home, and his account provides an interesting counterpoint to Mrs Hill's.

> Most folk in Shieldfield had a ticket man, and my mother was no exception. I remember he was called Mr Morton, and every Friday night my mother would put aside Morton's money. Doling out tickets was a prosperous business, and if the interest of a shilling in the pound does not sound much by today's standards, most of the ticket men flourished. It wasn't long before Mr Morton, who started his rounds on a bike, was calling on us in a smart motor car.[109]

Mrs Hill told me that she was aware that some of her customers sold their tickets for less than their face value to obtain ready cash when they were hard up. However, as she pointed out, she was still responsible to the shop for the amount on the ticket.[110] The ticket agent was in a similar position to the corner shopkeeper who offered groceries on credit. They had to be able to trust their customers to repay the debt.

It also seems likely that the area an agent traded in was very important. It must be remembered that Mrs Thompson and Mrs Hill were trading in quite poor parts of the west end of Newcastle during the Depression years. So it was not surprising that they ended up with a lot of bad debt.

Thomas Callaghan's autobiography is quite revealing on this subject. He was born in 1924 in Mill Lane, in the west end of Newcastle, and grew up in Benwell village (also in the west end). Apart from underlining the obvious poverty that many families lived in, he also describes the difficulties experienced by ticket men when they came to make collections. This could sometimes result in them being threatened with violence. Callaghan says that the family he had shared a landing with when he was a boy were customers of a ticket man from the Provident, who would call every Saturday lunch-time. The family would send their youngest boy out to deal with him:

> ...and he would shout out in this high pitched tone, 'Me muffer not in you.' And the poor little fat ticket man would fiercely retort, 'Your mother is in.' 'Me muffer not in, you.' 'Your mother is in — so don't give me that.' 'Me muffer not in, you.' This usually went on for about ten minutes without a pause, both participants becoming irritable; until finally the man went away in distress muttering to himself... Then one particular Saturday, my father had gone out to him and gave him ten seconds to vanish; the fat man disappeared in four.[111]

Callaghan says that when their own ticket man from another company called, his family would send his brother out to try get rid of him. This went on until their neighbour decided to intervene, in order to repay the favour that Callaghan's father had performed for him:

> Then once, our next door neighbour came out on to the landing, pretending to be in a furious mood: 'Stop bloody arguin' with the kid, if yer want to argue, al come doon th' stairs with yer.' And off went our ticket-man in a hurry![112]

Such tactics could be a only short-term solution to the problem of obtaining credit. It is clear from talking to Mrs Hill and other credit traders that they would not go on granting credit to a family that did not meet their repayments. When we add to this the threat of physical violence to the collector if they returned to a house, then it is apparent that these families would not be able to ask for more credit from the same creditor. They would also be likely to meet with difficulties if they applied to another creditor given the flow of information between credit companies and others dealing with the working class that I described above. Both the credit drapers interviewed (Mr Macrae and Mr Burton) belonged to the Newcastle Credit Traders Association. In fact they were both, at one time or another, presidents of that organisation. They also belonged to the National Association of Credit Traders. Any bad payers they dealt with would be blacklisted through one of these organisations.

It is clear from Mrs Hill's account that she encountered the same sort of difficulties as the collectors described by Callaghan (but without the threat of physical violence). She says,

> You could go for your money once, and you could go half-a-dozen times, 'cause we as children they used to send us for the money. You would be lucky if you got 3d. or 6d. off the debt. They didn't care whether they paid or not, you know? But you had all that lying out, 'cause all these bills had to be paid. It wasn't like the Provi. With them you don't have the responsibility, but you have when you're on your own.[113]

Mrs Hill was typical of a lot of part-time agents, as she belonged to the respectable working class but a lot of her customers did not. When I asked her about her customers she told me that they tended to be poorer and less respectable than her own family. An indicator for her of their lack of respectability was that they used the pawnshop. Their poverty was indicated by the fact that many of their children did not have shoes. She collected in various parts of the west end, including Scotswood and an area which no longer exists that she called 'The Tanyards', which housed miners. She singled out the people who lived in the latter area as being less respectable.

Mrs Hill's attitude towards her customers is highly ambiguous. On the one hand, as we have seen, she was highly critical of those customers who did not pay regularly (or at all). She says that they did not care whether they paid or not. On the other hand, she told me that she got on 'wonderfully' with her customers.

> No-one was better than another. The kettle was always on for a cup of tea, if you had time to sit and talk to them all. They used to like you calling, but they hadn't the money to pay you for it all, you know?[114]

Obviously, she tended to get on better with what she called 'good payers', but we can also see a degree of sympathy for her customers' plight in the above quote. This is partly to be explained by the fact that, like Mr Burton and Mr Macrae, she was brought into close contact with the people she dealt with and, as a result, was made aware of their lifestyle. However, there is a difference between Mrs Hill and these traders — Mrs Hill was herself from a working class family. Her father had been unemployed for several years after the General Strike of 1926. In other words, although she was respectable and considered herself to be a 'bit better' than the people she dealt with, her experience was not far removed from theirs.

It is being argued that, to some extent, this type of agent–customer relationship has a similar effect to that of the contradictory class location of small shopkeepers. In this case, though, we are not dealing with a question of class location, as both part-time agents and customers belong to the working class, but class fractionalisation. The effect of such relationships is contradictory. On the one hand it serves only to exacerbate existing divisions within the working class, thus contributing towards class fractionalisation. On the other hand, it tends to bring two disparate sections of the class together, thus contributing towards class integration.

The reasons for individual customers choosing to use the Provident, rather than a ticket agent such as Mrs Thompson, were straightforward. To begin with, the personality of the collector was not particularly important in drawing customers to the Provident. This was because the Provident was the most economically rational form of credit available to the Tyneside working class at that time. It simply made sense to use an agent of the Provident rather than one of the smaller ticket companies, as the Provident gave the customer access to more shops, and, consequently, better prices. This was the factor that drew the two women I quoted above, whom we shall call Mrs Perkin and Mrs Rowntree, to the Provident. Both women stressed the economic advantages of the Provident over the other firms that they could have dealt with at that time.

However, once they had actually started dealing with the firm, their relationship with their agent became an important factor in their continued use of that type of credit. Both Mrs Perkin and Mrs Rowntree told me that they liked their collectors. A third woman, Mrs Mason, who dealt with the Provident from about 1938 until 1975, told me that she 'enjoyed' visits from all the collectors that she had dealt with.[115] She emphasised the social aspect that the weekly transactions had for her. Another respondent, who used the Provident from 1943 to 1964, felt that one of the advantages of having collectors who knew their customers was that collectors were in a position to decide how much credit their customers could afford.[116] This particular woman had not adjusted to the more impersonal methods of credit (such as credit cards) that developed during the post-war period. She felt more comfortable with familiar methods of credit. It is also worth noting here that this respondent was quite explicit about the fact that the 'friendly' relationship between the customer and the agent continued after the war. According to her, the dynamics of the agent–customer relationship did not alter in the immediate post-war period. This is consistent with the other evidence from that period, as we will see in the following chapter.

Conclusion

This chapter has dealt with the relationship between agents of established credit firms and their customers before 1945. We have seen that one consistent feature of the use of credit by the working class is that those companies which offered them credit tended to rely upon agents, or collectors, to mediate between themselves and their customers. Some of the companies which traded in this way before the Second World War are still doing so today. The term 'agent' was used to refer to any individual, acting on behalf of any organisation which offers 'doorstep' credit to individual consumers, whose task it was to collect the regular instalments involved in this type of credit. The agent acted as the interface between the consumer and the organisation. For the credit agent, information-gathering was a crucial part of the job. They needed information on prospective customers, as well as personal details of their existing customers, which could help to create more business. In the interwar period, credit traders tended to use other credit traders, or insurance agents who dealt in the same district, as a source of information. One of the fundamental qualities of the relationship between the agent and the customer was that an agent's customers were usually loyal to the agent as an individual, rather than to the company. The importance of the close personal relationship that usually developed between the agent of a credit company and their customers has been acknowledged by various commentators. This close relationship continued to be a significant part of this type of trading after 1945, and it this remarkable continuity that we will go on to explore in the following chapter.

5

'Still One of the Family' the Role of the Agent and the Established Firm within Working Class Credit after 1945

The first point to consider in an analysis of the role of the agent and the established credit firm in the post-war period is that many of the old firms continued trading in the same way after 1945. We can find evidence for this in several of the immediate post-war studies. The authors of *Coal Is Our Life* say that many families continued to use credit drapers, partly because it was a method of purchase that they were accustomed to.[1] Richard Hoggart also felt that familiarity was important in maintaining the older forms of credit during this period.

> The clubs, or check-trading, tend to become a habit and the house-to-house agents are adept at persuading clients to 'keep the account open' continuously, so that in many cases more money is leaking away weekly in this way than can really be spared.[2]

Madeline Kerr says that most families used 'cheques' to buy clothing much as they did during the interwar years. There was also an indication that the next generation were going to carry on this tradition. As she says, 'Immediately children leave school they follow the Mum's example and buy on cheques.'[3]

Before considering the relationship between agents and their customers in the post-war period we need to consider the economic environment in which it occurred, and the general expansion of consumer credit in this period. After the Second World War, and the austerity that followed, the British people finally escaped from a world of shortages and rationing and entered the brave new world of a consumer society. Industrial production rose dramatically from 1953 to 1955 along with GDP, and the full-employment target was met. Expenditure on consumer durables also increased with annual increases in the number of cars, television sets and fridges purchased between 1953 and 1955.[4] Much of this consumer boom was funded by hire-purchase. The total hire-purchase debt outstanding in 1955, the first year in which the Board of Trade collected statistics, was in excess of £450 million.[5] After a slight drop, the volume of hire-purchase and other instalment credit outstanding rose quite sharply after 1957, reaching £935 million by 1960.[6]

Richard Hoggart noted working class participation in the post-war expansion of hire-purchase in the 1950s:

> Young couples like to go out and buy everything new when they 'set up' and the furniture salesmen often do their best to persuade them to buy, by hire-purchase, more new furniture than they need.[7]

The affluent workers studied by Goldthorpe *et al* in the 1960s also benefited from the consumer boom:

> In the sphere of domestic consumption, at least, there was little evidence at all of any restricting influence being exerted by traditional working-class norms. Considering, for example, refrigerators and cars — two high cost and characteristically 'middle class' possessions — the extent of ownership proved to be roughly comparable between our manual and non-manual samples: 58% of the former as against 56% of the latter had refrigerators and 45% as against 52% owned cars.[8]

Obviously, given their cost, such items would usually be obtained on hire-purchase. The issue of hire-purchase salesmen putting pressure on consumers to buy, which Hoggart mentions, had been a cause of concern since the interwar period.[9] This brings us to the negative side of the post-war expansion of consumerism.

In the years following the enactment of the *Hire Purchase Act* 1938 it became increasingly apparent that substantial extensions were needed if consumers were to be given sufficient protection. This concern resulted in further Acts in 1954, 1964 and 1965.[10] The *Hire Purchase Act* 1964 made the formal requirements of an agreement stricter, and introduced a 'cooling off' period, which gave the buyer the opportunity to cancel an agreement if it was signed outside commercial premises.[11] This latter safeguard 'was aimed at the door-to-door salesman who puts pressure, perhaps undue pressure, on customers in their own homes and induces them to sign binding agreements'.[12] MPs had been expressing concern over this issue for some time.[13] During one of the discussions preceding the Act, Mr W.T. Williams said,

... there cannot be any doubt that in the legislation as it now stands there is such confusion and so many abuses of the hire-purchase system that it is little short of a scandal.[14]

He was concerned about the number of people who were subject to warrant for non-payment of debt to hire-purchase companies.

Not only are many thousands of people paying their hire-purchase commitments under warrant, but, no fewer than 2,500 in the North-West alone are serving or have served terms of imprisonment for failure to pay hire-purchase debts.[15]

We can see that although it may have improved the situation, the *Hire Purchase Act* of 1938 did not completely eradicate all the problems it attempted to solve. One of the reasons for this was that the value of goods covered by the Act had continually to be raised to keep pace with increased standards of consumption. The other reason was that sellers simply continued to mislead their customers.

A good indication of the way such problems manifested themselves at a local level is the increase in the number of hire-purchase enquiries dealt with by the Citizens' Advice Bureau in Newcastle upon Tyne. In 1952–3 only 4 out of 188 enquiries to the Bureau were hire-purchase cases.[16] However, the 1961–2 report of the Bureau noted the increase in the intervening years.

A notable increase over the past years has been seen in the number of enquiries under the heading 'Trade.' In 1956 there were 181 enquiries and this had risen to 1,157 last year. The enquiries are mainly concerned with hire purchase difficulties and with unsatisfactory goods. Although this number is under 12% of the total enquiries, the amount of work is proportionately much greater. Other problems may often be referred to solicitors, welfare agencies, local authority departments etc., but there seems to be no other body which is able to deal with consumer complaints unless a clear breach of the law can be shown. We do our best to help. Some clients are able to deal with the problem themselves, after a reasonable explanation has been given, but others, especially the less educated and the elderly, need considerable help and often much correspondence is undertaken on their behalf.[17]

The bureau clearly felt that part of the answer to this problem was consumer education and subsequently distributed hundreds of leaflets on the '*Hire Purchase Act* 1965' and 'How to say No to a Doorstep salesman'.[18] Despite their best efforts, the number of enquiries in this category continued to gradually increase, reaching 1369 in the period 1966–7.[19] The personal unhappiness that lies behind such statistics is as much a part of the post-war consumer boom as the rise in the ownership of refrigerators and television sets.

Although by the 1960s the more affluent sections of the working class had begun to make more use of banks and building societies, their shift away from the old patterns of saving and borrowing was very gradual. Goldthorpe *et al* found that 40 per cent of the manual workers in their study had Post Office Savings Bank Accounts and that 64 per cent had money in a building society or the Trustee Savings Bank. These figures were comparable with those of the white-collar workers in their sample.[20] An interesting counterweight to this picture of increased affluence is provided by Hilary Land's study of 86 large families in London in the mid-1960s. She begins by acknowledging the greater financial pressures on large families but, even allowing for that, the picture that emerges is one of considerable hardship for some. The families in her study were drawn from all social classes, with only the richest being able to pay cash for clothing. The affluent workers in this study still bought most of their clothing through clothing clubs or Provident checks.[21] The poorer families were not always able to do even that. They often relied on jumble sales, second-hand clothes shops and charities to provide them with clothing, or simply went without. Parents would deprive themselves of clothing in order to provide for their children, and some mothers did not own any shoes other than a pair of slippers.[22] Those who did use the 'traditional' types of credit did not always do so out of choice, and some clearly felt exploited by the firms they were dealing with.[23]

In his 1975 article on the clearing banks and the 'new working class', Peter Willmott points out that a large proportion of the working class still clung to the old methods of credit, even in conditions of relative prosperity.[24] As he says, though, there were signs that this was beginning to change in the mid-1970s as, by this time, most employers and some workers favoured the payment of wages by non-cash means.[25] He advises the banks to make themselves more accessible to working class customers, and this was what they began to do at around this time. Berthoud and Kempson, the authors of the 1992 PSI report, point out that there was a particularly rapid expansion in the number of people with cheque accounts during the 1970s.[26] Tebbutt points out that a general appreciation of the choices available to them led many of the

more affluent customers of the established credit firms to turn away
from them. She cites one credit draper who estimated that they formed
a mere 15 per cent of his accounts by the early 1980s.[27]

What has happened during the post-war period is that the old doorstep
credit firms have been gradually usurped by other forms of consumer
credit. This is due to both the expansion of existing forms of credit and
the creation of new ones. In June 1966, the first credit card in Britain was
issued by Barclaycard. The 1994 PSI study of credit card use estimated that there were about 30 million credit cards in circulation at that
time.[28] Much of the growth in credit card use took place over the 1980s.
The authors of the PSI study say,

> Our national survey showed that credit cards were the most widely
> available credit facility. Almost 40 per cent of British households
> held a credit card — four times as many as there were when the
> National Consumer Council conducted its survey of credit in
> 1979.[29]

The NCC survey mentioned above made a comparison of the three
major credit surveys which immediately preceded it and found that,
since 1969, there had been considerable expansion in mail order, hire-
purchase and credit cards.[30] The volume of hire-purchase and other
instalment credit outstanding had reached £1384 million by 1970.[31]
The end result of all these changes is that the more prosperous sections
of the working class have now turned away from traditional forms of
working class credit. However, as has been indicated, the less affluent
sections of the working class are still excluded from the mainstream
credit market. This has led to the situation described in the previous
chapter with regard to restricted access to credit.

When we consider the contemporary research on doorstep credit, we
must remember the context in which it occurs. The working class is now
quite clearly divided between those who have access to mainstream
credit and those who do not. This is an important change that has
taken place gradually during the latter post-war period. It means that,
although in some ways very little seems to have changed in the relationship between the working class and doorstep creditors, there have
been great changes around that core relationship. There have been
several pieces of research which dealt with doorstep credit as part of
a more general survey of credit use which we could consider here. We
will focus on the two major surveys which deal with this area in depth:
Gillian Parker's research into indebtedness among Birmingham Money

Advice Centre clients, and the PSI research quoted above. Let us now consider each in turn.

Parker's research appeared in 1980 and dealt with Money Advice Centre (MAC) clients in Birmingham. She points out,

> Almost all MAC clients fall within the 'lower' categories of the Registrar-General's classification of occupations and, as such, constitute a very selective sub-group of the total population of debtors. As a corollary to this their incomes are low — most falling below the average for manual workers.[32]

This has implications for the type of credit available to them.

> Out of the possibilities of credit card, monthly account, option account, budget account, credit-sale, conditional sale, hire-purchase, shopping check or voucher, mail order catalogues and the 'club', the clients of the MAC are likely to have used or be using only the last four or five.[33]

The element of continuity with the pre-war era can be seen in the following quote from the same report.

> Despite the decline of hire purchase and the rise of the personal loan, check-trading companies have retained their hold on their traditionally working class market. Much of their success must be due to the personal way in which they conduct their business. Most of the 'callers' who visit MAC clients are from well-established 'family' firms and this often influences the way in which they are regarded by their customers. Women often do business with the same company used by their mothers or even grandmothers, and the callers come to be seen as family friends. Inevitably this personalisation of what is a business transaction makes it very difficult for customers who become financially distressed.[34]

Such a close personal relationship created a problem for MAC clients as they would almost invariably be advised to reduce their payments to all their creditors. However, they would often strongly resist the suggestion that they reduce payments to their doorstep collector. This was because they felt that they would be 'letting down' a friend. MAC clients will even give the weekly payments to the doorstep collector priority over rent and fuel bills.[35] As we will see below, this is precisely the point that money advice workers on Tyneside made.

Parker goes on to make an explicit comparison with the pre-war period, quoting Maud Pember Reeves to illustrate that little has changed in 66 years. She points out,

> ...when some 80 per cent of manual workers are still paid in cash and most of these on a weekly basis, and little more than half of the population have bank accounts, there can be little doubt that a weekly caller taking cash represents a much more convenient way of paying for credit.[36]

Most of the clients in her sample seem to have been using the Provident and, as she says, Provident agents are encouraged to call at a fixed time every week. This method of credit still fits in easily with a weekly pattern of budgeting. A final parallel with the pre-war period is that the MAC clients '... bought checks and sold them at less than their face value to friends, neighbours, relatives, even shopkeepers to raise cash'.[37]

Karen Rowlingson's study of moneylending, published in 1994 by the PSI, dealt with the activities of firms like the Provident, which provide small unsecured loans repaid in weekly instalments.[38] We have already considered some of her findings, but we shall now consider them in more detail. As we will see, although published 14 years after Parker's study, there are many similarities in the findings of the two reports.

Rowlingson's study demonstrates the continuing importance of the personal relationship between the agent and the customer. The best way to sell loans to customers was to be on friendly terms with them, and this was also the best way to recover repayments. Sometimes customers felt indebted to the agent, and this could help ensure repayment.[39] As we saw with debts to small shopkeepers, the amount owed will, in all probability, not be large enough for it to be worth taking a defaulting customer to court. This means that collectors try to conceal their anger from their customers in the hope that they can recover the money at a later date. It should be apparent by now that the evidence presented in the PSI study demonstrates the continuing significance of the interpenetration of rationalities in the operation of doorstep credit. However, there are three related theoretical issues that we also need to address. We might label these the three 'Rs': rationalisation, routinisation and reflexivity. Let us now look at each of these in turn, beginning with rationalisation.

Gerth and Mills say, 'The principle of rationalisation is the most general element in Weber's philosophy of history.'[40] What Weber means by rationalisation is the 'disenchantment of the world', or the debunking of magic. He felt that thought was becoming progressively more systematic in character. Rationality denotes systematicity, consistency and method. As Derek Sayer says, 'Rationality amounts to the calculated application of rules.'[41] Weber says, 'The "objective" discharge of business primarily means a discharge of business according to calculable rules and "without regard for persons".'[42]

We have seen that this thesis is, in part, contradicted by the importance of personal loyalty to a particular agent rather than to the credit company itself. This will be explored further. I indicated earlier that, despite their adoption of bureaucratic procedures in the 1970s, personal evaluation still played a significant role in the way mail order companies selected prospective agents. If we now turn to consider the evidence in the PSI study of other doorstep lenders, we will see that personal evaluation is even more important to those firms. The first point to consider in connection with this subject is that most forms of mainstream consumer credit are now highly bureaucratised. Applying for credit will now usually involve filling in a form and, on the basis of this, a potential customer will be given a credit score. The decision to lend will be based upon whether an applicant's credit score has reached the pass mark set by that particular company. However, as Rowlingson says, 'Becoming a customer of a moneylender is a much less formal process than it is for other customer credit.'[43]

Although they might sometimes use application forms and credit-reference agencies, moneylenders tend to be more interested in a customer's personal characteristics. 'These personal characteristics include honesty, trustworthiness and reliability.'[44] Rowlingson is quite clear about what their usual methods of recruiting customers are.

> Most managers and collectors agreed that the best way of recruiting good customers was through personal recommendation. As one manager said, 'We try to be very careful who we take on. We tend only to take on relatives of people on the books or friends. But if friends recommend it, the person recommending has to guarantee it to start off with.'[45]

In other words, business is not usually carried out 'without regard for persons'.

Once an agent has actually recruited a customer, routinisation plays a large part in maintaining the relationship between them. Rowlingson found that, when people first became customers of doorstep credit companies, it was usually because they had identified a need and then decided to borrow in order to fulfil it. In fact 17 of the 31 customers in her sample had become customers in that way. However, after they had been customers for a certain period, it just became a habit to borrow from that lender. A lot of customers were simply borrowing a set amount every 20 weeks and then deciding what to spend it on. Some people could not remember what their last loan was for.

While routinisation plays a part in sustaining the relationship between lender and borrower, another concept that Giddens attaches importance to is important in the termination of that relationship: reflexivity. Giddens sees reflexivity as an integral part of modernity.

> It is introduced into the very basis of system reproduction, such that thought and action are constantly refracted back upon one another. The routinisation of daily life has no intrinsic connections with the past at all, save in so far as what 'was done before' happens to coincide with what can be defended in a principled way in the light of incoming knowledge. To sanction a practice because it is traditional will not do; tradition can be justified, but only in the light of knowledge which is not itself authenticated by tradition.[46]

Doorstep credit is a traditional form of working class credit. I would argue that increased reflexivity, along with improved access to credit, has played an important role in drawing many people away from this traditional form of credit. Again, this is an issue that we will explore in more detail below, but there is some indication of this in the PSI research.

In the 1980 NCC report *Consumers and Credit* the authors say,

> The majority of respondents reported that they had 'never thought of comparing' credit facilities and that in fact their typical behaviour was to go to the same shop, consult the same mail order agent or obtain the usual Provident or clothing club cheque when they needed something.[47]

This illustrates the importance of the routinisation of transactions for customers of credit companies. The authors point out that people feel safer and life is simpler when they repeat the same pattern of behaviour. During the post-war period, this pattern has been disrupted for many people. This is due to the increased number of credit alternatives that have become available to members of the working class with a regular income. However, it does not matter what is available if people are not aware of the alternatives. This is where the reflexivity of modern life plays a role, as people become aware of what is available to them through advertising and the media.

Rowlingson points out that only current customers of doorstep credit firms were interviewed for *Moneylenders and their Customers*. So we have to look elsewhere to find accounts of individuals who had stopped using this type of credit. In fact, we can find such accounts in *Hard Times?*, the PSI study of how poor families make ends meet. If improved access to other forms of credit drew some people away from this type of credit, less fortunate members of the working class were still left with little alternative, as the following quote emphasises. The authors of *Hard Times?* interviewed a woman with £76 a week disposable income who was paying £150 interest on a £200 loan she had taken out for Christmas. She told them, 'It's disgusting isn't it? But they always come around at the right time, when you need money, and you've got no choice. I mean Christmas, there was nothing I could do.'[48] The tendency to weigh up the alternatives is clear:

> If I had got a loan [from a more reputable company] it would have been cheaper because this one works out to be 30 per cent interest . . . a friend in the same predicament told me.[49]

It is not being argued that people did not previously weigh up the alternatives available to them and choose from them. The point is simply that in conditions of late modernity people are much less inclined to continue doing the 'usual' thing just because it is the usual. As Giddens says, they need some other justification. This is a point we shall return to when we consider the evidence gathered for Tyneside.

Finally, we should consider the role of mail order in the post-war period. Many of the respondents interviewed for *Moneylenders and their Customers* had either used mail order in the past or were still doing so. Rowlingson says,

> Catalogues were used because they were convenient, gave a wide choice of goods and had no interest added to the price. Where the mail order agent was a friend, catalogues had all the advantages of weekly doorstep collection.[50]

Again, there was also an indication that an increased awareness of alternatives was having an impact upon people's use of this type of credit.[51]

Over half of the respondents interviewed for *Hard Times?* were currently paying for goods they had bought from a mail order catalogue. One of the attractions of this type of credit, as I said above is that, where an agent is involved in the transaction, it operates in exactly the same way as other forms of doorstep credit. This is exactly the point that the respondents in the PSI study dealing with an agent of a mail order company make. Because they are dealing with local agents, they are less likely to miss payments, and the agent is 'more like a friend'.[52] A BBC2 programme on mail order made an important point about the way the business has changed in the post-war period.

> Over the past 20 years changes in society have led to the decline of the agent system. With greater numbers of women out at work and more people moving away from their communities, running an efficient agency has become increasingly difficult.[53]

Don Garnett from Grattan Catalogues says,

> In the 1960s, an agent had about sixteen customers on average. Now it's considerably less than that. You get about three people purchasing from a catalogue. So it's changed in its nature, and the agents now are really using it as a means of shopping for their family and perhaps the next-door neighbour.[54]

This returns us to an issue addressed in previous chapters, again drawing upon the work of Anthony Giddens: the breakdown of trust. The argument is that the decline of the agent system was symptomatic of the decline of trust within working class communities.

The other major change in the nature of mail order in the post-war period is that the market has become more segmented than it formerly was. This point is made by Janet Ford:

> Mail order itself is now changing and moving up-market with special catalogues aimed at the more 'discerning.' Clothkits, ByMail (both selling clothes), Harrods, and recently Marks and Spencer, selling furniture direct through a mail order catalogue targeted to 250,000 of its charge-card customers, are just a few of the many moving in that direction.[55]

This expansion in the type of customers who deal by mail order has resulted in a growth in this type of trade.

> The amount of new credit granted by mail order firms has grown rapidly as has the amount of credit owed to them. In 1978 £513m was outstanding. By 1985 this had risen to approximately £980m.[56]

Having outlined the general situation in the post-war period, we are now in a position to consider the relationship between the agent and the customer on Tyneside during this period.

The role of the agent on Tyneside after 1945

There is, we have noticed, a great deal of continuity between the pre-war and the post-war periods. The first thing to point out is that the agent's customers are still often loyal to the agent as an individual rather than to the company. Here is how one woman began collecting for the Provident in 1954:

> My mother was in hospital and my husband was working in a factory, and I had two children that I couldn't get minded. So I went up and I says 'Could I be a Provident agent?' and then you had to find your own customers, they didn't give you any. Now they do, but then you didn't get a customer. So I was running a Kays catalogue and I was collecting about £8 a week, and they says, 'You're not allowed to start the Provident if you've got a catalogue,' and I says 'Well I promise you if you give me 20 weeks, as each customer finishes their account, I'll put them onto Provident, or drop them, and in 20 weeks I'll have got rid of the catalogue,' which I did.[57]

This story illustrates this point perfectly, as this woman was able to take all her customers with her from one firm to another.

Most women begin by dealing with their friends and relations, and then expand from there, as did the interviewee quoted above. She said,

> ...half of them was neighbours and relations and then I started picking up, getting friends from them. I would go and look up old friends and they would tell me about some of their friends. I never ever did a cold canvas knocking at doors...Then you found your friends' children were coming up. In the end, I was onto grandchildren![58]

As the following account shows, people were often quite willing to take on credit commitments just to 'help out' their friends or relatives. Mr Anderson, a retired shipyard worker now living in Byker, told me that during the 1940s and 1950s, 'I used to join things, like clubs, if anybody started to run a club and they wanted to get it off the ground I would join just to help.'[59] Mr Anderson was earning enough money to be able to pay cash for the goods he acquired through various doorstep credit firms. However he became involved in this type of trading as a result of his 'philanthropic' outlook. This is apparent from the following example of the type of credit he became involved in 'just to help'.

> I used to often get something out of a catalogue because me sister ran it. So I used to order something, and then I used to send her the money, and mostly I used to just send her the full whack.[60]

These two cases illustrate the point that there is often an existing bond between an agent and a customer, in which case the loyalty of the customer is ensured. Where it does not already exist, though, a personal relationship has to be established.

In the case of full-time agents of a company this relationship has to be built up over time. All the collectors, full or part-time, who I spoke to emphasised that they were 'one of the family'. In the case of part-time women collectors, though, they were quite likely to literally be one of the family to begin with. Full-time male collectors had to work harder to build up a relationship as they would not usually have an existing connection with their customers. Mr Parkin was a 'ticket man' for the Newcastle firm of McAdam's during the early 1950s. He said that he used to try to establish a common interest, particularly with the husband, as this would oil the wheels of business. So he would ask the man which club he went to because, as he put it, 'There were very very few working class men not interested in clubs.'[61]

A knowledge of the family meant more business for the full-time collector. Their attitude to their customers is more instrumental than that of the part-time collector. Like the woman mentioned above, Mr Parkin also dealt with several generations of the same family. He said,

> As soon as I got to know they'd started work I'd say, 'Look do you fancy a little one, just 5 bob or 10 bob a week,' or something like that. Then you had them on the books and, of course, once they were on the books then you had them right through till they got married, and then you would start on their children ... [62]

Although this is just what the part-time woman did, in effect, the attitude of the two collectors is quite different. For the full-time agent a knowledge of a family leads to more business. For the part-time agent the social interaction that goes with the job has an entirely different meaning. It can be one of the reasons that they continue to do the job.

For the firms involved, the advantage of using part-time women collectors was the same as the advantage of using Watch Clubs for the Fattorlnis in the nineteenth century. Collecting was a social occasion. Thus all the women who acted as agents described their collecting round as involving endless cups of tea with their customers. This meant that the social element was important to both customer and agent, in just the same way as paying their weekly subscription was an occasion to socialise over a drink for Watch Club members. So what happened when this cosy, social, relationship came under threat from a customer's unwillingness, or inability, to pay?

Mrs Joll was a Provident agent from 1972 to 1991. In difficult cases, she claims, section managers would visit the person and threaten them with court action.[63] She feels that more recently, however, many people have become aware that this is usually just a hollow threat, as it can cost the Provident more than the debt is worth to prosecute, so they are unlikely to be worried by this. What is interesting, though, is that the Provident sends a full-time worker to deal with this type of problem. There are two possible reasons for this. Firstly, the fact that someone with more authority and power than the agent has intervened is presumably meant to impress upon the erring customer the seriousness of their transgression. Secondly, it has the advantage, for the firm, of minimising the damage to the still potentially valuable customer–agent relationship. We will return to the difference between full and part-time collectors later. Having established the basic continuities in the relationship between agent and customer, we should now move on to consider the changes that have taken place in credit trading on Tyneside during the post-war period.

The fundamental change in doorstep credit trading in the post-war period on Tyneside has been the gradual disappearance of most of the smaller firms which traded in this manner. This is apparent from a search through the local directories, as well as from what my respondents have told me. Between the 1960s and the 1980s many of these firms began to experience difficulties and eventually closed down. We have already seen that Shephard's, of Gateshead, and Parrish's, of Byker, closed in 1980 and 1984 respectively. A lot of other firms were forced into closure before then. Another former collector with McAdam's, Mrs Moss, told me that McAdam's had been taken over by another credit firm, Beavans, in the early 1970s and, in the process, a lot of bad debt was written off.[64] Beavans, of Shields Road, Newcastle, was itself taken over by Great Universal Stores in about 1980, according to the current manageress of that shop. It is now a catalogue bargain shop and offers credit only through a finance company on large consumer durables.[65] The businesses of the two credit drapers that I interviewed no longer exist. Mr Burton ceased credit trading in 1975. He then opened an ordinary retailers in Blyth, to be nearer to his old customers, but was forced to close that in 1988. Mr Macrae opened a shop in Durham in 1947 but that closed in 1967. We could continue to trace the decline of countless other credit firms during the period, but this is not necessary for our purposes. It is more useful to consider the factors that led to the decline of this type of business.

Mr Macrae did not experience any great decline in custom during the 1960s. I asked him if he had lost customers to department stores and new types of credit during the 1960s? His reply was,

> They were always a competition, but I think the trust that we had with our customers was to our great advantage. I think that's where we succeeded, because of the trust. And all the credit traders were the same ... Some of the modern ones we lost, because when they got married some of the younger ones had different ideas. By and large, the families went on, and on our books you would find lots of people with the same names. They were just families you see. It was quite normal to go into a house and have three accounts in the house and collect money from everybody. There was a bit of tailing off, but it didn't affect us tremendously.[66]

He stopped trading only because Durham County Council placed a compulsory purchase order on his shop to make way for a new road development.

There seem to have been several factors contributing to the weakening of the relationship between the customer and the credit draper, and the subsequent decline of that type of trading. Mr Macrae acknowledges that he probably got out of the credit business at the right time. Credit drapers financed their own credit. They did not borrow from a financial institution. He said that as prices went up the business became increasingly difficult to fund independently.[67] Two comments Mr Parkin made also suggest reasons for the decline in the credit drapery trade. Firstly, he said that the areas he traded in had become increasingly dangerous by the end of his working life. Secondly, he felt that he was catering for men's reluctance to go shopping.[68] One factor that would have contributed to the decline of this type of business is the cultural shift in men's attitudes that allows them to take a greater interest in their appearance, and thus feel more comfortable shopping for clothes.

Changing patterns of consumption also figure largely in Mr Burton's explanation of the decline of his business. Mr Burton dates the decline of his type of credit trading from the formation of the National Coal Board in 1947. His explanation is: after the mines were nationalised, wages improved and this gave the young men increased spending power. So they no longer needed (or wished) to deal with a credit draper who carried a limited amount of stock. Now they could shop in the larger retail centres and take advantage of the greater choice. This also fitted in with young people's heightened interest in fashion. The ultimate result of this was the end of the credit trade as he had practised it.[69]

We should now consider the break with the established credit firm from the point of view of the customer. We can get a good idea of why individuals may have stopped trading with established companies if we look at the accounts of two people that broke with their traditional firm.

The first account comes from Mr Barker who was born in 1943 in South Shields. His father was a fitter's labourer in the shipyards and, in 1954, they moved to Jarrow. Mr Barker describes the importance of Shephard's of Gateshead to people living in Jarrow at that time. 'Shephard's was part of the community within Jarrow because ninety per cent of the people did shop at Shephard's. It was easy to access.'[70] His father used Shephard's, which he paid by Provident checks. It had been his aunt who had dealt with the Provident agent though. She held the payment cards for about five family members, and she would pay the collector for them. So Shephard's and the Provident were the traditional means of credit within Mr Barker's family. He initially continued this tradition when he started work in 1958.

> When I started work, you found it easier to stick with the Provident because you didn't have the cash when you first started. So if you bought a pair of shoes for £20 it would cost you a pound a week to pay it off.[71]

At this time he did not have enough money to pay cash for all of his immediate needs.

There was a significant difference between Mr Barker's attitude to credit and that of his father. Mr Barker's father did not see the Provident as a form of credit. Mr Barker said that he had tried to make his father aware of the alternative sources of credit that he could have used. He points out that his father could have bought items on hire purchase had he wanted to, but he had refused to.

He would rather stay with the Provident because it was hidden. He wasn't seen getting it...His belief was that, if you can't pay for it, don't get it. I said, 'Well what about the Provident?' He says, 'Well that's not the same.'[72]

This is obviously a somewhat bizarre consequence of the ideology of respectability. For Mr Barker's father, it meant that he did not see the Provident as a form of credit, which meant that he did not have to feel shame about buying on credit. It was also conveniently conducted well out of sight of the neighbours, particularly in his case as the collector did not call at his house. As Giddens says,

Human agents always know what they are doing on the level of discursive consciousness under some description. However, what they do may be quite unfamiliar under other descriptions, and they may know little of the ramified consequences of the activities in which they engage.[73]

What made Mr Barker break with the Provident, given that firm's embeddedness within his family?

When Mr Barker was 21, in 1964, his father died. As a result of this, for personal reasons, he left his old neighbourhood and moved to Gateshead. This was the point at which he broke with the Provident. He says,

So at that particular time I paid cash, because I had no other option. But again, I mean, I was earning a lot more money than I used to. I was earning about £37–8 pounds a week in 1965, which was a fair amount of money, and that allowed me to come out of the trap of the Provident. Which I would never use again mind.[74]

What emerges from this account is the crucial importance of economic factors in creating the break with the traditional firm. However, as is suggested in Mr Burton's account, economic factors are not sufficient in themselves. Both parents and children in the colliery districts Mr Burton traded in experienced an increase in their level of wages. However, it was initially only the children that had the motivation to reject this type of credit. Similarly with Mr Barker, his father was in a position to stop trading with the Provident if he had wished. He did not do so because it was a form of credit he had become accustomed to. We should also note that, in the above quote, Mr Barker begins by saying that he was compelled to start paying cash. This was because, in moving to Gateshead, he had removed himself from his family network, and consequently from the family credit arrangements.

The second account of the break with the established credit firm comes from Mrs Robinson. Mrs Robinson was a miner's daughter born in 1934 in the west end of Newcastle. She had a number of jobs, including nursing and cleaning, before getting married in 1955. Her husband worked in a foundry as a moulder. Unfortunately, in 1962, he was made redundant. Mrs Robinson used half of her husband's redundancy money to pay for all the items of clothing that the family urgently needed. Up until this point, Mrs Robinson had bought everything (on credit) from a ticket firm called J.R. Scott & Sons. Now she found that having the money in her hand made all the difference. As she says,

> I went into shops and I was asking 'How much off for cash?' And I mean I was amazed at how much I was saving by saying that. I did it in one shop, and when it worked, I did it in others. Because I didn't realise actually when you've got cash you can get things cheaper ... [75]

She went to the same wholesaler that she had been taking her tickets to and bought a coat for a third of the price she had been paying as a credit customer. After this experience, Mrs Robinson never used a doorstep credit firm again. One of the interesting things about Mrs Robinson's account is that she stopped using 'traditional' credit as soon as she became aware of the extent she had been exploited. Her behaviour was in no way facilitated by increased prosperity. After his redundancy, both she and her husband continued to experience spells of intermittent employment and a great deal of poverty. Despite this, Mrs Robinson managed not to return to the old types of credit. She managed this by a number of ingenious means, but basically through selling any valuables they had acquired.

These two accounts indicate the type of factors that could lead individuals to break with 'traditional' forms of credit during the 1950s and 1960s. Many people would have made the discovery Mrs Robinson had made — that it was cheaper to pay cash. A lot of people were also being drawn away from their communities, and consequently their old credit networks. Although many young people were turning away from the old types of credit, the older generation continued to use them.

Mrs Blackwell was born in South Shields in 1956. Her father was a miner, and they lived on a newly-built council estate in South Shields.

In her parents' case, the move to a new estate did not disrupt their old patterns of credit use. Mrs Blackwell said that her parents had used Provident orders for as long as she could remember, and they had a collector who used to call regularly for payments. Her parents continued to use the Provident throughout the 1960s, and stopped using it only in 1970. They managed to maintain a fairly traditional pattern of credit use throughout this period: the Provident, some hire-purchase, and credit from the local shops.[76] So why did they not make use of alternative sources of credit?

The basic reason they did not try new (and cheaper) sources of credit during the 1960s was that they had no knowledge of them. This will become apparent if we consider the circumstances which led them to eventually break with the Provident in 1970. In that year, Mrs Blackwell's older sister started work and the family found that they no longer had as much need for credit. The basic economic necessity for credit was removed. However, this does not explain why they continued to use the Provident until 1970, particularly when Mrs Blackwell's father's wages were being paid into a bank account. Mrs Blackwell told me that two things happened as a result of her sister starting work. Firstly, the family had more money coming into the house and, secondly, she brought a greater knowledge of financial institutions into the family.

> She was more aware of what you could do and what you couldn't do for credit. She was the one who got them to go down to the local bank (Barclays) where me dad's salary was paid in and they got a bank loan to buy a new car ... And it was a big surprise for me mam, because me mam never realised how easy it was to get credit.[77]

Her parents obtained this bank loan in 1972 but, until then, even though they had a bank account, it had not occured to them that their bank could be a source of credit.

The following account, from Mrs Hughes, shows us that, up until the 1970s, the old credit firms were still very embedded within working class communities. Mrs Hughes was born in 1947 and married her first husband in 1964. He worked as a panel beater, and they lived in Forest Hall in North Tyneside. Her description of the type of credit she used after she was married emphasises the importance of affectual rationality in the relationship between the agent and the customer.

> You would get a ticket and you would go to a wholesaler and buy something and, after that, a guy would come round once a week.

I mean, you had a really good relationship with these people, if you paid you did I don't know what it was like if you didn't pay. They were great friends. You used to wait for them coming for a cup of tea, and they'd run you to whatever wholesalers ... And they'd always want you to have more and more all the time. They were always happy for you to do that.[78]

Mrs Hughes offered some indication of what it was like if customers did not pay.

They [the collectors] used to talk about the Ridges (which is now classed as the Meadow Well) and they used to tell us of some horrific experiences they had with people: not wanting to pay, taking their car tyres off, and being punched on the nose. They were all friends when they came to our house anyway. A lot of them came years after we stopped getting tickets. We still actually kept in touch in some way or another. So it was actually quite nice.[79]

One of the fundamental conditions for the formation of a 'close' relationship between the agent and the customer is that the customer is a 'good payer'. The situation Mrs Hughes describes is not very different from that of the interwar years. As we saw from Thomas Callaghan's autobiography, even in 'the good old days', ticket men could still receive rough treatment from their customers, particularly in poorer districts.

Mrs Hughes, however, lived in a highly 'respectable' area and, as she worked in retailing, the couple had two incomes coming into the household. She was also aware of the fact that she could have got a bank loan if she had wanted to. However she still continued to use ticket agents. Here is her explanation why:

Because they'd come knocking on your door touting for it. We only got Howard's because one of the friends of ours [herself and her mother] over the way she always had this Howard's club and she used to go on and on about it. She sent this guy across who was really a nice guy this Thomas, in fact I'm still in touch with him today ... So we decided we would and, if I was going to have some, me mam might as well too, and we could go into town together and get it.[80]

It should be noted that Mrs Hughes did not weigh up the comparative rates of interest of different types of credit, and then choose this firm. She told me that she had 'no idea' of the rate of interest that she was being charged. As she says, 'I never thought about it, especially with something I wanted particularly.'[81] Mrs Hughes also used the Provident for a while. She was also asked why she had become a customer of that firm 'Oh, that was a girl who had just started working for the Provident and she wanted some customers. We knew her, so we got a Provident out.'[82]

We can see from Mrs Hughes' account that the old firms were still trading in the same way as they had been during the interwar period up until the 1970s. The first company she mentioned, Howard's Stores in North Shields, was a store Mrs Wrigley's mother had used to use before the Second World War (see above). Her account why she had begun trading with those firms is also remarkably similar to Mrs Samuel's family's pattern of credit use (see above). Mrs Hughes stressed that she really enjoyed using this type of credit. It seems that there were two elements to this enjoyment: the joy of having a spending spree (or the 'splurge' factor), and the pleasure of having regular callers coming to your house. She stopped using Howard's Stores in the early 1970s. The importance of the 'social' factor can be seen in her explanation of this. 'Thomas left the company, the guy who collected, and we didn't like the next fellow. So we just didn't bother getting any more. It was that simple.'[83]

An individual's attitude towards credit was formed by several factors. Chief among these was both their own and their families' previous experience of credit use. Mrs Johnson was born in 1924 in Shieldfield in Newcastle. Her father was an unskilled railway worker and her husband a printer. After she was married she lived on the Pendower council estate in the west end of Newcastle. She told me that during the 1950s a lot of people on that estate had used the Provident and Shephard's of Gateshead to buy clothing and other items. Mrs Johnson used both of these companies up until the late 1960s. In contrast to Mrs Hughes, she had stopped using this type of credit as soon as she was able to. As she says, 'Things got a little bit better and you stopped using it.' When I asked her why she said, 'There's no substitute for cash.'[84] After she broke with the 'traditional' forms of credit (that is, from the late 1960s onwards) Mrs Johnson never used credit again. She has never had hire-purchase, bank loans or credit cards. Part of the reason for this is her family's credit history. When Mrs Johnson was a little girl, the family had bought some furniture on hire-purchase and it had been repossessed. As a result of this, and the general poverty she had experienced as a child, she was very careful with her money. As she told me,

You still hesitate about buying anything, you know, even down to a few sweets. When you're brought up the way I was brought up, you think twice. If you've had the worry of seeing your mother worrying about how she's going to pay for things [bought on credit] you have a lifetime of fear of not being able to manage. It leaves a terrible impression on you.[85]

Mrs Johnson's account indicates just how important cultural predisposition can be in determining patterns of credit use. Like Mrs Hughes, she was aware of the fact that she would have been able to get a bank loan, a credit card or other forms of credit during the 1960s. However she chose not to make use of new forms of credit or continue with the 'traditional' types.

The final account of the break with the established firm comes from Mrs Mason, who was born in Newcastle in 1917. She began using the Provident after she was married, in 1940, and continued her relationship with the firm until 1975.[86] Her husband was a painter and decorator and the couple lived on the Cowgate council estate, in Newcastle, where Mrs Mason still lives. The Provident was the only source of credit Mrs Mason used during her married life. She told me that she was 'very friendly' with all her collectors and, 'I got on famously with the Provi.'[87] She furnished her whole house through the Provident. Shephard's and Parrish's were the main shops that she went to with her vouchers.

Mrs Mason said that her husband did not approve of her use of the Provident, but he could never openly object to it, as it was his fault that she had to resort to credit. She felt that she would not have had to use the Provident if her husband had given her more money. If he had objected, she says, 'I would have told him to mind his own damn business. I'd have said "Tip up more and I wouldn't need to do it".'[88] When I asked her if he was aware of her use of the firm she replied,

He had an idea, but he daren't say nothing. I'd have fettled him if he had. Because, I mean, if he didn't give me the money to get things, well how did he expect as to get them otherwise?... He knew they came but he didn't know why nor what for, nor how much I gave them or what have you.[89]

This is another reason women continued to use established credit firms like the Provident: the unequal distribution of income within the household which created a need for some form of credit. However, this still does not explain why Mrs Mason used this particular type of credit.

Mrs Mason also felt that she could have gone to a bank or obtained items on hire-purchase if she had wanted to. I asked her why she didn't use another form of credit instead? She replied, 'I like the Provi. That's all there was to it. If I take to a person, well that's it. I'd do anything to help them.'[90] This was why she would advise her collectors about lending money to her neighbours. She would tell them who would be able to repay their loans and who was having financial difficulties. Her account stresses the importance of affectual rationality in her continued relationship with the firm.

> You see I liked them, that was the main thing. I got on all right with them and they got on all right with me. They seemed to like me. One or two of them invited as to their houses for lunch and things like that.[91]

If she had disliked an individual collector she would have simply ended her relationship with the firm. However, as it happened, she was never allocated a collector she did not get on with. She stopped using the Provident only after she began to work full-time. Three things happened as a result of this. There was more money coming into the household, Mrs Mason was in control of this additional money as she had earned it, and it became increasingly difficult for her to be at home for collectors. The result was that she stopped using the Provident.

We should now attempt to summarise the evidence we have looked at so far. The doorstep credit firms we are considering here became successful, in the first instance, by offering credit trading to social groups that had previously been excluded from it. This process began with the Watch Clubs which offered credit to the labour aristocracy in the nineteenth century, and was extended to include the rest of the working class during the interwar period. After the Second World War, these companies remained embedded within working class communities due to their continued use of the system of agents. It seems that because people were approached by their friend, neighbour, or relative to take out an order, or buy something from a catalogue, this made it impossible to say 'no'. This turned a business transaction into an affectually motivated act. These established firms were the 'traditional' method of credit for many working class people. People felt comfortable using them because they were accustomed to them. As Giddens says, the routinisation of social practices creates a sense of ontological security. The established firms' position as the 'traditional' source of credit for the working class, and their concomitant embeddedness in the social networks of working class communities, is what kept such firms in business at a time when they were experiencing stiff competition from alternative sources of credit.

This was a state of affairs that could not last forever. We have identified a number of factors that contributed towards the decline of this type of credit. These include increased prosperity, changes in patterns of consumption, increased knowledge of new forms of credit, the increase in the employment of women, and the disruption of working class neighbourhoods. All of these factors taken together led to the decline of the 'traditional' credit firms during the 1970s. The underlying changes in the post-war period that caused this decline can be summarised as greater economic prosperity, and a higher degree of reflexivity in the way people lived their lives. However, this is still not the whole story. We also need to ask why some firms survived and others did not.

In the case of credit drapers, like Mr Burton and Mr Macrae, there are some fairly solid reasons for the decline of their business. They conducted a lot of their trade in relatively remote colliery villages. Improvements in public transport would be one factor that would damage their business. When we add to this the increased disposable income of young people and the attraction of the fashionable boutiques in urban centres, the credit draper's days were obviously numbered. However this does not explain the closure of shops like Shephard's and Parrish's, though, which still had the advantage of being close to their customers, and could carry a wide range of stock to keep pace with demand. Those two stores lasted right through the 1970s.

If we consider all the evidence presented so far, what seems to have happened was that the more affluent members of the working class turned away from 'traditional' forms of credit during the 1970s (for all the reasons already outlined). This change damaged the smaller firms most, as they did not have the flexibility of the larger, national companies, like Provident and Shopacheck. For example, many people bought Parrish's money through the Provident. From what the respondents for this study said, Parrish's seems to have been badly hit by the redevelopment of Byker in the 1970s. As pointed out in an earlier chapter, this resulted in the homes of 3000 people being demolished, and many had to leave the area. This seriously undermined the social networks that sustained Parrish's. If we add to this the fact that many of the people who remained in Byker would have been more able to pay cash and had access to other forms of credit we can begin to see why that store closed.

The Provident, on the other hand, has the ability to follow its customers wherever they move to. If individuals still wish to continue trading with them, the link with the firm can be maintained. Furthermore, the Provident cannot be damaged by the closure of a single shop, as all the company has to do is simply make an agreement with another shop. The most recent Provident publicity leaflet to be distributed on Tyneside lists 25 different retail outlets which accept Provident Shopping Vouchers. These include Argos, B&Q, Comet, Top Man, and What Everyone Wants. This illustrates the firm's ability to keep pace with changing patterns of consumption. As it says in the leaflet, 'You can buy practically anything with Shopping vouchers — clothes, shoes, electrical and household goods — even gifts for your family and friends.'[92]

There is another way in which the Provident has a greater degree of flexibility than other firms: it will physically take customers to shops which accept their vouchers. The Provident organises bus trips to shops that they deal with. The company seems to have begun this practice sometime after the Second World War, and it is continuing. Mrs Wilson worked for the Provident between 1954 and 1990, and went on many of these bus trips with her customers. Bus trips were organised by the local Provident office to various large retail outlets (usually clothing stores). Although they were not paid any extra to do it, agents were expected to drum up support for these trips and to accompany their customers. The bus would then make several designated stops along the way to pick up customers. During the 1950s and 1960s, trips were held during the day and in the evening. Daytime trips picked up customers at 10.00 in the morning and returned them at 3.00 in the afternoon so women could collect their children from school. Obviously, if trips were held in the evening, the shop would open (sometimes until midnight) just for Provident customers. Mrs Wilson says that the bus trips had the atmosphere of an outing. It was mainly women that went on them, and they were quite often used for bulk food shopping. The outings seem to have generated an atmosphere of frantic consumption. 'People would buy £200 worth of toys. They'd buy anything. You took them and they bought anything.'[93]

Mr Miller was a section manager for the Provident from 1988–9 in a mining district. He gave a similar account of the shopping trips as orgies of consumerism. Mr Miller told me that, by this time, they were usually held quite near to Christmas and only in the evening. Customers would be allocated about £100 of vouchers each and they'd be taken to a store to spend it. He says that, 'they'd have a certain length of time in the shop and run round and spend like crazy.'[94] There was a great deal of pressure on agents to get their customers to go on these trips. The Provident management expected coaches to be filled, and a lot of money to be spent.

In 1972 the Provident began to lend money. Before that they had dealt only in vouchers. Several Provident agents have expressed their concern over the large amounts of money they were given to lend. This can be up to £1000 at a time. For the agent there are several problems attached to this. Firstly, the agent often receives the money a day or two in advance, and they have to look after the cash until they distribute it. If it is lost or stolen the agent is responsible. Secondly, they then have to do their round with £1000 or so in cash. They are expected to unload this cash onto any customer who will take it. The general feeling was that the Provident was pushing people who could not afford it into debt.

This was the reason Mrs Joll gave for leaving the Provident. Mrs Joll felt uneasy about going into poor households with large sums of money to lend. She knew the people borrowing from her could not afford to pay the loan back, but there was pressure from the management to lend as much as possible. This particular agent became profoundly unhappy about her role within the communities she dealt with, and this led her to cease collecting. She was also acutely worried about her own personal safety, as collectors were attacked on occasion. Collectors make a fairly obvious target as they are known to the people in the area they collect in.

Mr Miller pointed out that, apart from being told to bank regularly, the Provident does not offer agents any guidance on personal security. As we will see, Mr Miller also became profoundly uneasy about some of the company's practices and this prompted him to leave the firm. Such discontent was not confined to part-time agents.

Mrs Wilson told me that during the 1960s the Provident gradually increased the interest rate on their vouchers. The interest rate went from a shilling in the pound in 1962 to 25p. in the pound. Cash loans earn a higher rate of interest. After they introduced cash loans the Provident began to move more and more of its business over to that type of loan. Now there are very few checks sold. Most of their business is in cash. The exact amount of interest charged varies according to the amount borrowed and the period it is borrowed over. The lowest APR in Provident's December 1989 *Tables of Charges* is 85.6% on a 100 week voucher, and the highest is 576.0% on a 13 week cash loan.[95] My respondents felt that the Provident does not just exploit their customers it also relies on the intensive intellectual and emotional labour provided by part-time agents.

Mrs Joll was asked if she thought it was worth it for the agent to perform such potentially difficult work? She replied that it was, but 'You put a lot of hours in book-keeping and going to the office.'[96] At the time she was employed by the Provident, the commission for agents was 8p. in the pound for vouchers and 7½ p. for cash loans.[97] This meant that if a customer took a £100 voucher the agent would receive £8. It is difficult to calculate whether this was a reasonable recompense, at this time, for an agent or not. It does not seem a very generous rate of pay if we consider the amount of time that would be spent collecting that loan back, keeping records of the repayments, and delivering the money to the local office. It would seem that the financial rewards of being an agent are not necessarily the primary benefits for the person involved. Mrs Wilson told me that, 'I loved it, I would still have been working, but I got thrown out at 65.'[98] Her husband said that she acted as an 'agony aunt' as she heard all her customers' troubles. Attachment to their customers, and the opportunity to socialise with them regularly, seems to be the main reason a lot of agents continue to do the job. We can see the operation of the interpenetration of rationalities here. Affectual rationality can not only create custom in the first instance, it can also provide a very real motivation for the agent to continue.

As has already been pointed out, the affectual element in the relationship between agent and customer usually works to the benefit of the firm. However there can also be a negative aspect to this for the companies involved, particularly with part-time agents. The agent can become the customer's personal debt counsellor. Mrs Wilson used to invite her customers over on Wednesdays (traditionally the agent's day off) if they needed help with their finances. Mrs Joll also helped her customers in this way. Mrs Wilson and Mrs Joll would sometimes advise customers experiencing financial difficulties to borrow less from the Provident. This kind of advice can benefit the customer, but it often runs counter to the interests of the company. So this is a case where affectual rationality can set limits on instrumental rationality in a real way.

Finally, we should consider the social status of Provident agents. Mr Miller suggests that the Provident recruited collectors from the 'respectable' working class who mainly dealt with people from more deprived parts of their own communities, which is consistent with the other information I have gathered about Provident agents.[99] This is perfectly illustrated by the case of two further Provident agents interviewed who have not been discussed so far. This is because, after only a brief discussion, they decided they did not want to answer any more questions. It seems that, unlike the other agents, they were still working for the Provident. These two agents lived in Heaton in the east end of Newcastle, were married to skilled manual workers, and collected in the west end of Newcastle.[100] In other words, they lived in a very respectable working class area and collected in a much more deprived part of the city, and this is typical of Provident agents generally.

The Full-Time agent

We should now turn to consider the relationship between the full-time agent of a firm and their customers in order to determine whether the different status of the agent has a significant impact on their relationship with their customers. The full-time collector tends to adopt a more instrumental approach to their customers, and we saw this in Mr Parkin's attitude towards his customers. On the surface, though, Mrs Moss had a different approach. She seems to have taken a responsible approach towards her customers and, like the part-time collectors, she also became involved in offering them financial advice. Every so often her supervisor would go out and sell items to Mrs Moss's customers. One Christmas he sold a lot of expensive toys to a family that she knew could not afford to pay for them until next Christmas. Understandably, she felt that this was highly irresponsible.

However, most of the other travellers did not share her outlook.

> And of course some travellers made quite a bit of commission, because they did sell much harder than I did. You know, every customer they went to, 'Do you want something else? Are you sure you don't need anything else? Do you want a bedding bale, or a towel bale?' I hadn't the heart to offer some people towels when they were looking for their last sixpence to give me what they could.[101]

Obviously one of the problems with this account is that Mrs Moss is offering a somewhat idealised image of herself. Is this indicative of a difference in attitude between herself and the other collectors? This is a difficult question to answer, as we have only her own account of her actions. She may have appeared quite differently to her customers. However, even if we accept her own version of events, she also claims that she had a particular ability to collect repayments where others had failed, and that would have found favour with the management. In this respect, Mrs Moss was an effective credit agent from the firm's point of view. As well as this, her own attitude to the job was important in conditioning her behaviour. She told me that she always regarded it as a temporary job, and not one that she wanted to make a career out of and, as a result, she held the job for only a year.

I feel that Mr Parkin's attitude was more typical of 'career-oriented' credit agents as he did, in fact, make a career in the credit business. He was well aware of the importance of his relationship with his customers in commercial terms. As he puts it:

> As a salesman-collector the first thing you had to sell was yourself! If customers didn't like you, they'd never buy anything off you. As time passed by you were just accepted, in the majority of cases, as one of the family.[102]

This is not to say that 'career-oriented' agents were careless about who they offered credit to. The full-time agent was put in a difficult position, as Mrs Moss suggests. Mr Parkin agrees that there was great pressure to open new accounts and make sales from McAdam's. The agents would receive commission on new accounts and sales, but they also had to collect the money. He said that, 'Nine times out of ten the traveller will not sell if they know they're not going to get the money.'[103] The management expected their agents to sell as much credit as possible, but the agent would also be blamed for bad debt. This put the full-time agents in an impossible position, which they had to resolve for themselves. Mr Parkin was also opposed to some of the individual sales that management wanted him to make, but this was because he knew he was likely to be blamed if those accounts fell into arrears. So, from the point of view of the credit company, the full-time agent fulfils essentially the same function as a part-time agent. However, there is a potential difference in the way they perceive their customers. They are more removed from them, and this can result in them being less sympathetic.

There would seem to be two types of full-time employees of credit firms: 'career-oriented' employees and 'short-term' employees. Mrs Moss and Mr Miller are both examples of the latter type of worker. This type of employee will not stay in the job long enough to internalise the firm's values to any great degree. It would seem to be a precondition of making the transition to a 'career' employee that an individual takes on board the ethos of the firm and forms a more instrumental attitude towards their customers. Full-time agents are more likely to consciously manipulate their customers than part-time agents. Full-time agents tend to cultivate techniques to deal with their customers in order to stimulate trade and 'keep them on the books'. Part-time agents also do this, but not always at the level of discursive consciousness.

Mail order

Finally, we should consider mail order on Tyneside during the post-war period. I pointed out above that where an agent is involved in a transaction, mail order operates in exactly the same way as other forms of doorstep credit. This was precisely the point that Graham Dixon, the manager of Newcastle CAB, made.[104] It is important to remember that agents of mail order catalogues recruit their friends and neighbours as customers on occasion. This was a point that three women members of Fenham Credit Union made to me during my interview with them.[105]

However, while the old pattern of agent and customer relationships is virtually unchanged within the other doorstep credit companies which survived into the post-war period, there has been a significant change in the way mail order is used by consumers. The role and the number of agents has declined quite dramatically during the post-war period. We have already seen some indication of this in the company history of Empire Stores. Beaver, writing in 1981, said that, 'Today Empire Stores deals with some 400, 000 part-time agents, each of whom serves an average of five customers and handles a turnover of £350 a year.'[106] It should be noted that this is a comparatively small amount of customers. This supports the assertion of Don Garnett, from Grattan Catalogues, that agents now have fewer customers than they used to have. He said,

In the 1960s, an agent had about sixteen customers on average. Now its considerably less than that. You get about three people purchasing from a catalogue. So it's changed in its nature, and the agents now are really using it as a means of shopping for their family and perhaps the next door neighbour.[107]

We have also seen that during the 1970s mail order companies changed the way they recruited agents. They switched from a method of personal recruitment by full-time agents to the use of postage-paid coupons. Empire Stores also adopted this approach in 1975. This is one reason for the decline in the number of customers supplied by individual agents, as now almost anyone can become an agent.

Tracy Armstrong, a debt counsellor at Newcastle CAB, described the way mail order catalogues were used by her clients. She said that unemployed people, people on income support and both male and female single parents all tended to use both the Provident and mail order catalogues, because the greater availability of these forms of credit to them. This was particularly true of catalogues.

> I don't know what sort of system they use for finding out whether people have had problems in the past, because you will always be able to get a catalogue, no matter what! They go on about the Consumer Credit Act and everything, but a lot of the catalogues, you don't even have to sign an agreement. If a friend introduces you, a can just say, 'Oh well, can you send a catalogue to them.' And if they make an order they can just ring up. So there's nothing in writing about it, although it's a form of verbal contract... and that would hold up in a court of law.[108]

In such cases, there is no written agreement. Under the *Consumer Credit Act* of 1974 there has to be a signed agreement by the client and the creditor. In the case of many catalogue purchases this may be legally acceptable, as credit transactions of less than £30 were excluded from much of the regulation. (There has been talk of rectifying this.)[109] However, it seems unlikely that all such purchases can be under £30, and the catalogue companies would seem to be taking advantage of a legal 'grey area'. Whatever the legal basis, though, the end result is, once again, the irresponsible promotion of indebtedness by creditors.

Tracey Armstrong said that the catalogues she had dealt with included Great Universal, Kays, Freemans, Janet Fraser, Brian Mills and Oxendales. These are some of the firms that promote credit in this way. We should also note that these firms actively promote the introduction of friends. Here is Tracey Armstrong's description of how this works.

> They have leaflets in with the catalogue, 'Introduce a friend and get £5 off your next order, or a free gift.' So this agent might say, 'Well me friend's interested in the catalogue can you send a catalogue to me friend.' Well the friend gets the catalogue, she has a look through it, inside the catalogue is a hotline number that you can ring. She rings and says, 'This is me first order and I'm interested in ordering this that and the other.' They get a certain amount of credit to start with. Then obviously, if they're a good payer, that credit limit will increase. And then they get the goods, they get an agency number, and it's done over the phone there's nothing in writing.[110]

This process of personal recommendation through existing agents could go on indefinitely. It certainly lessens the need for agents to act for customers. We should note that it introduces an instrumental element into what seems to be an affectual act, 'recommending a friend'. So the agent now has a financial incentive to find new agents for the company, and this is an incentive which may now look more attractive than running an agency. Although agents receive commission on sales, it seems that the problems that accompany running a catalogue agency in some areas may not make it seem worthwhile any more.

I interviewed a woman we shall call Mrs Ford who lives in Benwell in the west end of Newcastle. Mrs Ford was born in the west end of Newcastle in 1931, and she has lived in that area all her life. She has moved several times in her life, but Mrs Ford has lived at her current address for over 20 years. Very few of the original residents of her street still live there, as the area has quite a high turnover of people, and many of the properties are unoccupied and derelict. Mrs Ford has been divorced since 1973 and since then she has had various jobs including cleaning and shop-work. In 1992 she became an agent for Kays catalogue by mailing a coupon from a magazine. She had no intention of acting as an agent for any of her neighbours, even though she was on quite friendly terms with some of them. In fact, she actively tried to conceal the fact that she had a catalogue from the other people in the street because she did not trust them enough to offer them credit.[111]

Here is her account of what happened next:

I went away on a holiday and, when I came back, the little girl across the road came over and said, 'We've got a parcel for you.' So I went in and it was a parcel from the catalogue, and her mother told me to check everything was there ... That was how I got to speak to her because some of the new neighbours, I didn't bother with them. Then, I don't know when it was, a few months later, she asked if I took on customers for the catalogue. Well I didn't want people in the street to know but, when she asked, I thought she would be all right because I knew her. She got some tea towels, Christmas goods and a leather jacket ... I'd have to look at the order form to tell you what else. Anyway she wasn't that bad at the beginning, she paid. Then she stopped, and I warned her that I might have to speak to Kays to take the debt over from me. I wish I had. Then the payments started coming in again and then they stopped again. I tried to nag her a bit and I wrote her a letter and, on another occasion, I told her I wouldn't have let things go so far but I didn't like the idea of the bairn not getting stuff for Christmas.[112]

After her neighbour took in the parcel for her, the two women did become quite friendly. So ultimately Mrs Ford decided to clear the remainder of the debt herself for the sake of this friendship. However, Mrs Ford is now contemplating taking her neighbour to a small claims court, but she would do this only if she moved away from the area. As long as she still lives in the area she does not want to do take her to court for fear of reprisals. This illustrates the complexity of community relations in the current period. It is certainly significant that Mrs Ford did not originally intend to offer any of her neighbours goods from her catalogue and, after this experience, she will not do it again. Mrs Ford said that other women in her area also had catalogues and they did not usually act as agents for their neighbours either. They did not trust the people around them enough.[113]

The decline of trust within communities has been discussed, in earlier chapters, where I used the work of Anthony Giddens to argue that it is one of the ways in which the consequences of modernity have become radicalised. The change in the relationship between the shopkeeper and the community is an example of the erosion of locality as a source of ontological security, to borrow a phrase from Giddens.[114] As he says, trust can no longer be anchored in criteria outside the relationship itself.[115] So ties based on locality (for example) can no longer offer a sufficient basis, in themselves, for trust. The decline in the number of customers supplied by individual mail order agents would seem to be the result of the interaction of two factors. The first is the change in the way that such agents are recruited, which has made it much easier to become a catalogue agent. The second is the decline of trust within many communities, which means that the residents of those areas are increasingly unwilling to offer credit to their neighbours. This is part of the overall movement from Gemeinschaft-like relations to Gesellschaft-like relations which, as has been argued earlier, is the basic underlying movement in contemporary society.

Conclusion

This chapter has dealt with the relationship between agents of established credit companies and their customers after 1945. We have seen that, in the case of this particular type of credit, there is a great deal of continuity between the pre-war and the post-war periods. The central relationship upon which doorstep credit is based (between the customer and the agent) has remained largely unchanged. The basic change during the post-war period has been the decline in the number of companies trading in this manner. The biggest single decrease has been in the number of credit drapers.

We saw that there was an interpenetration of rationalities at work in the relationship between customers and agents generally. This was not just a business relationship. There was usually an affectual element present in the relationship as well. It has been argued that the actions of both customers and agents can be understood as manifestations of practical consciousness. In terms of the customers of doorstep agents, the element of routinisation is very important. They become accustomed to the same collectors calling at the same time every week. So they feel they are dealing with someone they can 'rely on'. This routinisation is enacted through the medium of practical consciousness. Credit agents were brought into close contact with the people they dealt with. This tended to contribute towards a certain amount of empathy and understanding of working class lives, which created highly ambiguous attitudes among all three types of credit agents. In the case of part-time agents, this is an issue of class fractionalisation and the effect of such relationships was contradictory.

We then went on to discuss concepts of rationalisation, routinisation, and reflexivity, arguing that Weber's thesis of the increasing progress of rationalisation in the modern world is partially contradicted by some of the practices of doorstep credit firms. This is because, as Karen Rowlingson points out, doorstep credit firms tend to recruit customers on the basis of personal recommendation. This was also one of the ways in which mail order catalogues recruited agents. In the case of mail order catalogues, they also manage to circumvent some of the legal restrictions about the administration of credit to consumers. The idea that business is carried out 'without regard to persons' is also contradicted by the importance of personal loyalty to a particular agent, rather than to the credit company itself. Once an agent has actually recruited a customer, routinisation plays a large part in maintaining the relationship between them. Reflexivity, on the other hand, plays an important role in the termination of that relationship. Anthony Giddens attaches importance to both of these concepts. It is argued that in conditions of late modernity people are much less inclined to continue doing the 'usual' thing just because it is the usual. As Giddens says, they need some other justification. When we considered the local evidence we found that this was one of the factors that drew people away from 'traditional' forms of credit. We have also seen that the decline of the agent system within mail order credit is partially the result of the breakdown of trust in communities. This notion is, again, borrowed from Giddens.

The fundamental change in doorstep credit trading in the post-war period on Tyneside was the gradual disappearance of most of the smaller firms which traded in this manner. I found that the decline of these firms was very gradual, as they continued trading in very much the same manner until the 1960s, when younger customers began to drift away. I then went on to consider the break with the established firm from the point of view of individual customers. Doorstep credit firms became successful, in the first instance, by offering credit to social groups that had previously been excluded from it. This process began with the Watch Clubs which offered credit to the labour aristocracy in the nineteenth century, and was extended to include the rest of the working class during the interwar period. After the Second World War, these companies remained embedded within working class communities due to their continued use of the system of agents. It seems that because people were approached by their friend, neighbour or relative to take out an order, or buy something from a catalogue, this made it impossible to say 'no'. This turned a business transaction into an affectually motivated act. These established firms were the 'traditional' method of credit for many working class people. This is what kept such firms in business at a time when they were experiencing stiff competition from alternative sources of credit.

This was a state of affairs that could not last forever. We have identified a number of factors that contributed towards the decline of this type of credit. These include increased prosperity, changes in patterns of consumption, increased knowledge of new forms of credit, the increase in the employment of women, and the disruption of working class neighbourhoods. All of these factors, taken together, led to the decline of the 'traditional' credit firms during the 1970s. The underlying changes in the post-war period that caused this decline can be summarised as greater economic prosperity, and a higher degree of reflexivity in the way people lived their lives. We also looked at the reasons for the survival of some firms and the decline of others and saw that the Provident had had a greater degree of flexibility than other firms. This, along with the aggressive promotion of expensive credit, helped it to survive in the post-war era.

The whole doorstep credit system is ultimately somewhat anachronistic. It is, in a sense, a survival from a previous era. Its methods of operation do not fit in with the predominant, highly bureaucratised methods employed in other sectors of the credit industry. It is also notably different from the other types of credit we have considered so far. They were largely dependent upon the existence of a relatively close and stable community. In the case of corner-shop credit or money clubs, for example, they needed a certain degree of trust to function. When communities were uprooted, or disrupted from within, in the post-war period those forms of credit began to disappear. This also happened to many of the small, locally based doorstep credit businesses, particularly those dependent in some way on the built environment. So, if they were largely dependent on a stable local population, they suffered if their customers' houses were demolished, as this disrupted their trade. Or they could suffer from having their own premises demolished.

It was those firms (particularly the Provident) which were not dependent upon the built environment or even embeddedness within a particular community (although they could also make use of it) which survived. As a national organisation, the Provident has the advantage of being able to follow their customers wherever they went. It is not locked into any particular retail outlet, so it can adapt to its customers' changing wants and needs. Of course, as we have seen, the Provident is still successful today because it is willing to take advantage of the fact that poor people are unable to obtain credit elsewhere. This means that part of their market is a captive market, but that is not the whole story. It has been argued that the Provident has also been sustained by the reciprocal ties between part-time agents and customers, which means that the Provident can function independently of the changes in the communities it trades in, because the agent system perpetuates its own personal ties. The personal relationship between agents and customers acted as a Trojan horse for the whole doorstep credit industry during the period of post-war affluence. This helped those firms to remain embedded within working class communities at a time when they were experiencing stiff competition from alternative sources of credit, many of which had become available to the working class for the first time. However, while smaller companies did not survive the social changes of the post-war era, companies like the Provident did. Aggressive marketing, a national presence, and the agent system has enabled the Provident to survive in the changed circumstances of the post-war world.

Conclusion

The debate about community has raised many questions about the nature of communities, the manners in which they have been depicted, and the extent to which they were characterised by either social solidarity or social division. The argument developed here has not sought to over-throw the notion of 'community' altogether, but to re-evaluate it. Prior to the Second World War, some sections of the working class appear to have been members of quite clearly delineated 'communities'. The members of those communities performed a diverse series of comple-mentary tasks and services for each other. This was the basis for a form of social cohesion. However, this was not necessarily true of all sections of the working class at this time, and the extent to which this resulted in social harmony within communities is also often exaggerated. Where neighbourhood sharing was a feature of working class life, there was also an element of calculation. The main division within working class communities was that of gender. Much of the mutuality between neighbours discussed in this study took place between women. The gender division within communities is particularly graphically illus-trated in the example of the illegal moneylenders, Mr Jones and Mrs Black, who lent almost exclusively to those of their own sex. It has been argued that an examination of the use of credit within working class communities, in the pre-war era, shows an interpenetration of the instrumental and affectual spheres of action. This is the basis of the norm of reciprocity that Abrams describes and it is also part of the central thesis of this research.

It has also been argued that some commentators have exaggerated the extent to which working class life has become privatised in the post-war era. Traditional social networks have been severely undermined in the post-war period for a number of reasons. These include the disruption

179

of traditional patterns of employment, an increase in the number of women in paid employment, the expansion of the welfare state, increased affluence, and the demolition of the old, inner-city areas. However, this does not mean that those networks have ceased to function altogether, or that communities do not have the ability to continually recreate themselves even in the most hostile conditions. Neighbourhood sharing is still a part of working class life, but in a much more limited manner than before. It has been argued that the social cohesion of working class communities has been increasingly undermined by the pressure of social change in the post-war period, so that it was eventually almost completely eroded in most communities.

This study has employed a theory of social change using the theories of Ferdinand Tönnies, Philip Abrams, and Anthony Giddens. The basic direction of the change in social relations can be described in terms of the movement from Gemeinschaft to Gesellschaft, as described by Tönnies. Philip Abrams' notion of modern neighbourhoodism indicates the points of continuity with the older neighbourhoods. In addition, there has been a restructuring of the relationship between the individual and the community. It has been argued that the first two developments apply to many working class neighbourhoods in the post-war era. However, the third development, a breakdown of trust within communities (as described by Giddens) is highly contingent. It has been argued that an examination of the use of credit within working class communities, in the post-war era, shows a much lesser degree of interpenetration of the instrumental and affectual spheres of action. This development can be discerned in most types of credit dependent upon social relationships in the locality.

Illegal moneylending is another practice which indicates that the solidaristic relationships that existed within the working class can also be seen to contain an instrumental element. Illegal moneylending within working class communities forms an interpenetration zone between the laws of utilitarian action and the ethics of the community. Moneylending took place within gendered affectual networks but was also a real form of exploitation. However, it was not always experienced as such by the participants for a number of reasons. Illegal moneylending in working class communities in the post-war era is much less likely to involve an affectual element than it previously was. It is no longer primarily carried out by members of local, gendered, networks. The 'street' moneylender has been partially supplanted by the 'loanshark'. The difference between street lenders and loansharks is not in their rates of interest or in their use of physical violence. Loansharks are illegal lenders who either come from outside the community they operate within or, if they live within it, operate solely by the use of terror. In either case there is no affectual element in the relationship between lender and borrower. There were violent street lenders during the earlier period, but these lenders were usually women who were part of a local social network, not male lenders with a known criminal background. The crucial development in the post-war period which has enabled the growth of loansharking has been the use of benefit books as collateral. This is vitally important because, as soon as this element is introduced into the relationship, the individuals involved no longer need to have any trust in each other.

Just as there was often an instrumental element involved in the solidaristic relationships within the working class, there was often an affectual element in the commercial relationships involved in the use of credit by the working class. This point can be illustrated by an examination of the relationship between small shopkeepers and their customers, and agents of credit firms and their customers. The relationship between small shopkeepers and their customers is conditioned, in the first instance, by the contradictory class location of small shopkeepers. In the past, they tended to be viewed as part of the communities that they exploited. This makes it difficult to explain the relationship between shopkeepers and their customers purely in terms of naked self-interest, or the cash nexus. This can best be explained in the way we explained illegal moneylending, in terms of the interpenetration of the instrumental and affectual spheres of action. We can certainly see evidence of some sort of affectual attachment on both sides of the counter. However, we can also see evidence of a certain amount of mistrust, particularly in the attitude shopkeepers had towards their customers. So we also have to consider the implications of the consistent use of deceit on the part of shopkeepers, most notably in the field of 'creative pricing'.

Small shopkeepers were an integral part of their communities. However, Hosgood notes the contradictory nature of the small shopkeepers' outlook, and this is echoed in the research of Bechhofer *et al.* The latter found that small shopkeepers have an attitude that is distinct from that of the working and the middle class. This distinctive attitude flows from their contradictory class location, and that this is the reason for the ambiguity in their behaviour towards their customers. This is why small shopkeepers can, almost at the same time, be both supporters and defrauders of the working class. So, we need to incorporate Hochschild's notion of emotional labour into our explanation of the particular version of the interpenetration of rationalities that this creates. This is the deliberate promotion of affectual attachment as part of a business transaction through the management of appearances. Emotional labour is a feature of various types of working class credit. However, there is a paradox at the heart of relationships that involve such an exploitation of emotions. The paradox is that quite often some sort of genuine affectual attachment coexists alongside the deliberate promotion or manipulation of such an attachment for 'business' reasons.

Not only has there been a gradual decline of corner shops in the post-war period, but there has also been a decline in the number of such shops which offer credit. It has been argued that the changing nature of working class communities has been a significant factor in the decline of the number of corner shops offering credit. The provision of small-scale credit in local shops is very much part of the informal economy. Debts incurred in this manner seem to have dubious legal status, even if they be pursued through the law courts. Corner-shop credit has to be based upon some type of mutual trust or understanding between the shopkeeper and the community. The change in the relationship between the shopkeeper and the community is another example of the breakdown of trust within communities discussed above.

It has been argued that the majority of credit-givers who deal with the working class are involved in a type of performance that is, in some way, 'cynical'. As we have seen, this is a complex issue as it can often be difficult to determine the extent to which the 'performance' of small shopkeepers is cynical or sincere. As Goffman says, performers tend to give an idealised impression of themselves. It has been argued that the actions of both customers and agents of doorstep credit firms can be understood as manifestations of practical consciousness. In terms of the customers of doorstep agencies, the element of routinisation is very important. They become accustomed to the same collectors calling at the same time every week. So they feel that they are dealing with someone they can 'rely on'. When the particular collector an individual has become accustomed to dealing with leaves the firm (for whatever reason) and a new collector takes over, there is still a link with the firm itself. The particular type of credit used by an individual becomes a means of sustaining that individual's sense of ontological security. As Giddens says, routine is psychologically relaxing. It must be remembered that this is part of the experience of doorstep credit for both customer and collector. For the collector, though, there is another aspect to the routinisation of their activities through the medium of practical consciousness. It places them at a distance from the consequences of their actions.

The relationship between agent and customer can be explained in terms of the interpenetration of the instrumental and affectual spheres of action. So in this respect it is similar to the other forms of credit we have considered so far. Unlike those forms of credit, though, there is a great deal of continuity between the pre-war and the post-war periods. In particular, the core relationship between the agent and the customer seems to have remained largely unchanged. However, this by no means contradicts what has been said so far about changes in working class communities after 1945. This is because, to a large extent, doorstep credit can survive independently of changes within communities. The central relationship between the agent and the customer endures, but that relationship now operates in a vastly changed context. Those elements of the trade dependent upon settled communities have been greatly eroded. There has been a decline in the number of customers supplied by individual mail-order agents, and one of the reasons is that people are less willing to offer credit to their neighbours. The smaller, self-employed, ticket agents in the interwar period (such as Mrs Hill) were in a similar position to the corner shopkeeper who offered groceries on credit, as they were personally responsible for any debt. They had to be able to trust their customers to repay the debt. After 1945, a lot of the smaller 'ticket' agencies began to disappear, and consequently this type of agent has become less common. Credit drapers (such as Mr Macrae) also suffered greatly as a result of social change. The 1970s saw the decline of many of the 'traditional' firms. The firms which survived, the most notable being the Provident, had the ability to follow their customers wherever they moved and adapt to their changing needs.

Many of the old, established credit firms continued trading in the same way after 1945. Although by the 1960s the more affluent sections of the working class had begun to make more use of banks and building societies, the shift away from the old patterns of saving and borrowing was very gradual. During the post-war period the old doorstep credit firms were gradually usurped by other forms of consumer credit. This was due to both the expansion of existing forms of credit and the creation of new ones. A lot of people were also being drawn away from their communities, and consequently their old credit networks. However, while some people, mainly the younger generation, were moving away from the old types of credit, the older generation maintained them. This was a state of affairs that could not last. We have identified a number of factors that contributed towards the decline of this type of credit. These include increased prosperity, changes in patterns of consumption, increased knowledge of new forms of credit, the increase in the employment of women, and the disruption of working class neighbourhoods. All of these factors, taken together, led to the decline of the 'traditional' credit firms during the 1970s. The underlying changes in the post-war period that caused this decline can be summarised as greater economic prosperity, and a higher degree of reflexivity in the way people lived their lives. We also looked at the reasons for the survival of some firms and the decline of others and saw that the Provident had a greater degree of flexibility than other firms. This, along with aggresive marketing, and exploitation of the agent system, helped it to survive in the post-war era.

The affectual element in the relationship between customers and agents of credit firms has not been eroded by the bureaucratisation of such companies. It was found that although there had been a gradual process of bureaucratisation within these companies, the use of personal contact was maintained at various organisational levels. We have discussed three related theoretical issues that appear in both my own evidence and the evidence in the PSI study. These were referred to as the three 'R's: rationalisation, routinisation, and reflexivity. Weber's thesis of the increasing progress of rationalisation in the modern world is partially contradicted by some of the practices of doorstep credit firms. This is because, as Karen Rowlingson points out, doorstep credit firms tend to recruit customers on the basis of personal recommendation. This was also one of the ways in which mail order catalogues recruited agents. In fact, in the case of mail order catalogues, they also manage to circumvent some of the legal restrictions about the administration of credit to consumers. The idea that business is carried out 'without regard to persons' is also contradicted by the importance of personal loyalty to a particular agent, not the credit company itself. Once an agent has actually recruited a customer, routinisation plays a large part in maintaining the relationship between them. Reflexivity, on the other hand, plays an important role in the termination of that relationship. Anthony Giddens attaches importance to both of these concepts. It has been argued that in conditions of late modernity people are much less inclined to continue doing the 'usual' thing just because it is the usual. As Giddens says, they need some other justification. When we considered the local evidence, we found that this was one of the factors which drew people away from 'traditional' forms of credit. The decline of the agent system within mail order credit is partially the result of the breakdown of trust in communities. This notion is, again, borrowed from Giddens.

One possible interpretation of the relationship between agent and customer is that it demonstrates the usefulness of Weber's ideas about the progress of rationalisation. Indeed, on one level, it does seem as if affectual rationality has been placed in the service of instrumental rationality. In other words, the affectual attachment between the customer and the agent seems to be working for the firm in sustaining business. However, while this is true, there is also still a 'ghost in the machine of modernity', to borrow a phrase from Derek Sayer. As we saw, the company can lose business if a customer does not take to an individual agent. As well as this, though, we also saw how some agents of the Provident could act as personal debt counsellors to their customers. In such cases affectual rationality can actually set limits on instrumental rationality in a very real way. The emotional ties that develop between agents and customers have helped sustain many of the old, established credit firms, but they do not always serve the commercial interests of those firms. This brings us to the final point. This book has focused on the individual experiences and personal perceptions of those involved. To paraphrase what was said at the beginning of this work: this focus on individuals has allowed us to see how broader impersonal (or historical) trends shape the lives of individuals, as well as the ways in which individuals themselves play a part in shaping the course of events.

Notes

Introduction

1. Tape: Elderly Gateshead Residents — 12.3.94 — 367.
2. Tebbut, Melanie *Making Ends Meet: Pawnbroking and Working Class Credit* (Leicester: Leicester University Press, 1983).
   Johnson, Paul *Saving and Spending: The Working Class Economy in Britain 1870–1939* (Oxford: Clarendon Press, 1985).
3. National Consumer Council *Consumers and Credit* (London: National Consumer Council, 1980).
   Berthoud, Richard and Kempson, Elaine *Credit and Debt: The PSI Report* (London: PSI, 1992).
4. Munch, Richard *Understanding Modernity: Toward a new perspective going beyond Durkheim and Weber* (London: Routledge, 1988) p. viii and pp. 224–7.
5. Crompton, Rosemary *Class and Stratification: An Introduction to Current Debates* (Cambridge: Polity Press, 1993) p. 71.
6. Marx, Karl and Engels, Friedrich *The Manifesto of the Communist Party* (London: Unwin, 1960) p. 17.
7. Gerth H.H. and Wright Mills C. (eds.) *From Max Weber: Essays In Sociology* (London: Routledge and Kegan Paul Ltd. 1974) p. 198.
8. Abrams, Philip *Historical Sociology* (Bath: Open Books, 1982) p. xviii.
9. Carr E.H. *What is History?* (Harmondsworth: Penguin Books, 1988) p. 16.
10. *Ibid.*
11. For balanced discussions of the advantages and disadvantages of using oral sources see:
    Portelli, Alessandro 'The Peculiarities of Oral History' *History Workshop* Autumn 1981 issue 12.
    Thomson, Alistair 'Unreliable memories? The use and abuse of oral history' in Lamont William (ed.) *Historical Controversies and Historians* (London: UCL Press, 1998).
12. Bourke, Joanna *Working-Class Cultures in Britain 1890–1960: Gender, class and ethnicity* (London: Routledge, 1994) p. 5.
13. Veit-Wilson J.H. 'Paradigms of poverty: a rehabilitation of B.S. Rowntree' in Englander David and O'Day Rosemary (eds.) *Retrieved Riches: Social Investigation in Britain 1840–1914* (Aldershot: Scolar Press, 1995) p. 201.
14. *Ibid.,* p. 220.
15. *Ibid.,* p. 222.
16. Kent Raymond A. *A History of British Empirical Sociology* (Aldershot: Gower, 1981) pp. 103–7.
17. George, Vic and Howards, Irving *Poverty Amidst Affluence: Britain and the United States* (Aldershot: Edward, Elgar, 1991) pp. 2–11.
18. Schenk Catherine R. 'Austerity and Boom' in Johnson Paul (ed.) *Twentieth Century Britain: Economic, Social and Cultural Change* (London: Longman, 1994) pp. 315–16.

Pollard, Sidney *The Development of the British Economy 1914–1990* (London: Edward Arnold, 1992) p. 278.

19. Bourke *op. cit.* p. 7.
20. Kent *op. cit.* pp. 131–2.
21. *Ibid.*, p. 132.
22. Hopkins, Eric *The Rise and Decline of the English Working Classes 1918–1990: A Social History* (London: Weidenfeld and Nicolson, 1991) p. 128.
23. Pollard, Sidney *The Development of the British Economy 1914–1990* (London: Edward Arnold, 1992) p. 272.
24. Ford, Janet *Consuming Credit: Debt & Poverty In The UK* (London: CPAG, 1991) pp. 6–10.
25. Pugh, Martin *State and Society: British Political and Social History: 1870–1922* (London: Arnold, 1994) p. 312.
26. Chinn, Carl *Poverty amidst Prosperity: the Urban Poor in England, 1834–1914* (Manchester: Manchester University Press, 1995) pp. 2–3.
27. Piachaud, David 'Poverty in Britain 1899 to 1983' *Journal of Social Policy* (1988) vol. 17, part 3 pp. 337–40.
28. *Ibid.*, pp. 340–9.
29. See, for example:
Andrews, Kay and Jacobs, John *Punishing the Poor: Poverty Under Thatcher* (London: Macmillan, 1992).
Ashley, Pauline *The Money Problems of the Poor: A Literature Review* (London: Heinemann Educational Books, 1983).
Cohen Ruth *et al Hardship Britain: Being Poor In The 1990s* (London: CPAG, 1992).
Ford, Janet *Consuming Credit: Debt & Poverty In The UK* (London: CPAG, 1991).
Kempson, Elaine *et al Hard Times?: How poor families make ends meet* (London: PSI, 1994).
Land, Hilary *Large Families in London: A Study of 86 Families* (London: G. Bell & Sons Ltd., 1969).
The numerous studies regularly produced by the CPAG are particularly revealing on this issue.
30. Ashley, Pauline *The Money Problems of the Poor: A Literature Review* (London: Heinemann Educational Books, 1983) p. 149.
31. Cohen, Ruth *et al Hardship Britain: Being Poor in the 1990s* (London: CPAG, 1992) p. 38.
32. Ashley *op. cit.* pp. 149–50.
33. Land, Hilary *Large Families in London: A Study of 86 Families* (London: G. Bell & Sons Ltd., 1969) pp. 50–2.
34. Ford *op. cit.* pp. 10–13.
35. Andrews, Kay and Jacobs, John *Punishing the Poor: Poverty Under Thatcher* (London: Macmillan, 1992) p. 211.
36. Hobsbawm E.J. 'Class consciousness in history' in Meszaros Istvan (ed.) *Aspects of History and Class Consciousness* (London: Routledge & Kegan Paul, 1971) p. 5.
37. Lyon, Larry *The Community in Urban Society* (Lexington, MA: Lexington Books, 1989) p. 7.
38. *Ibid.*, p. 19 and pp. 26–7.

39.   Giddens, Anthony *Modernity and Self-Identity* (Cambridge: Polity Press, 1991) p. 244.
40.   *Ibid.,* p. 3.

1 Credit, Kinship and Community: the Impact of Credit upon Working Class Social Networks

1.   Williamson, Bill *Class, Culture and Community* (London: Routledge & Kegan Paul, 1982) pp. 5–6.
2.   Williams, Raymond *Keywords* (London: Fontana Press, 1988) p. 76.
3.   Bourke, Joanna *Working-Class Cultures in Britain 1890–1960: Gender, class and ethnicity* (London: Routledge, 1994) pp. 136–8.
      For measured responses to Bourke's questioning of the notion of 'community' see:
      Gurney, Peter "Measuring the distance": D.H. Lawrence, Raymond, Williams and the quest for "community" in Laybourn Keith (ed.) *Social Conditions, Status and Community 1860–c.1920* (Stroud: Sutton Publishing, 1997) pp. 160–83.
      Colls, Robert 'Save our pits and communities!' *Labour History Review* 1995 Vol. 60 no. 2 pp. 55–66.
4.   *Ibid.,* p. 152.
5.   *Ibid.,* p. 154.
6.   Colls, Robert 'Save our pits and communities!' *Labour History Review* 1995 Vol. 60 no. 2 p. 65.
7.   Ross, Ellen 'Survival Networks: Women's Neighbourhood Sharing in London Before World War I.' *History Workshop* spring 1983 issue 15 p. 9.
8.   Chinn, Carl *They worked all their lives: Women of the urban poor in England, 1880–1939*(Manchester: Manchester University Press, 1988) p. 27.
9.   For challenges to the traditional image of the working class community see:
      Franklin A. 'Working-class privatism: an historical case study of Bedminster, Bristol.' *Society and Space* 1989 vol. 7 p. 93.
      Devine, Fiona *Affluent Workers Revisited: Privatism and the Working Class* (Edinburgh: Edinburgh University Press, 1992) p. 25.
      Bourke, Joanna *Working-Class Cultures in Britain 1890–1960: Gender, class and ethnicity* (London: Routledge, 1994).
10.   For depictions of 'traditional' working class communities see:
      Jackson, Brian *Working Class Community* (London: Routledge & Kegan Paul, 1968).
      Dennis, Norman *et al* *Coal is our Life* (London: Tavistock Publications, 1969).
      Williamson, Bill *Class, Culture and Community* (London: Routledge & Kegan Paul, 1982).
      Roberts, Robert *A Ragged Schooling* (Manchester: Manchester University Press, 1987).
      Roberts, Robert *The Classic Slum* (Harmondsworth: Penguin Books, 1988).
11.   Dennis, Norman *et al* *Coal is Our Life* (London: Tavistock Publications, 1969).
12.   Jackson, Brian *Working Class Community* (London: Routledge & Kegan Paul, 1968) p. 156.

13. *Ibid.*, p. 109.
14. Chinn *op. cit.* p. 34.
15. Goldthorpe, John H. *et al The Affluent Worker in the Class Structure* (Cambridge: Cambridge University Press, 1969) pp. 157–62.
16. Hoggart, Richard *The Uses of Literacy* (London: Chatto & Windus, 1971) p. 23.
17. *Ibid.*, p. 260.
18. *Ibid.*, p. 264.
19. Blackwell, Trevor and Seabrook, Jeremy *A World Still To Win: The Reconstruction of the Post-War Working Class* (London: Faber and Faber Limited, 1985) p. 26.
20. *Ibid.*, p. 50.
21. *Ibid.*, p. 107.
22. Campbell, Beatrix *Wigan Pier Revisited: Poverty and Politics in the Eighties* (London: Virago Press Limited, 1984) p. 224.
23. Williamson, Bill *The Temper of the Times* (Oxford: Basil Blackwell, 1990) p. 108.
24. Jackson *op. cit.* p. 150.
25. *Ibid.*, p. 163.
26. Young, Michael and Willmott, Peter *Family and Kinship in East London* (Harmondsworth: Penguin, 1969) p. 104.
27. *Ibid.*, p. 142.
28. Campbell *op. cit.* p. 41.
29. Willmott, Peter *The Evolution of a Community* (London: Routledge & Kegan Paul, 1963) p. ix.
30. *Ibid.*, p. 36.
31. *Ibid.*, p. 83.
32. *Ibid.*, p. 111.
33. Devine, Fiona *Affluent Workers Revisited: Privatism and the Working Class* (Edinburgh: Edinburgh University Press, 1992) p. 54.
34. Harrison, Paul *Inside The Inner City: Life Under the Cutting Edge* (Harmondsworth: Penguin, 1983) p. 403.
35. Campbell *op. cit.* p. 40.
36. *Ibid.*, pp. 50–1.
37. Harrison *op. cit.* pp. 404–5.
38. Campbell *op. cit.* p. 51.
39. Harrison *op. cit.* p. 405.
40. Campbell *op. cit.* p. 193.
41. *Ibid.*, p. 204.
42. Campbell, Beatrix *Goliath: Britain's Dangerous Places* (London: Methuen, 1993) p. 34.
43. *Ibid.*, p. 89.
44. *The Guardian* 19.6.93.
45. Campbell, Beatrix *Goliath: Britain's Dangerous Places* (London: Methuen, 1993) p. 186.
46. *Ibid.*, p. 188.
47. *Ibid.*, p. 319.
48. *Ibid.*, p. 201.
49. Tape: Mr Lewis — 15.9.94 — 045–057.

50. Tape: Mr & Mrs Wrigley — 7.10.94 — 140–50.
51. *Ibid.*, pp. 160–5.
52. Chinn *op. cit.* p. 35.
53. *Ibid.*, p. 37.
54. *Ibid.*
55. Ross *op. cit.* p. 11.
56. Tape: Mrs Johnson — 20.5.94 — Side 2: 200–15.
57. Tape: Mr Lewis — 15.9.94 — 080–5.
58. *Ibid.*, pp. 418–30.
59. *Ibid.*, pp. 379–85.
60. *Ibid.*, pp. 392–9.
61. *Ibid.*, p. 432.
62. *Ibid.*, p. 448.
63. LETS LINK U.K. Lets Info Pack (G.B. n.d.) p. 16.
64. LETS TRADELINK Leaflet p. 1.
65. Tebbut, Melanie *Making Ends Meet: Pawnbroking and Working Class Credit* (Leicester: Leicester University Press, 1983) pp. 43–4.
66. *Ibid.*, pp. 44–5.
67. Tape: Elderly Gateshead Residents — 12.3.94 — 304.
68. Letter from Byker resident in possession of author.
69. Letter from Gateshead resident in possession of author.
70. Tape: Fenham Credit Union (1) 30.3.93 — 253.
71. Tebbut *op. cit.* p. 50.
72. Tape: Mr & Mrs Wrigley — 7.10.94 — Side 2: 160–70.
73. Tape: Mrs Rowntree — 21.2.94 — 05.
74. *Evening Chronicle* 1.6.80.
75. Tape: Mrs Rowntree — 21.2.94 — 16–20.
76. Tape: Mr & Mrs Wrigley — 7.10.94 — 540–5.
77. Bowden, Sue 'The New Consumerism' in Johnson Paul (ed.) *Twentieth Century Britain: Economic, Social and Cultural Change* (London: Longman, 1994) p. 251. Tebbutt Melanie *Making Ends Meet: Pawnbroking and Working Class Credit* (Leicester: Leicester University Press, 1983) pp. 193–4.
78. Vallance, Aylmer *Hire Purchase* (London: Thomas Nelson and Sons Ltd. 1939).
79. Vernon, Betty D. *Ellen Wilkinson* (London: Croom Helm, 1982) pp. 147–51.
80. *Parliamentary Debates* 1937–8 vol. 330 Dec. 6–Dec. 23 (HMSO 1938) p. 730.
81. *Ibid.*, p. 731.
82. *Ibid.*
83. Vallance *op. cit.* pp. 68–9.
84. Tape: Mr & Mrs Wrigley — 7.10.94 — Side 2: 404–426.
85. Tape: Mrs Johnson — 20.5.94 — 135.
86. Bulmer, Martin *Neighbours: The Work of Philip Abrams* (Cambridge: Cambridge University Press, 1986) p. 3.
87. Ibid.
88. *Ibid.*, p. 8.
89. Ibid.
90. Tape: Mr Burton — 4.7.94 — 034–6.
91. *Ibid.*, pp. 147–57.

92. Roberts, Elizabeth 'Neighbours: North West England 1940–1970' *Oral History* Autumn 1993 p. 40 and 42.
93. *Ibid.*, pp. 320–5.
94. *Ibid.*, pp. 326–31.
95. Tape: Mrs Blake — 1.2.95 — 295–302.
96. *Ibid.*, Side 2: 25.
97. *Ibid.*, Side 2: 68–74.
98. Tape: Mark, Blake — 3.3.95 — 055.
99. *Ibid.*, p. 145.
100. Malpass, Peter and Murie, Alan *Housing Policy and Practice* (London: Macmillan, 1990) pp. 216–17.
101. *Ibid.*, p. 218.
102. *Ibid.*
103. Konttinen, Sirkka-Liisa *Byker* (Newcastle-Upon-Tyne: Bloodaxe Books, 1988) p. 125.
104. *Ibid.*
105. *Ibid.*
106. Tape: Byker Credit Union — 24.11.94 — 025.
     Ibid., pp. 526–8.
     Ibid., pp. 551–60.
     Ibid., pp. 382–400.
107. Tape: Byker Credit Union — 24.11.94 — 168–96.
     Ibid., pp. 321–32.
108. *Ibid.*, pp. 030–6.
     Ibid., pp. 164–6.
109. *Ibid.*, pp. 355–67.
110. *City News* December 1972.
111. *Cowgate Profile: Statistical Information* (Cowgate Family, Health and Community Project July 1994) p. 2.
112. *The Guardian* 26.5.87.
113. Tape: Ian Poole — 29.11.94 — Side 2: 593–9.
114. *Fenham, Spital Tongues and Cowgate — Miscellaneous Articles* (File held at: Newcastle Central Library L942.82 N537F) p. 8.
115. Interview conducted by author with Mo O'Toole 6.3.95.
116. Tape: Fenham Credit Union (3) — 18.11.94 — 343–53.
117. *Ibid.*, pp. 354–60.
118. *Ibid.*, pp. 361–5.
119. *Ibid.*, pp. 375–82.
     Ibid., pp. 383–7.
120. *Ibid.*, pp. 388–90.
121. *Ibid.*, pp. 398–400.
122. *Ibid.*, pp. 464–70.
123. Tape: Tracey Armstrong — 9.11.94 — 278–297.
124. Malpass, Peter *Rebuilding Byker: Twenty Years Hard Labour* (U.K. 1976) Publisher Unknown. Held at Newcastle Central Library. p. 13.
125. *Ibid.*, p. 16.
126. Bulmer, Martin 'The rejuvenation of community studies? Neighbours, networks and policy.' *Sociological Review* August 1985 vol. 33 no. 3 p. 439.
127. Giddens, Anthony *Modernity and Self-Identity* (Cambridge: Polity Press, 1991) p. 6.

2 'Taking an Interest in your Neighbours, or just Taking Interest from your Neighbours?' Illegal Moneylending and the Working Class

1. Tebbutt, Melanie *Making Ends Meet: Pawnbroking and Working Class Credit* (Leicester: Leicester University Press, 1983) p. 51.
2. Booth, Charles *Life and Labour of The People in London* (Final Volume: Notes On Social Influences and Conclusion) (London: Macmillan and Co. 1903) p. 82.
3. *Ibid.*
4. *Ibid.*, p. 83.
5. De Vesselitsky V. and Bulkley M.E. 'Money-lending among the London poor' *Sociological Review* 1917 Vol. 1 Part 9 p. 129.
6. *Ibid.*, p. 130.
7. *Ibid.*, p. 131.
8. *Ibid.*
9. Booth *op. cit.* p. 83.
   Pember Reeves, Maud *Round about a Pound a Week* (London: Virago Limited, 1979) p. 73.
10. De Vesselitsky and Bulkley *op cit.* p. 132.
11. Benson, John *The Penny Capitalists: A study of Nineteenth century working-class Entrepreneurs* (London: Gill And Macmillan, 1983) p. 90.
12. Williamson, Bill *Class, Culture and Community* (London: Routledge & Kegan Paul, 1982) p. 128.
13. De Vesselitsky and Bulkley *op. cit.* p. 132.
14. Vincent, David *Poor Citizens: The State and the Poor in Twentieth Century Britain* (London: Longman, 1990) p. 92.
15. Chinn, Carl *They worked all their lives: Women of the urban poor in England, 1880–1939* (Manchester: Manchester University Press 1988) p. 78.
16. De, Vesselitsky and Bulkley *op. cit.* p. 137.
17. *Ibid.*
18. Tebbutt *op. cit.* p. 52.
19. *Ibid.*
20. *Ibid.*, p. 53.
21. *Ibid.*
22. Chinn *op. cit.* p. 78.
23. Tebbutt *op. cit.* p. 54.
24. *Ibid.*
25. *Ibid.*
26. Callaghan, Tom *Those were the Days* (Newcastle Upon Tyne: Newcastle Upon Tyne City Libraries & Arts, 1992) p. 5.
27. Letter in possession of author.
28. *Ibid.*
29. Tape: Mr Jones — 15.9.93 — 082–092.
30. *Ibid.*, p. 117.
31. *Ibid.*, p. 119.
32. *Ibid.*, p. 458.
33. *Ibid.*, Side 2: 555–65.

34. *Ibid.*, Side 2: 347.
35. Tape of interview with elderly residents of Byker — 13.9.93 — Side 2: 350
36. Tape: Mr & Mrs Wrigley — 7.10.94 — 289–99.
37. Tape: Mr Jones — 15.9.93 — Side 1: 568.
38. *Ibid.*, p. 416.
39. *Ibid.*, Side 2: 508–18.
40. *Ibid.*, Side 2: 215.
41. Munch, Richard *Understanding Modernity: Toward a new perspective going beyond Durkheim and Weber* (London: Routledge, 1988) p. viii and pp. 224–7.
42. Samuel, Raphael *East End Underworld: Chapters in the life of Arthur Harding* (London: Routledge & Kegan Paul, 1981) p. 237.
43. Vincent *op. cit.* p. 186.
44. Tebbutt *op. cit.* p. 165.
    Tebbutt *op. cit.* p. 196.
45. Reuter, Peter *Disorganized Crime* (Cambridge, MA: The MIT Press 1986) p. 88.
46. Andrews, Kay and Jacobs, John *Punishing the Poor: Poverty under Thatcher* (London: Macmillan, 1990) pp. 191–211.
47. *The Times* 4.3.89.
48. Bolchever, S. *et al* 'Consumer Credit: Investigating the Loansharks' *Trading Standards Review* 1990 Vol. 98 no. 1 p. 18.
49. Bolchever *et al op. cit.* p. 18.
50. Crossley, Michael 'Tackling the scandal of illegal money lenders' *Municipal Review & AMA News* June 1984 no. 647 p. 56.
51. *Loansharks* (Fact Sheet produced by the Channel 4 Television series 'Cutting Edge' 1992) p. 2.
52. Bolchever *et al op. cit.* p. 22.
53. *Evening Chronicle* 18.8.69.
54. *Ibid.*
55. *Sunday Sun* 12.6.77.
56. Crossley *op. cit.* p. 56.
57. *Shop Around* (Tyne And Wear County Council Consumer Services Department News Sheet n.d.) no. 3.
58. Tape: Ian Poole — 29.11.94 — 295–300.
59. Tape: Money Matters Project — 15.8.93 — 020–040.
60. Tape: Mrs Flannery — 20.2.95 — 015–030.
61. *Ibid.*, pp. 33–40.
62. *Ibid.*, p. 45.
63. *Ibid.*, p. 65.
64. *Evening Chronicle* 14.12.92.
65. Tape: Margaret Nolan — 13.12.93 — 15–45.
66. Tape: Graham Dixon — 4.11.94 — 410–20.

3 'The Changing Fortunes of a Petit Bourgeois Chameleon' the Relationship between Small Shopkeepers and Working Class Communities

1. Kent David A. 'Small Businessmen and their Credit Transactions in Early Nineteenth Century Britain.' *Business History* vol. 36 no. 2 1994 p. 51.

2. *Ibid.,* p. 52.
3. *Ibid.,* p. 56.
4. *Ibid.,* p. 57.
5. Engels, Friedrich *The Condition of the Working Class in England* (Harmondsworth: Penguin Books, 1987) p. 106.
6. Marx, Karl and Engels, Friedrich *The Manifesto of the Communist Party* (London: Unwin Books, 1960) p. 22.
7. Roberts, Robert *The Classic Slum* (Harmondsworth: Penguin Books, 1988) p. 81.
8. *Ibid.,* p. 82.
9. Roberts, Robert *A Ragged Schooling* (Manchester: Manchester University Press, 1987) p. 17.
10. Roberts, Robert *The Classic Slum* (Harmondsworth: Penguin Books, 1988) p. 81.
    Roberts, Robert *A Ragged Schooling* (Manchester: Manchester University Press, 1987) p. 17.
11. Roberts, Robert *A Ragged Schooling* (Manchester: Manchester University Press, 1987) p. 71.
12. *Ibid.,* p. 17.
13. Kent *op. cit.* p. 60.
14. Roberts, Robert *The Classic Slum* (Harmondsworth: Penguin Books, 1988) p. 110.
15. *Ibid.,* pp. 17–18.
16. *Ibid.,* p. 132.
17. Roberts, Robert *A Ragged Schooling* (Manchester: Manchester University Press, 1987) p. 15.
18. Williamson, Bill *Class, Culture and Community* (London: Routledge & Kegan Paul, 1982) p. 128.
19. Tape: Elderly Gateshead Residents — 12.3.94 — 80–100.
20. *Ibid.,* p. 110.
21. Beales H.L. and Lambert R.S. (eds.) *Memoirs of the Unemployed* (London: Victor Gollancz Ltd. 1934) p. 86.
22. *Ibid.,* p. 166.
23. Tebbutt, Melanie *Making Ends Meet: Pawnbroking and Working Class Credit* (Leicester: Leicester University Press, 1983) p. 17.
24. *Ibid.,* pp. 20–1.
25. *Ibid.,* p. 60.
26. Johnson, Paul *Saving and Spending: The Working Class Economy in Britain 1870–1939* (Oxford: Clarendon Press, 1985) p. 145.
27. Benson, John *The Rise of Consumer Society in Britain, 1880–1980* (London: Longman, 1994) p. 62.
28. *Ibid.,* p. 61.
29. Levy, Hermann *The Shops of Britain* (London: Kegan Paul, 1947) p. 7.
30. Booth, Charles *Life and Labour of the People in London* First Series: Poverty (London: Macmillan & Co. Ltd. 1902) p. 142.
31. Chinn, Carl *They worked all their lives: Women of the urban poor in England, 1880–1939* (Manchester: Manchester University Press, 1988) p. 74.
32. Levy *op. cit.* p. 8.
33. Scott, Peter *Geography and Retailing* (London: Hutchinson & Co. 1970) p. 55.
34. *Ibid.,* p. 71.

35. Hughes, Anne and Hunt Karen 'A culture transformed? Women's lives in Wythenshawe in the 1930s' in Davies, Andrew and Fielding, Steven (eds.) *Workers' Worlds: Cultures and communities in Manchester and Salford, 1880–1939* (Manchester: Manchester University Press, 1992) p. 85.
36. Tebbutt *op. cit.* p. 173.
37. Roberts, Elizabeth 'Neighbours: North West England 1940–1970' *Oral History* Autumn 1993 p. 42.
38. Wallman, Sandra *Eight London Households* (London: Tavistock Publications, 1984) p. 149.
39. Cohen, Ruth *et al Being Poor in the 1990s* (London: CPAG, 1992) p. 103.
40. Kempson, Elaine *et al Hard Times? How Poor Families Make Ends Meet* (London: PSI, 1994) p. 221.
41. Tape: Mr Barker — 29.3.93 — 185.
42. National Consumer Council *Consumers and Credit* (London: National Consumer Council, 1980) p. 282.
43. Tape: Mr Barker — 29.3.93 — 205.
44. The *Guardian* 5.5.95.
45. NETTO Publicity Leaflet (1995).
46. Tape: Ian Poole — 29.11.94 — 101–18.
47. The *Guardian* 30.10.93.
48. *Ibid.*
49. Rowntree B. Seebohm *Poverty and Progress: A Second Social Survey of York* (London: Longmans, 1942) p. 60.
50. Levy *op. cit.* p. 216.
51. Crompton, Rosemary *Class and Stratification: An Introduction to Current Debates* (Cambridge: Polity Press, 1993) p. 69.
52. *Ibid.*, p. 71.
53. Wright, Erik Olin *Classes* (London: Verso, 1989) p. 77.
54. Edgell Stephen *Class* (London: Routledge, 1993) p. 20.
55. Wright *op. cit.* p. 89.
56. Crossick, Geoffrey and Haupt, Heinz-Gerhard 'Shopkeepers, master artisans and the historian: the petite bourgeoisie in comparative focus' in Crossick Geoffrey and Haupt Heinz-Gerhard (eds.) *Shopkeepers and Master Artisans in Nineteenth Century Europe* (London: Methuen, 1984) p. 6.
57. Wright *op. cit.* p. 8.
58. *Ibid.*, p. 54.
59. *Ibid.*, p. 87.
60. Samuel, Raphael *et al* (eds.) *The Enemy Within: Pit Villages and the miners' strike of 1984–5* (London: Routledge & Kegan Paul, 1986) p. 170.
61. *Ibid.*, p. 196.
62. *Ibid.*, p. 180.
63. Young, Michael and Willmott, Peter *Family and Kinship in East London* (Harmondsworth: Penguin, 1969) p. 94.
64. Vigne, Thea and Howkins, Alun 'The Small Shopkeeper in Industrial and Market Towns' in Crossick Geoffrey (ed.) *The Lower Middle Class in Britain 1870–1914* (London: Croom Helm, 1977) p. 184.
65. *Ibid.*, p. 185.
66. *Ibid.*, p. 188.
67. *Ibid.*, p. 189.

68. Vigne and Howkins borrow from Roberts, Robert *The Classic Slum* (Harmondsworth: Penguin Books, 1988).
69. *Ibid.*, p. 193.
70. Foster, John *Class Struggle and the Industrial Revolution* (London: Weidenfeld and Nicolson, 1974) p. 238.
71. Hosgood Christopher, P. 'The 'Pigmies of Commerce' and the Working-Class Community: Small Shopkeepers in England, 1870–1914.' *Journal of Social History* 1989 vol. 22 no. 3p. 440.
72. *Ibid.*, p. 439.
73. Crossick, Geoffrey 'The petite bourgeoisie in nineteenth-century Britain: the urban and liberal case' in Crossick Geoffrey and Haupt Heinz-Gerhard (eds.) *Shopkeepers and Master Artisans in Nineteenth Century Europe* (London: Methuen, 1984).
74. Hosgood *op. cit.* p. 443.
75. *Ibid.*, p. 445.
76. *Ibid.*, p. 447.
77. *Ibid.*, p. 448.
78. *Ibid.*, pp. 450–1.
79. *Ibid.*, p. 453.
80. Bechhofer, Frank and Elliot, Brian 'Petty Property: the Survival of a Moral Economy' in
Bechhofer, Frank and Elliot, Brian (eds.) *The Petite Bourgeoisie: Comparative Studies of the Uneasy Stratum* (London: The Macmillan Press Ltd. 1981) p. 187.
81. Bechhofer, Frank *et al* 'The Petit Bourgeois in the Class Structure: the case of the Small Shopkeepers' in Parkin Frank (ed.) *The Social Analysis of Class Structure* (London: Tavistock, 1974) p. 103.
82. Bechhofer, Frank *et al* 'Small Shopkeepers: Matters of Money and Meaning.' *The Sociological Review* (1974) vol. 22 no. 4p. 479.
83. Bechhofer, Frank *et al* 'Small Shopkeepers: Matters of Money and Meaning.' *The Sociological Review* (1974) vol. 22 no. 4p. 471.
84. Parkin (ed.) *op. cit.* p. 120.
85. *Ibid.*, p. 121.
86. Bechhofer, Frank and Elliot Brian 'The Voice of Small Business and the Politics of Survival.' *The Sociological Review* (1978) vol. 26 no. 1p. 73.
87. Tape of interviews with elderly residents of Byker — 13.9.93 — 343.
88. Benwell CDP *From Blacksmiths to White Elephants* (Newcastle-Upon-Tyne: Benwell CDP, 1979) p. 11.
89. *Ibid.*, p. 10.
90. *Ibid.*
91. Roberts, Robert *The Classic Slum* (Harmondsworth: Penguin Books, 1988) p. 15.
92. Johnson *op. cit.* p. 147.
93. *Ibid.*, pp. 146–7.
94. Blackman, Janet 'The Development of the Retail Grocery Trade in the Nineteenth Century' *Business History* (1967) vol. ix p. 111.
95. *Ibid.*
96. *Ibid.*, p. 110.
97. Engels *op. cit.* p. 106.
98. Robinson, Joe *The Life and Times of Francie Nichol of South Shields* (London: George Allen & Unwin Ltd. 1975) pp. 167–8.

99. *Ibid.*, p. 169.
100. Byrne, David 'Working Class Owner-Occupation and Social Differentiation on Inter-War Tyneside' in Lancaster Bill (ed.) *Working Class Housing on Tyneside 1850–1939* (Whitley Bay: Bewick Press, 1994) p. 103.
101. Interview with elderly resident of Heaton 17.9.93.
102. *Ibid.*
103. Johnson, Paul 'Credit and thrift and the British Working Class, 1870–1939' in Winter Jay (ed.) *The Working Class in Modern British History: Essays in honour of Henry Pelling* (Cambridge: Cambridge University Press, 1983) p. 154.
104. Letter (13).
105. Tape of interviews with elderly residents of Byker — 13.9.93 — 325.
106. *Ibid.*, p. 337.
107. Tape: Mr Jones — 15.9.93 — Side 2: 460–70.
108. Letter (12).
109. Tape: Mrs Wrigley — 7.10.94 — 387–90.
110. *Ibid.*, pp. 395–410.
111. *Ibid.*, pp. 448–55.
112. Letter (1).
113. Letter (15).
114. Tape: Mr Lewis — 15.9.94 — 278–294.
115. *Ibid.*, pp. 220–30.
116. Booth *op. cit.* p. 142.
117. Tape: Mr Lewis — 15.9.94 — 294 300.
118. *Ibid.*, pp. 330–34.
119. Hochschild Arlie, Russell *The Managed Heart: Commercialization of Human Feeling* (Berkeley, CA: University of California Press, 1983).
120. Goffman Erving *The Presentation of Self in Everyday Life* (Harmondsworth: Penguin Books, 1972) p. 32.
121. *Ibid.*, p. 29.
122. *Ibid.*, p. 31.
123. Dennis, Norman *et al Coal is our Life* (London: Tavistock Publications, 1969) p. 197.
124. Tape: Mrs Blackwell — 10.9.94 — Side 2: 020–060.
125. Parker, Gillian *Getting and Spending: Credit and Debt in Britain* (Aldershot: Avebury, 1990) p. 8.
126. Tape: Heaton Shopkeeper — 12.8.93 — 015–045.
127. Tape: Ian Poole — 29.11.94 — Side 2: 090–100.
128. Tape: Heaton Shopkeeper — 14.7.95 — 060–070.
129. Interview with Walker Shopkeeper — 3.8.94.
130. Interview with Byker Shopkeeper — 14.6.95.
131. *Ibid.*
132. Tape: Heaton Shopkeeper — 14.7.95 — 100–10.
133. Kempson *et al op. cit.* p. 221.
134. *Ibid.*, p. 222.
135. *Ibid.*
136. *Ibid.*
137. *Ibid.*, p. 223.
138. Home Office Report *The Response to Racial Attacks: Sustaining the Momentum* (Home Office, 1991) p. 1.

139. *The Journal* 18.3.94.
140. Newcastle City Council *Racial Equality in Newcastle: Action Plan 1990* (Newcastle City Council, 1990) p. 4.
141. Newcastle City Council *A Way of Life?: The Experience of Racial Harassment in Newcastle* (Newcastle City Council, 1990).
142. Interview with Mo O'Toole 6.3.95.
143. *Evening Chronicle* 27.5.93.
144. *Ibid.*
145. Campbell, Beatrix *Goliath: Britain's Dangerous Places* (London: Methuen, 1993) pp. 24–5.
146. *Ibid.*, p. 7.
147. *Ibid.*, pp. 60–2.
148. *Ibid.*, p. 62.
149. *Ibid.*, p. 63.
150. *Evening Chronicle* 27.8.94.
151. *Ibid.*
152. Giddens, Anthony *The Consequences of Modernity* (Cambridge: Polity Press, 1990) p. 103.
153. Giddens, Anthony *Modernity and Self-Identity* (Cambridge: Polity Press, 1991) p. 6.

4 'Just Like One of the Family' the Agent, the Established Firm and Working Class Credit before 1945

1. Rowlingson, Karen *Moneylenders and their Customers* (London: PSI, 1994) p. 23.
2. *Ibid.*
3. Jefferys, James *Retail Trading in Britain 1850–1950* (Cambridge: Cambridge University Press, 1954) p. 334.
4. Great Universal Stores *Great Universal Stores: Years of Progress* (Great Universal Stores, 1957) p. 7.
5. Great Universal Stores PLC *Annual Report for the Year Ended 31st March 1992* (Great Universal Stores, 1992) p. 22.
6. Ford Janet *Consuming Credit: Debt & Poverty in the UK* (London: CPAG Ltd. 1991) p. 33.
7. NCC *Consumers And Credit* (London: NCC, 1980) p. 28.
8. Berthoud, Richard *Credit, Debt and Poverty* (London: PSI, 1989) p. 15.
9. *Ibid.*, p. 20.
10. Berthoud, Richard and Kempson, Elaine *Credit and Debt; The PSI Report* (London: PSI, 1992) p. 82.
11. Bradshaw, Jonathan and Holmes, Hilary *Living on the Edge: a study of the living standards of families on benefit in Tyne & Wear* (London: Tyneside CPAG, 1989) p. 44.
12. Glendinning, Caroline and Millar, Jane (eds.) *Women and Poverty in Britain* (London: Wheatsheaf Books Ltd. 1987) p. 252.
13. Beaver P. *A Pedlar's Legacy: The Origins of Empire Stores* (London: Henry Melland, 1981) *Ibid.*, p. 32.
14. *Ibid.*, p. 34.

15. *Ibid.*, p. 38.
16. *Ibid.*, p. 46.
17. *Ibid.*, p. 64.
18. *Ibid.*, p. 65.
19. *Ibid.*, p. 84.
20. *Ibid.*, p. 85.
21. *Ibid.*, p. 111.
22. Gerth H.H. and Mills C. Wright (eds.) *From Max Weber: Essays in Sociology* (London: Routledge & Kegan Paul Ltd. 1974) p. 198.
23. Beaver *op. cit.* p. 11.
24. *Ibid.*
25. *Ibid.*, p. 12.
26. *Ibid.*, p. 13.
27. *Ibid.*
28. *Ibid.*
29. Baldwin, Sally 'Credit and class distinction' in Jones Kathleen (ed.) *The Year Book of Social Policy In Britain 1973* (London: Routledge & Kegan Paul Ltd. 1974) p. 191.
30. Berthoud, Richard and Kempson, Elaine *Credit and Debt; The PSI report* (London: PSI, 1992) p. 82.
31. *Provident's 90 Years of Service* souvenir issue published by Colonnade on behalf of the Provident Clothing and Supply Company Ltd. (1980) p. 2.
32. *Ibid.*, p. 6.
33. *Ibid.*, p. 7.
34. *Ibid.*, pp. 8–9.
35. *Ibid.*, p. 8.
36. *Ibid.*
37. Johnson, Paul *Saving and Spending: The Working Class Economy in Britain 1870–1939* (Oxford: Clarendon Press, 1985) p. 39.
38. Tebbutt, Melanie *Making Ends Meet: Pawnbroking and Working Class Credit* (Leicester: Leicester University Press, 1983) p. 21.
39. *Ibid.*
40. *Ibid.*, p. 180.
41. *The Retail Credit World* August 1928 vol. 1 no. 5.
42. *Ibid.*
43. *The Retail Credit World* September 1928 vol. 1 no. 6.
44. Warren, Edward C. *Credit Dealing* (London: Sir Isaac Pitman & Sons Ltd. 1939) pp. 33–34.
45. *The Credit World* 25 July 1930 vol. 12 no. 64.
46. *The Credit World* 30 August 1929 vol. 4 no. 2.
47. *Ibid.*
48. *The Credit World* 26 June 1931 vol. 19 no. 112.
49. *The Credit World* 30 August 1929 vol. 4 no. 2.
50. *Ibid.*
51. Warren *op. cit.* p. 16.
52. *Ibid.*
53. *The Retail Credit World* October 1928 vol. 2 no. 7.
54. *Ibid.*
55. *Ibid.*

56. BBC2 *Shopping* 31 July 1995.
57. Rowlingson *op. cit.* p. 3.
58. *The Credit World* 20 March 1931 vol. 17 no. 98.
59. *The Credit World* 18 December 1931 vol. 22 no. 127.
60. Bell Florence *At the Works* (London: Virago Press, 1985) pp. 70–1.
61. *The Drapers' Record* 22 December 1906.
62. Tebbutt *op. cit.* p. 187.
63. This being redolent of Benson's 'penny capitalists.' See: Benson John *The Penny Capitalists: A Study of Nineteenth century working-class Entrepreneurs* (London: Gill And Macmillan, 1983).
64. *Shephard Ltd.* Gateshead Central Library Class No. L658.871 (Private Publication n.d.).
65. *Evening Chronicle* 1 June 1980.
66. *Ward's Directory Newcastle, Gateshead, North & South Shields, Jarrow, Sunderland and the adjacent villages* (R. Ward & Sons. Printers and Publishers 1879/80) p. 483.
67. *Ward's Directory* 1881/82 p. 446.
68. *The North East Times* November 1984.
69. Tape: Mr Parkin — 19.2.94 — 280–290.
70. *Ward's Directory* 1934 p. 891 (Wenger's).
    Ward's Directory 1925 p. 653 (McAdam's).
    Ward's Directory 1911/12 p. 1140 (Woolf's).
71. *Ward's Directory* 1923 p. 545.
72. Tape: Mr Parkin — 19.2.94 — 290–305.
73. *Ward's Directory* 1937 p. 711.
74. *Ward's Directory* 1893 p. 957.
75. Tape: Mrs Perkin — 4.2.94 — 425–35.
76. *Ibid.,* p.430.
77. Tape: Mrs Rowntree — 21.2.94 — 99–103.
78. *Ibid.,* p. 25.
79. Tape: Mr Burton — 4.7.94 — 084–100.
80. Tape: Mr Macrae — 15.6.94 — 140–50.
81. *Ibid.,* pp. 000–052.
82. Tape: Mr Burton — 4.7.94 — 450–5.
83. Tape: Mr Macrae — 15.6.94 — 303–10.
84. *Ibid.,* pp. 269–80.
85. Tape: Mr Burton — 4.7.94 — 56–8.
86. *Ibid.,* pp. 240–60.
87. Tape: Mr Macrae — 15.6.94 — 445–50.
88. *Ibid.,* pp. 451–5.
89. *Ibid.,* pp. 456–60.
90. *Ibid.,* pp. 312–14.
91. Rowlingson *op. cit.* p. 43.
92. Giddens, Anthony *The Constitution of Society* (Cambridge: Polity Press, 1984) p. xxiii.
93. *Ibid.*
94. Giddens, Anthony *The Consequences of Modernity* (Cambridge: Polity Press, 1990) p. 98.
95. Giddens, Anthony *The Constitution of Society* (Cambridge: Polity Press, 1984) p. 26.

96. See: Tape: Mr Macrae — 15.6.94 — 269–80. Also: (84)
     Tape: Mr Burton — 4.7.94 — 393–413.
97. Tape: Mr Burton — 4.7.94 — 564.
98. Rowlingson *op. cit.* p. 79.
99. Tape: Mrs Wrigley — 7.10.94 — 571–80.
100. *Ibid.,* Side 2: 000–050.
101. *Ibid.,* pp. 560–70.
102. Tape: Mrs Rowntree — 21.2.94 — 515.
103. Tape: Mrs Samuel — 12.7.94 — 278–92.
104. *Ibid.,* pp. 395–400.
105. Tape: Mrs Hill/Joll — 26.2.94 — 000–060.
106. *Ibid.,* pp. 182–92.
107. Tape: Mrs Rowntree — 21.2.94 — 007–010.
108. *Ibid.,* pp. 166–8.
109. Hind, Joe *A Shieldfield Childhood* (Newcastle-Upon-Tyne: Newcastle-Upon-Tyne City Libraries and Arts, 1994) pp. 99–100.
110. Tape: Mrs Hill/Joll 26.2.94 — 080–100.
111. Callaghan, Thomas *A Lang Way to the Panshop* (London: Butler Publishing, 1987) *Ibid.,* pp. 10–11.
112. *Ibid.,* p. 11.
113. Tape: Mrs Hill/Joll — 26.2.94 — 139–50.
114. *Ibid.,* pp. 314–18.
115. Tape: Mrs Mason — 1.7.94 — 090.
116. Tape: Elderly Gateshead Residents — 12.3.94 — Side 2: 160–70.

5 'Still One of the Family' the Role of the Agent and the Established Firm within Working Class Credit after 1945

1. Dennis, Norman *et al Coal is Our Life* (London: Tavistock Publications, 1969) pp. 200–1.
2. Hoggart, Richard *The Uses of Literacy* (London: Chatto & Windus, 1971) p. 44.
3. Kerr, Madeline *The People of Ship Street* (London: Routledge & Kegan Paul Ltd. 1958) p. 92.
4. Schenk, Catherine R. 'Austerity and Boom' in Johnson, Paul (ed.) *Twentieth Century Britain: Economic, Social and Cultural Change* (London: Longman, 1994) pp. 315–16.
5. *Board of Trade Journal* 21 April 1956 vol. 170 no. 3090 (London: HMSO, 1956) pp. 424–5.
6. *Annual Abstract of Statistics* no. 100 1963 (London: HMSO, 1963) p. 285.
7. Hoggart, Richard *The Uses of Literacy* (London: Chatto & Windus, 1971) pp. 30–1.
8. Goldthorpe, John H. *et al The Affluent Worker in the Class Structure* (Cambridge: Cambridge University Press, 1969) p. 39.
9. Lewis, Jane (ed.) *Labour & Love: Women's Experience of Home and Family 1850–1940* (Oxford: Basil Blackwell, 1987) p. 205.
10. Furmston M.P. *Cheshire, Fifoot & Furmston's Law of Contract* (London: Butterworths, 1986) p. 133.
    Goode R.M. *Hire-Purchase Law and Practice* (London: Butterworths, 1970) p. 12.

11. Goode R.M. *Hire-Purchase Law and Practice* (London: Butterworths, 1970) p. 15.
12. *Parliamentary Debates* 1963–4 vol. 689 Feb.10–Feb.21 (London: HMSO, 1964) 1039.
13. *Parliamentary Debates* 1961–2 vol. 650 Nov. 27–Dec. 8 (London: HMSO, 1962) 1779.
14. *Ibid.*, p. 1717.
15. *Ibid.*, p. 1718.
16. *Newcastle upon Tyne Council of Social Service Annual Report and Statement of Accounts* Newcastle Central Library Class 1949/50–1960/61, vol. 1 no. L360 Annual Report 1953 p. 10.
17. *Newcastle upon Tyne Council of Social Service Annual Report and Statement of Accounts* Newcastle Central Library Class 1961/62–1970/71, Vol. 2 No. L360 Annual Report 1962 p. 10.
18. *Newcastle upon Tyne Council of Social Service Annual Report and Statement of Accounts* Newcastle Central Library Class 1961/62–1970/71, vol. 2 No. L360 Annual Report 1966 p. 13.
19. *Newcastle upon Tyne Council of Social Service Annual Report and Statement of Accounts* Newcastle Central Library Class 1961/62–1970/71, vol. 2 No. L360 Annual Report 1967 p. 9.
20. Goldthorpe John H. *et al* The *Affluent Worker in the Class Structure* (Cambridge: Cambridge University Press, 1969) p. 37.
21. Land, Hilary *Large Families in London: A Study of 86 Families* (London: G. Bell & Sons Ltd., 1969) p. 50.
22. *Ibid.*, pp. 50–2.
23. *Ibid.*, p. 51.
24. Willmott, Peter 'A Working Relationship? The clearing banks and the 'new working class." *The Bankers' Magazine* September 1975 Vol. CCIX no. 1578 p. 8.
25. *Ibid.*, p. 7.
26. Berthoud, Richard and Kempson, Elaine *Credit and Debt: The PSI report* (London: PSI, 1992) p. 14.
27. Tebbutt, Melanie *Making Ends Meet: Pawnbroking and Working Class Credit* (Leicester: Leicester University Press, 1983) pp. 199–200.
28. Rowlingson, Karen and Kempson, Elaine *Paying With Plastic: A study of credit card debt* (London: PSI, 1994) p. 1.
29. *Ibid.*
30. Ashley Pauline *The Money Problems of the Poor* (London: Heinemann Educational Books, 1983) p. 72.
31. *Annual Abstract of Statistics* no. 108 1971 (London: HMSO, 1971) p. 350.
32. NCC *Consumers and Credit* (London: NCC, 1980) p. 307.
33. *Ibid.*, p. 319.
34. *Ibid.*, pp. 319–20.
35. *Ibid.*, pp. 322–3.
36. *Ibid.*, pp. 321–2.
37. Parker, Gillian *Getting and Spending: Credit and Debt in Britain* (Aldershot: Avebury, 1990) p. 33.
38. Rowlingson, Karen *Moneylenders and their Customers* (London: PSI, 1994) p. 23.
39. *Ibid.*, p. 116.
40. Gerth H.H. and Mills C. Wright (eds) *From Max Weber: Essays in Sociology* (London: Routledge & Kegan Paul Ltd. 1974) p. 51.

41. Sayer, Derek *Capitalism & Modernity: An excursus on Marx and Weber* (London: Routledge, 1991) p. 114.
42. *Ibid.*, p. 142.
43. Rowlingson, Karen *Moneylenders and their Customers* (London: PSI, 1994) p. 62.
44. *Ibid.*
45. *Ibid.*, p. 57.
46. Giddens, Anthony *The Consequences of Modernity* (Cambridge: Polity Press, 1990) p. 38.
47. NCC *op. cit.* p. 282.
48. Kempson, Elaine *et al Hard Times?: How poor families make ends meet* (London: PSI, 1994) p. 212.
49. *Ibid.*, p. 213.
50. Rowlingson, Karen *Moneylenders and their Customers* (London: PSI, 1994) p. 85.
51. *Ibid.*, pp. 85–6.
52. Kempson, Elaine *et al Hard Times?: How poor families make ends meet* (London: PSI, 1994) pp. 225–9.
53. BBC2 *Shopping* 31 July 1995.
54. *Ibid.*
55. Ford, Janet *The Indebted Society: Credit and Default in the 1980s* (London: Routledge, 1988) p. 16.
56. *Ibid.*
57. Tape: Mrs Wilson — 17.2.94 — 291–9.
58. *Ibid.*, pp. 305–10.
59. Tape: Byker Community Centre — 13.9.93 — 125–30.
60. *Ibid.*, pp. 140–50.
61. Tape: Mr Parkin — 19.2.94. — 255–60.
62. *Ibid.*, pp. 275–80.
63. Tape: Mrs Hill/Joll — 26.2.94 — 336–40.
64. Tape: Mrs Moss — 1.7.94 — 387–97.
65. Tape: Manageress, Beavans — 1.11.95 — 10–50.
66. Tape: Mr Macrae — 15.6.94 — 305–20.
67. *Ibid.*,pp. 260–5.
68. *Ibid.*, pp. 100–10.
69. Tape: Mr Burton — 4.7.94 — 315–31.
70. Tape: Mr Barker — 29.3.93 — 158–60.
71. *Ibid.*, pp. 345–50.
72. *Ibid.*, pp. 404–14.
73. Giddens, Anthony *The Constitution of Society* (Cambridge: Polity Press, 1984) p. 26.
74. Tape: Mr Barker — 29.3.93 — 445–55.
75. Tape: Mrs Robinson — 6.4.93 — Side 2: 000–033.
76. Tape: Mrs Blackwell — 10.9.94 — Side 2: 082–094.
77. *Ibid.*, Side 1: 533–8.
78. Tape: Mrs Hughes — 26.5.94 — 350–8.
79. *Ibid.*, pp. 360–70.
80. *Ibid.*, pp. 428–40.
81. *Ibid.*, p. 408.

82. *Ibid.*, pp. 518–20.
83. *Ibid.*, pp. 510–15.
84. *Ibid.*, Side 2: 122.
85. *Ibid.*, Side 2: 166–80.
86. Tape: Mrs Mason — 1.7.94 — 210–20.
87. *Ibid.*, pp. 100–10.
88. *Ibid.*, pp. 334–6.
89. *Ibid.*, pp. 337–40.
90. *Ibid.*, pp. 223–5.
91. *Ibid.*, pp. 262–70.
92. Provident Personal Credit Leaflet (n.d.).
93. Tape: Mrs Wilson — 17.2.94 — 114–16.
94. Tape: Mr Miller — 3.3.94 — Side 2: 470.
95. Tape: Mrs Wilson — 17.2.94 — 010–020 .
    Provident Personal Credit Limited Tables of Charges December 1989.
96. Tape: Mrs Hill/Joll — 26.2.94 — 370.
97. *Ibid.*, p. 375.
98. Tape: Mrs Wilson — 17.2.94 — 400.
99. *Ibid.*, Side 1: 100–10.
100. Tape: Two Provident Agents — 2.8.94 — 000–050.
101. Tape: Mrs Moss — 1.7.94 — 360–70.
102. Tape: Mr Parkin — 19.2.94. — 230–5.
103. *Ibid.*, p. 540.
104. Tape: Graham, Dixon — 4.11.94 — 270–90.
105. Tape: Fenham Credit Union — 18.11.94 — 464–70.
106. Beaver P. *op. cit.* p. 13.
107. BBC2 *Shopping* 31 July 1995.
108. Tape: Tracey Armstrong — 9.11.94 — 157–72.
109. Gillian Parker *op. cit.* p. 8.
110. Tape: Tracey Armstrong — 9.11.94 — 176–96.
111. Tape: Mrs Ford — 22.8.94. — 000–050.
112. *Ibid.*, pp. 110–30.
113. *Ibid.*, pp. 135–45.
114. Giddens, Anthony *The Consequences of Modernity* (Cambridge: Polity Press, 1990) p. 103.
115. Giddens, Anthony *Modernity and Self-Identity* (Cambridge: Polity Press, 1991) p. 6.

Bibliography

Oral Sources

Taped Interviews

Margaret Nolan	8.3.93.
Mr Barker	29.3.93.
Fenham Credit Union (1)	30.3.93. (Mrs Robinson)
Fenham Credit Union (2)	6.4.93. (Mrs Robinson & two credit union members)
Margaret Nolan	26.4.93.
Meadowell Credit Union (1)	4.5.93. (Three credit union members)
Heaton Shopkeeper	12.8.93.
Money Matters Project	15.8.93.
Two Elderly Byker Residents	13.9.93.
Mr Jones	15.9.93.
Margaret Nolan	13.12.93.
Mrs Perkin	4.2.94.
Mrs Wilson	17.2.94.
Mr Parkin	19.2.94.
Mrs Rowntree	21.2.94.
Mrs Hill/Joll	26.2.94.
Mr Miller	3.3.94.
Three Elderly Gateshead Residents	12.3.94.
Mrs Johnson	20.5.94.
Mrs Hughes	26.5.94.
Mr Macrae	15.6.94.
Mrs Moss	1.7.94.
Mrs Mason	1.7.94.
Mr Burton	4.7.94.
Mrs Samuel	12.7.94.
Two Provident Agents	2.8.94
Mrs Ford	22.8.94.
Mrs Blackwell	10.9.94.
Mr Lewis	15.9.94.
Mr & Mrs Wrigley	7.10.94.
Graham Dixon	4.11.94.
Tracey Armstrong	9.11.94.
Fenham Credit Union (3)	18.11.94. (Three credit union members)
Byker Credit Union	24.11.94. (Five credit union members)
Ian Poole	29.11.94.
Mrs Blake	1.2.95.
Mark Blake	3.3.95.
Mrs Flannery	20.2.95.

Heaton Shopkeeper	14.7.95.
Manageress, Beavans	1.11.95.
Meadowell Credit Union (2)	2.12.95. (One credit union member)

Interview Notes

Interview with elderly resident of Heaton	17.9.93.
Interview with Walker Shopkeeper	3.8.94.
Interview conducted by author with Mo O'Toole	6.3.95.
Interview with Byker Shopkeeper	14.6.95.

Television Programmes

BBC2 *Shopping* 31 July 1995 'Mail Order'.
C4 *Cutting Edge* 2 November 1992 'Loansharks'.

Written Sources

Letters

Correspondence from various Tyneside residents. Material in possession of author. 42 letters written in response to newspaper appeals (see text).

Newspapers

City News (Newcastle Central Library).
The Credit World (The British Library).
The Drapers' Record (The British Library).
Evening Chronicle (Newcastle Central Library).
The Guardian (Newcastle Central Library).
The Journal (Newcastle Central Library).
The North East Times (Newcastle Central Library).
The Retail Credit World (The British Library).
Sunday Sun (Newcastle Central Library).
The Times (Newcastle Central Library).

Printed Primary Sources

Annual Abstract of Statistics 1963 No. 100 (London: HMSO, 1963).
Annual Abstract of Statistics 1971 No. 108 (London: HMSO, 1971).
Board of Trade Journal 21 April 1956 vol. 170, No. 3090 (London: HMSO, 1956) 3.
Cowgate Profile: Statistical Information (Cowgate Family, Health and Community Project July 1994).
Fenham, Spital Tongues and Cowgate — Miscellaneous articles (File held at: newcastle Central Library L942.82 N537F).
Great Universal Stores *Great Universal Stores: Years of Progress* (Great Universal Stores, 1957).
Great Universal Stores PLC *Annual Report for the Year Ended 31st March 1992* (Great Universal Stores, 1992).

Home Office Report *The Response to Racial Attacks: Sustaining the Momentum* (Home Office, 1991).
LETS LINK U.K. Lets Info Pack (G.B. n.d.).
LETS TRADELINK Leaflet.
Loansharks (Fact Sheet produced by the Channel 4 Television series 'Cutting Edge' 1992).
NETTO Publicity Leaflet (1995).
Newcastle City Council *Racial Equality in Newcastle: Action Plan 1990* (Newcastle City Council, 1990).
Newcastle City Council *A Way of Life?: The Experience of Racial Harassment in Newcastle* (Newcastle City Council, 1990).
Newcastle upon Tyne Council of Social Service Annual Report and Statement of Accounts Newcastle Central Library Class 1949/50–1960/61 Vol. 1 No. L360.
Newcastle upon Tyne Council of Social Service Annual Report and Statement of Accounts Newcastle Central Library Class 1961/62–1970/71 Vol. 2 No. L360.
Parliamentary Debates 1937–8 Vol. 330 Dec. 6–Dec. 23 (London: HMSO, 1938).
Parliamentary Debates 1961–2 Vol. 650 Nov. 27–Dec. 8 (London: HMSO, 1962).
Parliamentary Debates 1963–4 Vol. 689 Feb. 10–Feb. 21 (London: HMSO, 1964).
Provident's 90 Years of Service souvenir issue published by Colonnade on behalf of the Provident Clothing and Supply Company Ltd. (1980).
Provident Personal Credit Limited Tables of Charges December 1989.
Provident Personal Credit Leaflet (n.d.).
Shephard Ltd. Gateshead Central Library Class No. L658.871 (Private Publication n.d.).
Shop Around (Tyne And Wear County Council Consumer Services Department News Sheet n.d.) no. 3.
Ward's Directory Newcastle, Gateshead, North & South Shields, Jarrow, Sunderland and the adjacent villages (R. Ward & Sons. Printers and Publishers 1877–1937).

Manuscripts

Malpass Peter *Rebuilding Byker: Twenty Years Hard Labour* (U.K. 1976) Publisher Unknown. Held at Newcastle Central Library.

Books and Articles

Abrams, Philip *Historical Sociology* (Bath: Open Books, 1982).
Andrews, Kay and Jacobs, John *Punishing the Poor: Poverty under Thatcher* (London: Macmillan, 1990).
Ashley, Pauline *The Money Problems of the Poor: A Literature Review* (London: Heinemann Educational Books, 1983).
Beales H.L. and Lambert R.S. (eds.) *Memoirs of the Unemployed* (London: Victor Gollancz Ltd. 1934).
Beaver P. *A Pedlar's Legacy: The Origins of Empire Stores* (London: Henry Melland, 1981).
Bechhofer, Frank *et al* 'Small Shopkeepers: Matters of Money and Meaning.' The *Sociological review* 1974 vol. 22 no. 4 pp. 465–82.
Bechhofer, Frank and Elliot, Brian 'The Voice of Small Business and the Politics of Survival.' *The Sociological Review* 1978 vol. 26 no. 1 pp. 57–88.
Bechhofer, Frank and Elliot, Brian (eds.) *The Petite Bourgeoisie: Comparative Studies of the Uneasy Stratum* (London: The Macmillan Press Ltd. 1981).
Bell, Florence *At the Works* (London: Virago Press, 1985).

Benson, John *The Penny Capitalists: A study of Nineteenth century working-class Entrepreneurs* (London: Gill And Macmillan, 1983).

Benson, John *The Rise of Consumer Society in Britain, 1880–1980* (London: Longman, 1994).

Benwell CDP *From Blacksmiths to White Elephants* (Newcastle-Upon-Tyne: Benwell CDP, 1979).

Benyon, Huw 'Jeremy Seabrook and the Working Class' *Socialist Register* 1982 pp. 285–301.

Berthoud, Richard *Credit, Debt and Poverty* (London: PSI, 1989).

Berthoud, Richard and Hinton, Teresa *Credit Unions in the United Kingdom* (London: PSI, 1989).

Berthoud, Richard and Kempson, Elaine *Credit and Debt: The PSI Report* (London: PSI, 1992).

Blackman, Janet 'The Development of the Retail Grocery Trade in the Nineteenth Century' *Business History* 1967 vol. ix pp. 110–17.

Blackwell, Trevor and Seabrook, Jeremy *A World Still To Win: The Reconstruction of the Post-War Working Class* (London: Faber and Faber Ltd. 1985).

Bolchever S. *et al* 'Consumer Credit: Investigating the Loansharks' *Trading Standards Review* 1990 Vol. 98 no.1 pp. 18–22.

Booth, Charles *Life and Labour of the People in London* First Series: Poverty (London: Macmillan & Co. Ltd 1902).

Booth, Charles *Life and Labour of the People in London* (Final Volume: Notes On Social Influences And Conclusion) (London: Macmillan and Co. 1903).

Bourke, Joanna *Working-Class Cultures in Britain 1890–1960: Gender, class and ethnicity* (London: Routledge, 1994).

Bradshaw, Jonathan and Holmes, Hilary *Living on the edge: A study of the living standards of families on benefit in Tyne & Wear* (London: Tyneside CPAG, 1989).

Bulmer, Martin 'The rejuvenation of community studies? Neighbours, networks and policy.' *Sociological Review* August 1985 vol. 33 no. 3 pp. 430–48.

Bulmer, Martin *Neighbours: The Work of Philip Abrams* (Cambridge: Cambridge University Press, 1986).

Bulmer, Martin (ed.) *Working-Class Images of Society* (London: Routledge & Kegan Paul Ltd. 1975).

Burnett, John *et al The Autobiography of the Working Class: An Annotated Critical Biography* (London: The Harvester Press, 1984).

Byrne, David *Beyond the Inner City* (Milton Keynes: Open University Press, 1989).

Byrne, David 'Dangerous Places? A Response.' *North East Labour History Society Bulletin* 1993 No. 27 pp. 75–81.

Callaghan, Thomas *A Lang Way to the Panshop* (London: Butler Publishing, 1987).

Callaghan, Tom *Those were the Days* (Newcastle-Upon-Tyne: Newcastle-Upon-Tyne City Libraries & Arts, 1992).

Campbell, Beatrix *Wigan Pier Revisited: Poverty and Politics in the Eighties* (London: Virago Press, 1984).

Campbell, Beatrix *Goliath: Britain's Dangerous Places* (London: Methuen, 1993).

Carr E.H. *What is History?* (Harmondsworth: Penguin Books, 1988).

Chinn, Carl *They worked all their lives: Women of the Urban Poor in England, 1880–1939* (Manchester: Manchester University Press, 1988).

Chinn, Carl *Poverty amidst Prosperity: The Urban Poor in England, 1834–1914* (Manchester: Manchester University Press, 1995).

Cohen, Ruth *et al Hardship Britain: Being Poor In The 1990s* (London: CPAG, 1992).

Colls, Robert 'Save our pits and communities!' *Labour History Review* 1995 Vol. 60 no. 2.

Colls, Robert and Lancaster, Bill (eds.) *Geordies* (Edinburgh: Edinburgh University Press, 1992).

Crompton, Rosemary *Class and Stratification: An Introduction to Current Debates* (Cambridge: Polity Press, 1993).

Crossick, Geoffrey (ed.) *The Lower Middle Class in Britain 1870–1914* (London: Croom Helm, 1977).

Crossick, Geoffrey and Haupt, Heinz-Gerhard (eds.) *Shopkeepers and Master Artisans in Nineteenth Century Europe* (London: Methuen, 1986).

Crossley, Michael 'Tackling the scandal of illegal money lenders' *Municipal Review & AMA News* june 1984 No. 647 p. 56.

Davies, Andrew and Fielding, Steven (eds.) *Workers' Worlds: Cultures and communities in Manchester and Salford, 1880–1939* (Manchester: Manchester University Press 1992).

Dennis, Norman *et al Coal is our Life* (London: Tavistock Publications, 1969).

De Vesselitsky V. and Bulkley M.E. 'Money-lending among the London poor' *Sociological Review* 1917 Vol. 1 Part 9 pp. 129–38

Devine, Fiona *Affluent Workers Revisited: Privatism and the Working Class* (Edinburgh: Edinburgh University Press, 1992).

Edgell, Stephen *Class* (London: Routledge, 1993).

Engels, Friedrich *The Condition of the Working Class in England* (Harmondsworth: Penguin Books, 1987).

Englander, David and O'Day Rosemary (eds.) *Retrieved Riches: Social Investigation in Britain 1840–1914* (Aldershot: Scolar Press, 1995).

Ford, Janet *The Indebted Society: Credit and Default in the 1980s* (London: Routledge, 1988).

Ford, Janet *Consuming Credit: Debt & Poverty In The UK* (London: CPAG, 1991).

Foster, John *Class Struggle and the Industrial Revolution* (London: Weidenfeld and Nicolson, 1974).

Franklin A. 'Working-class privatism: an historical case study of Bedminster, Bristol.' *Society and Space* 1989 Vol. 7 pp. 93–107.

Furmston M.P. *Cheshire, Fifoot & Furmston's Law of Contract* (London: Butterworths, 1986).

George, Vic and Howards, Irving *Poverty Amidst Affluence: Britain and the United States* (Aldershot: Edward Elgar, 1991).

Gerth H.H. and Mills C. Wright *From Max Weber: Essays In Sociology* (London: Routledge & Kegan Paul, 1974).

Giddens, Anthony *Capitalism and modern social theory: an analysis of the writings of Marx Durkheim and Max Weber* (Cambridge: Cambridge University Press, 1971).

Giddens, Anthony *The Constitution of Society* (Cambridge: Polity Press, 1984).

Giddens, Anthony *The Consequences of Modernity* (Cambridge: Polity Press, 1990).

Giddens, Anthony *Modernity and Self-Identity* (Cambridge: Polity Press, 1991).

Glendinning, Caroline and Millar, Jane (eds.) *Women and Poverty in Britain* (London: Wheatsheaf Books Ltd. 1987).

Goffman, Erving *The Presentation of Self in Everyday Life* (Harmondsworth: Penguin Books, 1972).

Goldthorpe, John H. *et al The Affluent Worker in the Class Structure* (Cambridge: Cambridge University Press, 1969).

Goode R.M. *Hire-Purchase Law and Practice* (London: Butterworths, 1970).

Harrison, Paul *Inside The Inner City: Life Under The Cutting Edge* (Harmondsworth: Penguin, 1983).

Hind, Joe *A Shieldfield Childhood* (Newcastle-Upon-Tyne: Newcastle-Upon-Tyne City Libraries and Arts, 1994).

Hochschild, Arlie Russell *The Managed Heart: Commercialization of Human Feeling* (Berkeley, CA: University of California Press, 1983).

Hoggart, Richard *The Uses of Literacy* (London: Chatto & Windus, 1971).

Hopkins, Eric *The Rise and Decline of the English Working Classes 1918–1990: A Social History* (London: Weidenfeld & Nicolson, 1991).

Hosgood, Christopher P. 'The 'Pigmies of Commerce' and the Working-Class Community: Small Shopkeepers in England, 1870–1914.' *Journal of Social History* 1989 vol. 22 no. 3 pp. 439–53.

Jackson, Brian *Working Class Community* (London: Routledge & Kegan Paul, 1968).

Jefferys, James *Retail Trading in Britain 1850–1950* (Cambridge: Cambridge University Press, 1954).

Johnson, Paul *Saving and Spending: The Working Class Economy in Britain 1870–1939* (Oxford: Clarendon Press, 1985).

Johnson, Paul (ed.) *Twentieth Century Britain: Economic, Social and Cultural Change* (London: Longman, 1994).

Jones, Kathleen (ed.) *The Year Book of Social Policy in Britain 1973* (London: Routledge & Kegan Paul Ltd., 1974).

Kempson, Elaine *et al Hard Times? How Poor Families Make Ends Meet* (London: PSI, 1994).

Kent, David A. 'Small Businessmen and their Credit Transactions in Early Nineteenth Century Britain.' *Business History* 1994 vol. 36 no. 2 pp. 47–64.

Kent, Raymond A. *A History of British Empirical Sociology* (Aldershot: Gower, 1981).

Kerr, Madeline *The People of Ship Street* (London: Routledge & Kegan Paul Ltd., 1958).

Konttinen, Sirkka-Liisa *Byker* (Newcastle-Upon-Tyne: Bloodaxe Books, 1988).

Lamont, William (ed.) *Historical Controversies and Historians* (London: UCL Press, 1998).

Lancaster, Bill (ed.) *Working Class Housing on Tyneside 1850–1939* (Whitley Bay: Bewick Press, 1994).

Land, Hilary *Large Families in London: A Study of 86 Families* (London: G. Bell & Sons Ltd., 1969).

Laybourn, Keith (ed.) *Social Conditions, Status and Community c.1860–c.1920* (Stroud: Sutton Publishing, 1997).

Levy, Hermann *The Shops of Britain* (London: Kegan Paul, 1947).

Lewis, Jane (ed.) *Labour and Love: Women's Experience of Home and Family 1850–1940* (Oxford: Basil Blackwell, 1987).

Lyon, Larry *The Community in Urban Society* (Lexington, MA: Lexington Books, 1989).

Malpass, Peter and Murie, Alan *Housing Policy and Practice* (London: Macmillan, 1990).

Marx, Karl and Engels, Friedrich *The Manifesto of the Communist Party* (London: Unwin Books, 1960).

Meszaros, Istvan (ed.) *Aspects Of History and Class Consciousness* (London: Routledge & Kegan, Paul, 1971).

Munch, Richard *Understanding Modernity: Toward a new perspective going beyond Durkheim and Weber* (London: Routledge, 1988).

National Consumer Council *Consumers and Credit* (London: National Consumer Council, 1980).

Parker, Gillian *Getting And Spending: Credit and debt in Britain* (Aldershot: Avebury, 1990).

Parkin, Frank (ed.) *The Social Analysis of Class Structure* (London: Tavistock, 1974).

Pember Reeves, Maud *Round about a Pound a Week* (London: Virago Limited, 1979).

Piachaud, David 'Problems in the Definition and Measurement of Poverty ' *Journal of Social Policy* (1987) vol. 16, part 2 pp. 147–64.

Piachaud, David 'Poverty In Britain 1899 to 1983' *Journal of Social Policy* (1988) vol. 17, part 3 pp. 335–49.

Pollard, Sidney *The Development of the British Economy 1914–1990* (London: Edward, Arnold, 1992).

Portelli, Alessandro 'The Peculiarities of Oral History' *History Workshop* autumn 1981 issue 12 pp. 96–107.

Pugh, Martin *State and Society: British Political and Social History: 1870–1922* (London: Arnold, 1994).

Reuter, Peter *Disorganized Crime* (Cambridge, MA: The MIT Press, 1986)

Roberts, Elizabeth *A Woman's Place: An Oral History of Working Class Women 1890–1940* (Oxford: Basil Blackwell, 1984).

Roberts, Elizabeth 'Neighbours: North West England 1940–1970' *Oral History* Autumn 1993 pp. 37–45.

Roberts, Robert *A Ragged Schooling* (Manchester: Manchester University Press, 1987).

Roberts, Robert *The Classic Slum* (Harmondsworth: Penguin Books, 1988).

Robinson, Joe *The Life and Times Of Francie Nichol of South Shields* (London: George, Allen & Unwin Ltd., 1975).

Ross, Ellen 'Survival Networks: Women's Neighbourhood Sharing in London Before World War I.' *History Workshop* Spring 1983 issue 15 pp. 4–27.

Rowlingson, Karen *Moneylenders and their Customers* (London: PSI, 1994).

Rowlingson, Karen and Kempson, Elaine *Paying With Plastic: A study of credit card debt* (London: PSI, 1994).

Rowntree B. Seebohm *Poverty and Progress: A Second Social Survey Of York* (London: Longmans, 1942).

Samuel, Raphael *East End Underworld: Chapters in the life of Arthur Harding* (London: Routledge & Kegan Paul, 1981).

Samuel, Raphael *et al* (eds.) *The Enemy Within: Pit villages and the miners' strike of 1984–5* (London: Routledge & Kegan Paul, 1986).

Sayer, Derek *Capitalism & Modernity: An excursus on Marx and Weber* (London: Routledge, 1991).

Scott, Peter *Geography and Retailing* (London: Hutchinson & Co. 1970).

Tebbutt, Melanie *Making Ends Meet: Pawnbroking and Working Class Credit* (Leicester: Leicester University Press, 1983).

Vallance, Aylmer *Hire Purchase* (London: Thomas Nelson and Sons Ltd., 1939).

Vernon, Betty D. *Ellen Wilkinson* (London: Croom Helm, 1982).

Vincent, David *Poor Citizens: The State and the Poor in Twentieth Century Britain* (London: Longman, 1990).

Wallman, Sandra *Eight London Households* (London: Tavistock Publications, 1984).

Warren, Edward C. *Credit Dealing* (London: Sir Isaac Pitman & Sons Ltd., 1939).

Weber, Max *The Theory of Social and Economic Organization* (New York: The Free Press, 1964).

Williams, Raymond *Keywords* (London: Fontana Press, 1988).

Williamson,Bill *Class, Culture and Community* (London: Routledge & Kegan Paul, 1982).

Williamson, Bill *The Temper of the Times* (Oxford: Basil Blackwell, 1990).

Willmott, Peter *The Evolution of a Community* (London: Routledge & Kegan Paul, 1963).

Willmott, Peter 'A Working Relationship? The clearing banks and the 'new working class.'' *The Bankers' Magazine* September 1975 Vol. CCIX no. 1578 pp. 7–9.

Winter, Jay (ed.) *The Working Class In Modern British History: Essays in honour of Henry Pelling* (Cambridge: Cambridge University Press, 1983).

Wright, Erik Olin *Classes* (London: Verso, 1989).

Young, Michael and Willmott, Peter *Family and Kinship in East London* (Harmondsworth: Penguin Books, 1969).

Zweig, Ferdynand *The Worker in an Affluent Society* (London: Heinemann Educational Books, 1961).

Index